Encountering islam

Encountering Islam

Christian–Muslim Relations
in the Public Square

Richard Sudworth

scm press

© Richard Sudworth 2017

First published in 2017 by SCM Press
Editorial office
3rd Floor, Invicta House,
108–114 Golden Lane,
London EC1Y 0TG

Hymns Ancient & Modern* is a registered trademark of Hymns Ancient and Modern Ltd.

SCM Press is an imprint of Hymns Ancient & Modern Ltd
(a registered charity)
13A Hellesdon Park Road, Norwich,
Norfolk, NR6 5DR, UK

www.scmpress.co.uk

British Library Cataloguing in Publication data

A catalogue record for this book is available
from the British Library

978 0 334 05518 1

Printed and bound in Great Britain by
CPI Group (UK) Ltd, Croydon

Contents

v

In memoriam

Bishop Kenneth Cragg
1913–2012

Acknowledgements

The evolution of the research for this book has been marked by the generosity of a great many people who have given of their time, shared reflections or made themselves available for interview. I would like to name specifically Luke Bretherton, Michael Ipgrave, Graham Kings, Christopher Lamb, Theresa Lawton, Philip Lewis, David Marshall, Lucinda Mosher, Oliver O'Donovan, Patrick Riordan, Julian Rivers and Rowan Williams. The structured conversations of the Georgetown University-sponsored. 'Campion Hall study group' came at a crucial juncture in my research so I would also like to express my thanks to Gavin D'Costa, Lucy Gardner, Damian Howard, Catriona Laing and Daniel Madigan for their rich reflections on Christian–Muslim encounter.

Anthony O'Mahony, my supervisor at Heythrop College where I conducted my research, has modelled generosity and patience, with a seemingly inexhaustible store of knowledge. It has been my privilege to have found in Anthony the ideal person to explore research that traverses Christian–Muslim relations, theology, history and politics. In the process, as I have frequently admitted to Anthony, I have become a much better Anglican through my engagement with the traditioned environment of Heythrop College. When asked 'What tradition do you seek to retrieve in answering your research question?', this Anglican priest has learned from his supervisor something of the riches of the Eastern and Latin Churches in ways that I would never have anticipated. My gratitude encompasses the recognition of a debt that is both intellectual and spiritual.

Thanks are due too to Guy Wilkinson for his foresight in

endorsing the resourcing of an Anglican in the Jesuit 'theology and philosophy' climate of Heythrop College. This foresight has been given material form in financial support from Church House, Ministry Division, enabling this research to take place. To David Hewlett and the community of Birmingham's Queen's Foundation, including Michael Gale that most outstanding of librarians, I am immensely grateful to work with colleagues who stimulate me by blurring the boundaries of systematic and practical theologies; disciplines that are all too often prised apart. In the Anglican Diocese of Birmingham, I would like to thank Faith Claringbull, Mark Pryce, Bishop David, Bishop Andrew, Steve Simcox and the congregation of Christ Church, Sparkbrook. They have all recognized that this research has been part and parcel of the priestly vocation.

Finally, I would like to thank Fiona, Nellie and Dylan. Their love and partnership help put all studies and ministry in proper perspective.

This book is dedicated to the Revd Frank Sudworth and Jenny Sudworth. Their formative influence rooted me in an evangelical tradition of Scripture reading and prayer. Without those roots this engagement with broader Christian tradition and Christian–Muslim relations would have been impoverished.

Foreword

A casual glance at Islam – and Christians seldom take any other kind of glance, save perhaps for a fearful one – might suggest a religion problematic in three respects. First, that it has a supersessionist mindset: it's simply newer and better than first Judaism and then Christianity, and will eventually envelop both – and much else besides. Second, that it has no notion of the separation of Church and state: it assumes a holistic unity where religion and public life are inseparable and invariably indistinguishable. Third, it has had no Enlightenment: it never, unlike Christianity, turned to the subject, and placed human experience prior to external truth; and it never developed a critical faculty, perceiving scrutiny of historical sources as enriching rather than destructive.

In short, Islam does not know its place. In the first sense, Islam doesn't grasp that it's supposed to be part of the backward culture that the colonialists civilized, and part of the non-Western shroud that immigrants to the West should shuffle off if they are to be assimilated into the advanced society of late modernity. In the second sense, Islam doesn't understand that there is a fundamental distinction between the public and the private, and that religion can only find a home in Western culture if it concentrates on the private. It can keep its headcoverings because they're private, but it can't have its courts because they're public; and when it claims outrage due to alleged blasphemy, it's simply mistaking what is merely a private offence by regarding it inaccurately as a public crime. In the third sense, Islam can't seem to comprehend Immanuel Kant's argument that we can only know the information that can be garnered by our five senses. Anything beyond that, such as the 'word of God', is simply speculation and can never be asserted as public truth. The more Muslims, particularly radical Islamists, vigorously assert the validity of their claims, the more the West retreats into the habits of Kantian thought.

Into this stand-off the churches in the West in general, and England in particular, have some delicate and challenging choices to make. Historically the Church has defaulted rather too often to the first assumption: incapable of extricating itself from the superiority of its colonial mindset, it has been waiting in vain for Muslims to realize their faith is a limited and in some degree distorted assortment of insights and traditions of which a better and fuller embodiment is found in Christianity, especially of the Western, liberal Protestant kind. As secularization has taken hold and church engagement has diminished, the least the Church could expect was that many of the same assaults would afflict Islam too, and the two religions would decline together. When this common downward trajectory has not proved so evident, the Church has rather too easily switched to the second assumption, and taken common cause with secular advocates in demanding that Islam restrict its ambitions to the so-called private sphere. In doing so the danger is that the Church comes close to defining itself by race or culture rather than by faith and ecclesial identity; by which I mean, scratch the surface of the Church and underneath you find, not a lively network of practising believers united in the habits of counter-cultural engagement, but people whose formation lies in liberal democracy and who turn to church to find stimulation for the soul. Pushed to explain why it has lined up with the secular state and against fellow followers of a tradition of faith, the Church spills into the third assumption – that we can't any longer describe Christianity as true, simply as worthy and useful and reasonable: in short, a religion Immanuel Kant would be content with. Islam, by infuriatingly still claiming to be true, simultaneously yields the desire to be worthy, useful and reasonable, and thus becomes a problem.

But look what has happened to the Church. In its alarm about

Islam it has distorted its own identity to such a degree that it has lost its true nature. For sure, there's a supersessionist dimension to Christianity that's hard to slough off, but that is about Jesus and the way Christians see Jesus as fulfilling all the promises of Israel and anticipating all the glories of the Last Day. It's not about cultural dominance or racial purity. Without doubt the agonies of the divergent paths faith took after the Reformation has taught the Church to limit its aspiration to control government and demand uniformity from a population, but that doesn't have to mean spinelessly accepting the public–private distinction, where the state gets the body and the Church is left with the somewhat contested and insubstantial consolation prize of the soul. Of course Christianity has been enriched by critical scrutiny and made wiser by being able to distinguish between traditioned and dispassionate reasoning, but that's not to sell the pass and forget that all reasoning is, in the end, traditioned, and that all enquiry has to begin somewhere, with conviction and trust, rather than a blank sheet of paper.

Once the church begins to recognize what it has jettisoned by its knee-jerk anxiety about Islam, it gets into shape to take on a humbler, more receptive conversation and encounter. This is the place Kenneth Cragg reached through his gentle walk with Muslim friends and cultures, and that Rowan Williams charts in his public theology that seeks a way for Christianity truly to enrich the public sphere and at the same time deepen its own identity.

This is the starting point for Richard Sudworth's admirable book. Steeped in personal practice, relationship and partnership, percolated through years of reflection and strengthened by careful exploration of existing theological wisdom, his essay seeks a path through the thicket I've described and a bond worthy of those who seek God with all their heart. The destination for which he strives is not well populated, but it is urgently necessary – not just because peace in the world cannot be found without peace between the world religions, but because in Islam and perhaps more precisely in Muslims, God is presenting the Church with a gift for the renewal of its life. And if the Church experiences its life as scarcity, while disregarding or rejecting the abundance God is meanwhile presenting to it, whose fault, and whose loss, is that?

The Revd Dr Samuel Wells

Introduction

In February 2008, the then Archbishop of Canterbury Rowan Williams was interviewed on BBC Radio 4 about an esoteric lecture he had presented at the Royal Courts of Justice the evening before. The resulting furore garnered headlines that put both the Church of England and Islam under the spotlight. The *Daily Mail* described Williams as a 'batty, old booby', *The Sun* covered their front page with the title, 'What a Burkha' and *The Star* called Williams 'a prize chump'.[1] In the charged emotions that were produced in response to Williams' complex musings on the place of Shari'a law in Britain, deep fissures and questions were at stake. The controversy revealed sensitivities around the place of religion in public life, about Islam in particular and the role of the established Church in speaking about the 'other'. Such will be the interface of this book.

It seems that not a day goes by without Islam featuring directly or indirectly in news headlines. As I write this, the 2016 Rio de Janeiro Olympics are underway, and a US fencer has 'made Olympic history' by being the first American athlete to compete in a hijab (headscarf). The American fencer Ibtihaj Muhammad, it seems, is a microcosm of continuing fascination and fear of Islam.[2] This is just another headline that brings the place of 'public religion' to the fore, and says as much about the aspirations and insecurities of non-Muslims as it does about the nature of Islam in the West.

Islam is news and it would seem Islam is fiercely contested. When beginning to address the issue of Islamist violence, for example, one has to pick through the nuances of what can properly be regarded as 'Islamic'. Is the use of the name 'ISIS' (denoting the

'Islamic State of Iraq and Syria'), as some would say, colluding with the agenda of those terrorists who actually have nothing to do with Islam and associating the vast majority of peaceable Muslims with violence? Or, as others argue, is Islam at heart fated to present this violent, totalizing tendency? Whether the issues revolve around the particularities of head coverings, religiously sanctioned war, ritual slaughter or values in education, what these and other controversies reveal is a struggle to make sense of religion in the public square. This struggle is one that is both internal to Muslim communities and a wider one for the whole of society.

This book is an attempt to navigate some of this struggle as a Christian priest and theologian. I will not attempt to offer an account of Islam, per se, to judge what is or is not Islamic. I am not qualified as an Islamic scholar and I have always been rather more persuaded by Wilfred Cantwell Smith's dictum that 'Islam is what Muslims say it is'. What I will be offering, though, is an account of how Christians have engaged with Muslims and Islam across traditions, contexts and ages, in all their diversity, and to suggest some patterns and trajectories to those encounters. I write as an Anglican Christian and my presenting context is as a parish priest in a Muslim-majority area of Birmingham. Prior to ordination, I was a Church Mission Society mission partner in Birmingham, before that in North Africa, and have been energized by questions of Christian–Muslim relations and their associated political implications for over 17 years. In many ways, the book represents the fruit of a very personal journey where my handle on concepts of mission, social justice and spirituality have all been refashioned, deepened and at times disturbed by the engagement with Islam. In essence, my own encounter with Islam has been a formative path of discipleship where the serious engagement with the other has pushed me back to a reinvigorated encounter with my own faith.

So while this book gathers together material from PhD research, it is interspersed with 'Anecdotes from the field' in this spirit of bringing the theological in conversation with the rooted and the practical. I find myself in the position of being someone who enjoys the philosophical abstractions, wants to ask 'the big questions', but the passion to do so comes from encounters and conversations, and from a wish to model reflective practice as a parish priest in Birmingham. This book should be read, then, as a theological resource, where the 'anecdotes' offer illustrations of what the theological trajectories may look like in practice.

Though the earliest recorded legal reference to British Muslim presence was in 1764, when it was decided that a Muslim could swear his oath on the Qur'an, settled communities only began to be established from the end of the nineteenth century.[3] From being small communities in British ports, Muslim presence began to grow in scale with the economic immigration from the Indian subcontinent to industrial towns and cities after the Second World War.[4] By the 2011 national census, there were up to 2.7 million Muslims in England and Wales, representing about 4.8 per cent of its total population.[5] This book is concerned to explore the Church of England's account of Islam and how it configures space for Islam in the public realm. With the growing reality of religious diversity, what historical, theological resources enable the Church of England to move from the unitary church–state model to an engagement with Islam as a religious other?

I will propose that an *ecclesial turn* has taken place in contemporary Anglican reflections on Islam that seeks to root relations with Islam in the prior identity of the Church as a participatory community within the life of the trinity. This turn draws from historical and ecumenical resources of Christian–Muslim encounter. The motif of hospitality will be seen to be a key theme for this ecclesial turn, which has echoes within the wider Church. The work of Kenneth Cragg and Rowan Williams are vital influences on this ecclesial turn, which seems to eschew the novel schema of theologies of religions that were entertained in Anglican documents during the 1980s and 1990s. Instead, a *retrieval* of traditions will be seen to have shaped the contemporary understanding of relations with Islam. This retrieval amounts to a consolidation of traditional Anglican themes, reinterpreted for the contemporary reality of religious diversity, exemplified in Cragg's adaptation of the kenosis theology of the *Lux Mundi* school. This retrieval is also a widening of the canon in the recovery of other Christian traditions. Thus, Williams retrieves the contemplative tradition of the Desert Fathers and the Eastern Orthodox sensibilities of the Russian émigré movement in his account of Islam. Both theologians, representative of the Anglican ecclesial turn in interfaith relations, will be seen to situate themselves within the retrieval and renewal of sources exemplified by the Catholic Church in Vatican II, which was vital to its own reappraisal of other faiths. The ecumenical vista of the ecclesial turn will be confirmed by the extent to which reflections on Islam from the wider Anglican Communion have shaped Christian–Muslim relations too.

The logic of my analysis then builds on studies of formative early Christian–Muslim encounters, and the broader Christian tradition, where Catholic encounters with Islam particularly post-Vatican II offer a model for Anglican engagement. I will then assess the history of Anglican Christian–Muslim encounters, focusing especially on three Lambeth Conferences – 1988, 1998 and 2008 – to suggest the ecclesial turn that draws from the pattern of Vatican II. It will be apparent that the works of Kenneth Cragg and Rowan Williams contribute significantly to contemporary accounts of Anglican Christian–Muslim encounter, and I will conclude by focusing on the resources they offer for relations in the public square.

The Church of England and 'Anglicanism'

The Church of England's self-identifying sense of continuity with the pre-Reformation Church in England and its evident interweaving of ecclesial and national identities are exemplified in the ongoing relevance of pre-Reformation canon law to the state and the Church.[6] The Church of England has never seen itself beginning *ab initio* in 1534. The original reformers were not 'anti-Catholic', they 'merely wished to renew the one Church in Christ by removing abuses … and to return to the faith and practice of what they described as the "primitive" church'.[7] Anglican theologies of Christian–Muslim encounter, then, cannot reckon without the confluence of Catholic tradition in its midst. Thus, the earliest historical encounters between Christians and Muslims and the broader Catholic and ecumenical experience all inform the specific theologies that will be assessed in this study.

It must be acknowledged that the challenges of diversity are especially creative for the exploration of an ecclesial tradition's theology. As Paul Avis says, 'Self-conscious identity has not been required where Anglicanism has been the norm.'[8] Whether we are talking of the Catholic Church's appraisal of ecumenical and global realities at Vatican II, or the Anglican Communion's struggles with its own internal diversity, intentional ecclesiology seems to proceed from the challenge of *difference*:

> Ecclesiology, one might suggest, is a response to need – where there was little major division and few international problems there was little need for reflection on the nature of the worldwide church.[9]

It may be added, as Avis asserts, that 'Anglicanism' as a subject for ecclesiological discussion has only recently deepened in intensity: 'when national ties had been weakened, pluralism of religious expression was becoming acute, and the social and political aspects of religious belief and practice were beginning to grip the attention of theologians'.[10] It must be acknowledged, then, that this effort to assess the Church of England's relations with Islam in the public square occurs at a time when the Anglican Communion's internal bonds are strained and when fundamental questions about the nature and vocation of Anglicanism are being asked.

Grace Davie has summed up something of the ambiguities of the Church of England in the twenty-first century as being situated in a context of 'persistent paradox'. While a process of secularization continues unabated, jeopardizing the sustainable future of the Church of England,[11] the profile of religion in public life has risen inexorably.[12] So what Muslims and Christians do and say receives attention, and matters, but the actual influence on wider societal structures of religious groups is likely to be weaker than it has ever been. Significantly, too, the embeddedness of cultural and political commentators in religious traditions is rarer than in previous ages and the corresponding religious literacy harder to come by. The paradoxical state of religion in British public life makes for genuine complexity in assessing Christian–Muslim relations. Even a cursory assessment of some of the contours for Islam's understanding of politics as I will suggest would encourage us to eschew simplistic and reductive conclusions. It is apparent that there are many different perspectives within Islam, and Christian theologies of engagement must therefore be able to reckon with a diverse Islam.

The irony of the parallel process of secularization and growing public profile of religion is that the Church of England has increasingly to see itself as pushed to the edge of society alongside a British Muslim community that is itself marginalized by colonial history and Islamophobia. The shifting power relations affecting the Church of England will become more apparent when we look at the historic nature of Christian–Muslim encounters. Threaded through this book, though, is a recognition that the controversies stirred by Williams' Shari'a law speech unearthed a need to reflect on how the encounter with Islam probes both a Christian's understanding of the 'other' that is the Muslim, and the 'other' that is the realm of the political.

Islam and the political

For the purposes of this book's analysis of theologies of the public square, I am taking a broad understanding of what is termed 'political theology',[13] utilizing the definition of Peter Scott and William T. Cavanaugh in their introduction to *The Blackwell Companion to Political Theology* as an 'analysis and criticism of political arrangements ... from the perspective of differing interpretations of God's way with the world'.[14] Thus, from the theologies of Christian–Muslim relations and an articulation of 'God's way with the world' through the interreligious encounter, what political arrangements might then follow? What space within the body politic does the Church of England envisage for Islam?

The vigour of British Islam has prompted contemporary questions of the Church of England and wider society that make this question of particular note. As Mona Siddiqui has said, 'for many people the debate about religion and society is essentially a debate about Islam and society'.[15] Muslims have witnessed their transition from being migrants to being citizens[16] and gradually developed sophisticated tools and forums for interacting with the British political system as religious communities.[17] This presence, though, has challenged deeply held assumptions about the nature of religion in public life, raising issues for the Church of England as an established Church.

For many commentators, reaction to the publication of *The Satanic Verses* in 1989 epitomized the hitherto hidden difficulties that British society had in accommodating Islam.[18] On the one hand, as Kylie Baxter has argued, 'the Rushdie affair spoke intensely of a Muslim sense of identity and place in British society'.[19] British Muslims were asserting their freedom to be at home in a country where their religion should not be blasphemed by portrayals of Muhammad in a novel. On the other hand, the burning of books and the fatwa issued on the author, Salman Rushdie, scandalized a liberal society that assumed the rights of freedom of expression. That the private realm of religious devotion might have public import seemed to be the great shock of the Rushdie affair. The Church of England was no mere bystander to this debate, at that time benefitting from the privilege of a blasphemy law that could theoretically have protected it from similar literary defamations of Jesus. The Church was caught between a Muslim community that was calling for an 'equalizing upwards'[20] and a secularizing agenda that would revoke all such privileges such that there would be a legal and political system that was religiously neutral.[21] Is the

Church of England a partner with Islam in protecting the ideal of religion in British public life? Are the freedoms of speech and religious liberty so tied into the Anglican, ecclesial influence on the state that Islamic protestations to the state are alien intrusions potentially dangerous to British culture? Or is the role of the Church of England to help steer, as gatekeeper to the religious impulse, a tolerant diversity accommodating secularist and religious sensibilities? These are among the questions brought to the fore by the Rushdie affair.

This book will not include an examination of the arguments for and against the establishment of the Church of England.[22] Rather, taking the present reality of a vestigial establishment, Christian–Muslim relations are set in the context of the Church of England's role in Britain's public life. As Julian Rivers argues in his *The Law of Organized Religions*, 'In spite of increasing levels of religious diversity, this book could almost have been called "the law of church and state".'[23] The residual marks of Anglican establishment on the state's understanding of religion are woven through the British political and legal system. Thus, there is no definitive pristine establishment *or* disestablishment; rather, there is a continuum from the Elizabethan Settlement that equated citizenship with Anglicanism, to a wholly secularized polity where all faiths are privatized with a neutral legal and public square. The contemporary Church of England operates along this continuum.

'Secularism' can be a process that fosters the distinction between the private and public spheres, matters of religion discretely kept within the community of faith: 'secularism-as-separation'. It can also be 'secularism-as-indifference' where the state operates with a single body of law that makes no allowances for religion. Religion here effectively operates 'in the gaps', giving way to the priority of a purportedly neutral state.[24] The reality for Britain is that it inherits a history with Christian, and indeed Anglican, fingerprints evident throughout, and subject to the pressures of both secularism-as-separation and secularism-as-indifference. The Anglican 'fingerprints' are evident in such public structures as the independent canon law of the Church of England, the legal duties of clergy as clerks in holy orders, the existence of church schools and chaplain-cies, or the presence of bishops in the House of Lords. In all these structures and more, the Church of England has modelled a way of being 'religious' in public. As Sophie Gilliat-Ray has noted, non-Christian religions have followed the pattern of the Church of England in integrating their faith into British public life.[25] Muslims have mirrored the example of the Church of England in the setting up of Muslim schools, for example, or prison chaplaincies under-lying the importance of the Church of England to other faiths, even as a 'broker' of the expansion of other religions.[26]

Seeing that Britain exists in this in-between of establishment and secularism, there is a more pragmatic question facing the Church of England about how it conceives of the public presence of Islam. The possibilities of partnership or exclusion depend on the prior Christian understanding of what Islam is in relation to the Church. Since the Rushdie affair, there have been a number of other notable landmarks that have made the image of comfortable coexistence seem overly optimistic. The Islamist – inspired atro-cities of 9/11 and 7/7 have raised the profile of Islam's own potential to exist with plurality: to make space for their own 'other'. As Philip Lewis contends, there is a 'frank supercessionism written into Islam' that inhibits curiosity of the 'otherness of the other', and especially Christianity.[27] The 'resurgence of religion' that Mona Siddiqui hinted at as a largely Islamic theme is energized by its self-understanding as a wholly political religion: Islam offers a total system for living that unites legal government with religious direction.

The unity of religion and state, the *dīn wa-dawlah*, of Islamic aspiration is traditionally crystallized in the Medinan polity of Muhammad's success. Thus, minority status and plurality, in this economy, are incomplete stages towards the full realization of Islamic power. For the purposes of this study, I will be concentrating on, for the most part, the political implications to Christian–Muslim relations of the Sunni Islamic tradition from which the Medinan polity obtains as archetype, and not Shi'ism.[28] Internally, Islam is engaging with vigorous reappraisals of how this may translate into the diversity of Western democracies. Tim Winter's explorations of British Muslim identity encourage a creative retrieval of historic strands of Islam conducive to an embedded identification with a dominant culture.[29] Abdullahi An-Na'im proposed a reformation of the Shari'a so as to present an Islamic basis for universal human rights.[30] Farid Esack responds to the question of authorization in Islam by using the Qur'an as a manifesto for a preferential option for the poor and the oppressed much as Christian liberation theologians began to do in the interaction with Marxism in the 1960s.[31] Tariq Ramadan has famously sought a reconfiguration of the dichotomies of *dār-al-Islām* and *dār-al-harb*. For him, the pre-Medinan sense of Islam being a minority community as *dār-al-da'wa*, abode of invitation or mission, is much more pertinent to modern self-identity and peaceful coexistence.[32] We shall see later in this study how Kenneth Cragg has also sought to highlight the importance of a Medinan sensibility within Islam, a trajectory of political dominance that needs to reckon with contemporary realities of religious diversity and democratic government. For the Sudanese leader of the 'Republican Brothers' and religious thinker Mohamed Taha (1909–85) (and mentor of An-Na'im), Medina was a historical concession rather than an ongoing political aspiration for Muslims.[33] The Mecca to Medina shift of Islamic political identity that Cragg identifies as so crucial to the politico-theological question is thus a substantive debate among Muslims.[34]

Even *within* Islamist groups, there are efforts at revisionism such that *dhimmitude* is superseded by citizenship as the most appropriate framework within which to view cooperative life with non-Muslims in an Islamic state.[35] The project 'Critical Muslim', fostering open and diverse debate on 'the great debates of our times', would suggest that the largely stillborn 'Arab Spring' represents the spilling over of the crisis of this internal debate within Islam.[36]

The realities of those strands of Islam prohibitive of coexistence alongside the creativity of reforming tendencies means that the Church of England's understanding of Islam must reckon with its diversity. Any consequent political theology must be able to engage

10

publicly with Islam as a potential agent or obstacle of shared citizenship while being conscious that Islam represents just one among many other faiths that must be engaged with. It will be apparent from this study that a widening of the canon to the breadth of encounters with Islam historically and globally gives the Church of England this empirical experience of diversity. Underlying the proposal of the ecclesial turn is a proposal that the Christian–Muslim endeavour is a necessarily ecumenical task. Thus, a preliminary exploration of Christian–Muslim relations will involve an analysis of resources available to the Church of England in the wider Christian tradition, as well as that of the Anglican Communion.

Anecdotes from the field: 'Trojan Horse'

In the spring of 2014, an anonymous letter was received by a number of media outlets that seemed to suggest a conspiracy by Islamist groups in Birmingham to infiltrate schools with a conservative, *Salafi*-inspired agenda. Subsequent reports and allegations emerged of takeovers of school governing bodies by Islamists, bullying of head teachers, gender separation, suppression of music and the visual arts, and favouritism for staff sympathetic to more conservative Muslim values. Following a number of local and national investigations, the original Trojan Horse letter is deemed to be a fake but a number of the concerns seem to have been warranted, such that specific governors and governing bodies have been sacked and stricter regulations for the deployment and training of governors instituted. Here in Sparkbrook, as chair of governors of a church school where the majority of our children are Muslim, the controversy has not been without impact. The drip-drip of negative coverage of inner-city communities with significant British Muslim presence has undermined confidence that Muslims can and should engage in their community and made it difficult to attract good candidates from elsewhere to work professionally in Sparkbrook. In addressing the wrongs in some Birmingham schools that the Trojan Horse letter evoked, the government conflated conservative religion with extremism and terrorism. Michael Gove, as then Education Secretary, appointed Peter Clarke, the ex-head of Counter Terrorism Command, to lead the Department of Education's investigation. Subsequent government policy has mirrored this tendency by shifting the activities of community cohesion from the Department of Communities and Local Government to the Home Office. The practical implication in our local primary school is that a concern over a child's comment, say, about the role of women or the status of homosexuality is likely to produce an alert that requires follow-up under the auspices of extremism and anti-terrorism concerns.

The investigations found no evidence of a link between the Islamist factions in certain of the schools and terrorism, yet the government policy veered in a direction that raised the spectre of extremist violence being fostered in state schools with significant Muslim populations. Arguably, the episode illustrates something of the religious illiteracy prevalent in public life. There were evidently problems in a number of schools, and conspiracies hatched out of a desire to improve inner-city schools that had often failed local pupils. In a climate where 'choice' has become the shibboleth proffered to parents by successive governments, many local Muslims were doing what they thought was best for their children's improved outcomes. The issues that had not been addressed and are only beginning to be articulated now the Trojan Horse circus has left town are what space is given to parental sensitivities over such topics as sex education, dress-code and music.

The complexities I have summarily outlined over Islamic approaches to the political mean that essentialist approaches need to be rejected. There *were* problems in some of the schools. These problems were generally not of an extremist nature but rather concerned the appropriateness of certain conservative religious values in British schools. Islam in Britain is neither a huge source of danger and repression nor a pristine model of spiritual life entirely committed to the common good. That this should be the case should not surprise us Christians, as neither are we. However, essentialist approaches in the media and in government policy have tended to engage with Islam in binary terms: if it is not benign then it is oppositional; if it is not peaceable then it is violent.[37] It means that more difficult conversations in education policy are required that can withstand pressures by some conservative religionists, and this is where all religious communities are implicated, without having to label these pressures as extremist or terrorist.

The complexities and diversities that Christians responding to Islam need to take seriously become not just a hedge against untruthful labelling and prejudice but a protection for those Muslims who are as equally exercised by the reactionary approaches of some in their own community. In the next chapter, we shall be exploring some of the historic resources for Christian–Muslim encounter, especially as they help reinforce such nuance.

PART 1

CONTEXTS AND BACKGROUNDS

1

What do Christians Say Islam is? Formative Christian–Muslim Encounters

Having outlined some of the context for religion and public life and the particular challenges posed to the public square by Islam, there remains the Church's fundamental task of identifying and locating the essence of Islam. As Jacques Waardenburg has said, 'The first issue is simply that of identity: who are the Christians and the Muslims about whose relations we speak?'[38] Because the originating story of Islam draws from the Christian narrative, it suggests that a historical perspective to this quest is necessary.[39] If, as Sydney Griffith believes, Islam is a 'template and foil'[40] of Christian and Jewish religions, the earliest encounters between the respective faiths should contribute significantly to this question of identity.

James Sweetman notes some of the common worship practices of Christians and Jews in seventh-century Arabia, exhibiting a rich pattern of public faith recognizable among the nascent community forming itself around Muhammad.[41] The perception that the original form of Islam was deeply shaped by the Christian and especially Jewish faiths has been more recently underlined by Gerald Hawting.[42] It is perhaps not surprising then that one of the earliest Christian assessments, by John of Damascus (645–753 CE) in his *De Haeresibus*, attributes Islam as a Christian heresy. John of Damascus views Islam entirely through the lens of the Christian faith;[43] as a distortion of the Christian tradition. The trajectory of revelation, initiated by God towards humanity in Scripture and through his servants the prophets, marks shared features of familial resemblance. The corresponding responsibility of humanity to a creator God, in humanity's role as viceregent or steward, under the shadow of a final judgement, likewise posits Christianity and Islam as decisively missionary and global faiths, albeit with differently conceived 'missions'.

John of Damascus provides us with an ambiguous admission of that family resemblance in his labelling of Muslims as 'Ishmaelites' and 'Hagarites',[44] nomenclature that evokes a common heritage traced back to Abraham but also the derogation represented by Islam's perceived waywardness. Ishmael is the son of promise but the fruit of Abraham's unfaithful grasping; Hagar, the second-best bearer of covenant future. Whether one acknowledges 'Hagarite' as a Christian insult to Islam or self-styled indebtedness to Abrahamic roots, as Patricia Crone and Michael Cook have suggested, the title suggests something of what Kenneth Cragg terms the 'de-ethnicizing' nature of Islam.[45] The followers of Islam are monotheists in the tradition and pattern of Hagar whose legacy runs as counterpoint to the aspiration of the ethnic nation in Judaism. Hers is a privilege that is not constrained by a territorial inheritance nor identified with a specific chosen people. Hagar, who was decidedly 'not chosen', did not bear the risk of a God invested in the prospects of a nation. Here one can see already an understanding of God that works to split divine providence from the vagaries of the human community. Therefore, at the origins of Islam there is the universalizing potential without the apparent 'divine fellow-feeling' of election intrinsic to the biblical tradition.[46]

However, it would be misleading to regard Islam as fully formed entirely in response to the Christian and Jewish faiths at the time of Muhammad. As Wensinck points out, it was over three centuries later that a coherent system of Islamic theology and jurisprudence became apparent.[47] But if Islam was developing as a religion in contradistinction to Judaism and Christianity in this intervening period, the resonance of so many of the theological disputes to today is remarkable. The celebrated exchange between Caliph Mahdi and Timothy I, Patriarch of the Church of the East (728–

823), results in a Muslim accusation that the Christian worships three gods and the innuendo that God had sexual intercourse with Mary. The mockery in the Caliph's questioning of the Christian belief in the crucifixion of Jesus seems to point to a persistent thread that delineates the frontiers between Christian and Muslim theology to this day.[48] In the Caliph's rejection of the plausibility of Timothy's faith is both an affirmation of that which is distinctive to Islam and a refusal to accept the Christian's own self-understanding. The doctrine of God's unity, *tawhīd*, prioritizes the victory and potency of God over any notion of suffering and vulnerability. In this economy, the Jesus that is prophet can never be Christ crucified. The Christian sees God's unity in the self-giving love of the cross, however, and the incarnation as the creator's generous and supernatural identification with his creation. For Muslims, these are beliefs that are refused by distortion.

Much as John of Damascus' writings helped provide a Greek apologetic for Christians encountering Islam, Theodore bar Koni in his *Scholion* (*c.*792) was at pains to affirm the reasonableness of the Christian faith for Syriac-speaking Christians in the eighth century.[49] It is evident from this work that Christology, the Scriptures and the crucifixion, with the all-pervading doctrine of the trinity, were vital themes needing to be explained and justified to Muslims. Michael Ipgrave believes that both Arabic and Greek Christians were forced to reflect on the *hypostases* of God in Christ the Word among their burgeoning Muslim neighbours in this period as central to the philosophical challenge presented by Muslims.[50] Thus, even at this earliest stage, Islam's acceptance of God's immutability rejects the Christian inflection on this doctrine; an inflection that allows for an outpouring without which God remains 'sterile in His inaccessible height'.[51]

The first known Christian composition in Arabic *On the Triune Nature of God* (*c.* 755) affirms boldly 'that God and his Word and his Spirit are one God'[52] as a clear rebuff to Q 4:171 with its accusation that Christians worship more than one God. This repeated recourse to the Christian orthodoxy of the trinity required the prior dismantling of misperception (idolatry) and highlights the significance of respective understandings of Scriptures. The New Testament account of Jesus' death and resurrection, his embodiment of the fullness, as *logos*, of the creator God, let alone the Hebrew Scriptures' covenant between YHWH and the Jewish people, are necessarily redundant to Islam. As Jacques Jomier observes, 'For Muslims, Islam is not simply God's final revelation but also God's first.'[53] The implications are that Islam does not merely supersede the Christian revelation but negates it *ab initio*:

> What Jews and Christians now recognise as their scriptures do not coincide with the Qur'an, God's full and final revelation. Since God's word does not change, this lack of consonance must result from more or less intentional alteration or corruption of the text.[54]

In drawing from tradition to present itself as the original revelation, there is then, in turn, an abrogation of that tradition.

The inference in Islam that Christian and Jewish Scriptures are corrupted is reflected on by Peter the Venerable (1094–1156) and dismissed summarily as 'a tradition without any foundation, and without proof, the author of which is unknown'.[55] The essential dilemma is that the 'inference' that has produced this tradition rests with Muhammad and the qur'anic account of the Christian's story.

Anthony O'Mahony proposes that there is a formative 'objectively deficient understanding' of the Christian faith by Islam and wonders whether that understanding can be rehabilitated within contemporary Muslim–Christian dialogue.[56] There has been a tendency to blame that formative distortion on the confusion and sectarianism of the Eastern Churches in the seventh century.[57] Sidney H. Griffith's work, however, suggests a richer and more creative responsiveness to the challenges of Islam in the seventh century that retains the elevated Christology and trinitarian hue. For Christian apologists writing in Arabic, the inevitable consequence of the Islamic negation of the Bible as authoritative was an appropriation of Islamic idiom and even referencing of the Qur'an as support for the reasonableness of the Christian faith. The *Summary of the Ways of Faith in the Trinity of the Unity of God, and in the Incarnation of God the Word from the Pure Virgin Mary*[58] reveals Christians utilizing the first phrase of the *shahadah* in the confession of their faith and the existence of 'secret Christians' whose Christology sets them apart from their Muslim counterparts. Even where Christian theological language accommodates to Islamic frameworks, the author continues to assert the doctrine of the trinity, believing that 'once Christians have given way on this issue, the distinctiveness of their faith is eclipsed.'[59] This picture of Christian contextualization, as opposed to syncretism, is reinforced by the Eastern, Arabic Christian theology of Theodore Abu Qurrah (*c*.755– *c*.830), who defends the practice of the veneration of icons from the accusation of idolatry by Muslims. The context was plainly one where Christians were accommodating their Christian worship to the external pressures of the Muslim community. Abu Qurrah provides a Christian theological justification in Arabic that is responsive to the questions raised by Islamic misunderstanding. In that sense, then, we have 'the beginnings of Christian theology in Arabic.'[60]

The Arabic Christian milieu in the early Islamic period also witnessed the development of an apologetic in the idioms of Islamic discourse. For example, the doctrines of the trinity and the incarnation were defended in terms of the Qur'an's beautiful names for God.[61] Almost without exception, though, the doctrines of the trinity and the incarnation were seen as vital beliefs to be conveyed as reasonable and in a language that was accessible to Islamic sensibility.[62] This echoes the Greek Christian sentiments of John of Damascus for whom 'the Muslim idea which separates from God that which is essential to His being and life, namely Word and Spirit, is a mutilation of God.'[63]

A popular Christian apologetic of the time, *Kitab al-masa'il wa l-ajwibah* (the 'Book of Questions and Answers'), by Ammar al-Basri (*c*.850), deploys the idioms of Islamic texts and defers respectfully to the Muslim Caliph's role in support of true religion.[64] In laying this groundwork of cultural and political sensitivity, the question and answer format is used to commend the Christian faith's inner coherence and logic at the expense of Islam. Contemporary Anglican articulations of the trinity as a basis for relations with Islam, configured contextually to Islamic interlocutors, will be seen to characterize two major lectures by Rowan Williams and be indicative of the ecclesial turn I propose, consistent with a wider canon of tradition.[65]

One of the earliest known Christian texts on Islam emphasizes the violent and sensual nature of Islam, distinguishing it from the true religion of the Christian faith, and thus providing a foretaste of later assessments.[66] An unholy trinity of 'bloodshed, Antichrist, the sensual nature of paradise'[67] serves to underline the essential otherness of Islam and to prefigure the apocalyptic framing from which the subsequent surrender of Jerusalem in 637 was viewed.

The Christian–Muslim exchange between Timothy I and Caliph al-Mahdi reveals further insights into the nature of theological debate between Christians and Muslims in the formative years of Islam. This became an 'apologetic catechism'[68] for the Syriac-speaking Christians living among Muslims but was translated and became a resource for Arabophone Christians too. As with the pattern of so many of the apologetic works of the time, there is a question and answer challenge to the Christian from the Muslim. Central to this encounter is the vital role of Muhammad as prophet: 'How is it that you accept Christ and the Gospel from the testimony of the Torah and of the prophets, and you do not accept Muhammad from the testimony of Christ and the Gospel?'[69] The flip side of a defence of the trinity and the incarnation would seem to be the refusal of Muhammad's prophethood, bearing as it does a message that denies Jesus' divinity, death and resurrection.

Timothy's reply consolidates the prophetic vocation of Jesus in sacred Scripture, this revelation amounting to a 'mirror'[70] of God, contrasting Muhammad, as being 'from the earth', with the Holy Spirit, who comes from God. Timothy even quotes the Qur'an in invoking the limitations of Muhammad, exhibiting a sophisticated contextual engagement that affirms the doctrine of the trinity. Throughout the discourse, the repeated basis for authority is sacred

Scripture, with counter-challenges proffered by Muslims to argue for the corruption of the Bible. The natural progression of the debate leads to the definitive challenge from the Caliph, 'What do you say about Muhammad?'[71] The sophistry of Timothy's reply – 'Muhammad is worthy of all praise, by all reasonable people, O my Sovereign. He walked in the path of the prophets, and trod in the track of the lovers of God'[72] – betrays the balance of the power equation in the conversation and 'more than a hint of political compromise'.[73] The delicacy with which Timothy felt obliged to deal with the question of Muhammad likewise sets a recurring pattern through history, arguably epitomized in the omission of any assessment of Muhammad from Vatican II's treatment of Islam within *Nostra aetate*.[74]

The rapid military expansion of Islam in its formative years created reverberations that were to begin a process of setting Christian and Muslim states in opposition to each other.[75] It is interesting to note Agapus writing of the fall of Damascus to Muslims in the reign of the Byzantine Emperor Heraclius (*c*.575–641):

When Heraclius saw the routing of the Greeks and news reached him at Antioch of what the Arabs had done to the Persians, he was seized with wrath and indignation and was utterly discouraged. He wrote to Egypt, Syria, Mesopotamia and Armenia, ordering them not to fight with the Arabs any longer and no more to oppose the will of God.[76]

The casting of Muslims as instruments of God in judgement against the Church would be a motif that recurs in later centuries when Christian Europe is conscious of its borders besieged by Islam.[77] It led Louis Massignon in the twentieth century to characterize Muhammad as a 'prophèt negatif': the vehicle of God in calling out the errors and omissions of the Church.[78]

Perhaps understandably, the heightening polarization between the Christian and Islamic empires served to deepen the insecurity of the Eastern Church for which Arabic was becoming the lingua franca. As the Christian–Muslim interface increasingly took on a political hue, the minority Eastern Church in formerly Christian lands became largely detached from the wider Church family. As Kenneth Cragg notes, the cultural Islamization that resulted, supremely realized in the medium of Arabic, led to the Eastern Church being 'bound over to a language that is bound over to Islam'.[79] In Sweetman's view, there was a gradual weakening of the theological resilience of the Eastern Church in the eleventh and twelfth centuries, occasioned by the simultaneous Islamic cultural dominance and detachment from and by the Latin Church and Byzantine Churches.[80] The effective annexation of the Eastern Church was welcomed and encouraged by Muslim rulers, who would view a Christian religion that felt bound to Byzantium and Rome as outpost of a rival state.[81]

Yohanan Friedmann describes the complex of juristic approaches to the various non-Muslim minorities; Eastern Christians becoming a marginal and vulnerable group within Islamic hegemony. Christians and Jews were generally treated less harshly than polytheists but if someone had converted from Islam then the protection of *dhimmitude* could be negated, for example. Additionally, the special regard given to Arabia as home of the prophet Muhammad tended towards the expulsion of all non-Muslims from cities such as Mecca and Medina.[82] Friedmann's conclusion from the array of Hadith and juristic discussions is that 'frequently the impression [is] that the humiliation of the unbeliever is more important than his conversion'.[83] The emphasis seemed to be on heightening the disparity between the superior Islamic faith in the realm of daily, practical and public acts rather than in religious persuasion. The public debasement of non-Muslims was manifest in regulations that stipulated the superior height of Muslim dwellings and riding postures as much as it reinforced the priority of Muslims in positions of actual governance.

Uncompromising attitudes to those who converted from Islam, reflected in the common Shari'a injunction to execute the apostate,[84] and the daily humiliation of qualified Christian citizenship[85] under Islamic rule combined to undermine the resilience of the Eastern

Church in the Middle East and to hasten its introversion. Within Arabia, the Islamic predominance that permitted the pursuit of a sacred vocation to rid the region of idolatry was, according to Friedmann, also motivated by the aspiration of religious uniformity.[86] Being the final revelation complete with a text and a law, Islam within its formative territories had no need of the 'other'. Interestingly, as Islam expanded, the juristic debate would witness inevitable questions about the status of non-Muslims in non-Muslim lands; cities with mixed governance or what were termed 'frontier' towns. Here, the Islamic discourse is far more pragmatic and allows for the expedience of shared citizenship where Islam is held to be faithfully observed and in the interests of the expansion of the faith.[87] What is clear, though, is that Islam is regarded as a total system that would, and should, inexorably supersede other systems of religion and law. The ferocity reserved for apostates, epitomized in Ibn Taymiyya's dictum that 'the apostate is more crude in his infidelity than an original unbeliever',[88] reflects a theological trajectory that presumes that the lived experience of Islam, both personally and geographically, demands obeisance.

There was thus a religious and a political momentum pushing the Eastern Church in the Middle East to the margins. As the Christian and Islamic communities hardened into respective territorial empires, Islam 'was destined to be a geographic as well as a spiritual "other", for Christendom could hardly find room for so potent an adversary in its midst'.[89] The widening distance between the two faiths fuelled the growth of apocalypse and legend as literary responses to the actual and perceived threat of Islam that was engendered by the totemic fall of Jerusalem. Pope Urban II's announcement in 1095 of the First Crusade to free the Holy Land from Muslim rule, liberating Eastern Christians and protecting pilgrim routes, thus brought into sharp relief an already burgeoning mutual hostility. As Jules Michelet notes:

For a long time Europe and Asia, the Christian and the Muslim religions, two sisters, two halves of humanity, had lost sight of each other. With the Crusades they found themselves face to face once more. Their first glance at each other was one of horror.[90]

For some of the Christians living under Muslim rule, the harsh realities of *dhimmī* status[91] were coupled with the inevitably isolating effects of the mistrust often felt by the Crusaders to their fellow Christians. Youssef Courbage and Philippe Fargues quote one Crusader's sentiments thus: 'We expelled the Turks and the pagans, but we could not expel the heretics, Greeks and Armenians, Syrians and Jacobites.'[92] The Eastern Church therefore faced the dilemma of demonstrating loyalty to their Muslim authorities while exhibiting a religious affinity with a foreign invading force that was in turn theologically and culturally alien.[93]

It would be wrong to view the period of the Crusades as an essentially bipolar conflict between Christian and Islamic civilizations, however. Benjamin Kedar reveals a far more nuanced complex of relations that suggests evidence of pockets of communities of thriving Eastern Christians prior to the arrival of the Crusaders.[94] Some of these Eastern Christians were employed in subsequent Frankish administrations as Arabic-writing clerks,[95] and the Latin Church achieved a union with the Maronite Church in the twelfth century that exists to this day. Perhaps most significantly for the purposes of this study, though, Kedar notes the variety of experiences of Christian–Muslim encounter under Frankish rule that belies the caricature of consistent conflict. There is evidence of conversion to the Christian faith by Muslims[96] and even spying by Muslims against sultan Baybars on behalf of the Franks.[97] It seems that where Christian rule was obtained peacefully, there were precedents for the exercise of religious freedoms[98] and even comparative prosperity for some Muslims who had otherwise suffered from penal tax regimes under Muslim, Syrian rule.[99]

There is evidence that Muslims under Latin rule in Sicily were granted religious freedoms and a degree of prosperity.[100] This may have shaped the more constructive approach to coexistence by Tancred, a leading Norman Crusader from southern Italy,[101] in his treatment of Muslims in some regions of the Levant. The complexity under the apparent surface of hostility of the Crusades may also be relevant in considering the frequently lauded harmony of the Andalusian *convivencia*. Within the realities of nearly 300 years of peaceful shared citizenship of Christians and Jews under Muslim rule, are the stories of mutual mistrust and tension and the persistent efforts at erecting cordons sanitaires between the corrupting influences of the respective outsiders.[102] Indeed, before the Christian reconquest of Spain in 1492, '*convivencia* was already moribund' under the militant rule of Islamic Almorávides and Almohades tribes.[103] Conversely, if all Islamic governance in Andalusia was not tolerant, neither was all Christian rule repressive of religious diversity. Thus, the Christian reconquest of Toledo offered patterns of the *convivencia* found in the popularly celebrated Muslim rule of Cordoba.[104] It would seem that the Iberian peninsula's isolation from the rest of Europe inhibited the ability of Christendom Europe to reflect fully on the lessons of Christian–Muslim coexistence,[105] much as the Eastern Church's experiences also failed to be incorporated.

Set against the well-documented atrocities of the Frankish conquest of Jerusalem in 1099, we must recognize the positive patterns of Latin Christian encounter with Islam in order to move beyond what Sydney Griffith describes as the 'mutual invective and recrimination'[106] between Christians and Muslims that seems to have been set in this period. That much of the Latin Church's discourse on Islam became increasingly subject to caricature and ignorance,[107] however, and framed in political rather than theological terms, meant that the wealth of the Eastern Church's formative engagement with Islam was largely lost to the West.[108]

The history of Christian–Muslim relations through the lens of the Crusades is well documented and their impact on the contemporary scene will not be repeated in this study.[109] However, the patterns from the experiences of the Eastern Church in the preceding period under Islamic rule suggest some worthwhile inquiries for the Church of England's encounter with Islam today. These inquiries offer a resource for a contextual articulation of the trinity that permits a retrieval from history and a widening of the canon integral to this study of Anglican Christian–Muslim relations.

Conclusion

The earliest Christian judgements on Islam suggested that it was a Christian heresy, but very quickly the separate theological shape to Islam became apparent.[110] The theological discourse is remarkable for its resonance with ongoing interreligious controversies and in the study of the nature of God's revelation to humanity. The primary point of contention with Christianity for Muslims was the nature of the godhead. Much of the available evidence suggests a profound attention to the significance of the doctrine of the trinity in the earliest encounters with Islam, even while in positions of considerable vulnerability. The status of respective sacred texts, too, is vital to issues of authority in the course of debate, as is the prophethood of Muhammad. There is an evident process of theological enculturation of Christian theology, both in the Arabicization of language and in the cultural and religious adaptation of Christian doctrines and concepts to an Islamic audience.

As the gulf widened between Christian and Muslim empires and the Eastern Churches became increasingly isolated and marginalized, the coherence and resilience of this theological adaptation weakened. This marginalization was both the result of the hardened resolve of political Islam, especially in the heartlands of Arabia, and in the growing gulf between the Eastern Churches and Latin Christendom. While the Eastern Churches in the Middle East were pushed away from the Latin Church, they still exhibited a deep understanding of Muslim rule and religion. This knowledge was largely absent from a Latin Church that launched the project of the Crusades against an enemy it often chose to know through legend and hearsay rather from the encounters of shared citizenship in its midst or elsewhere in Christendom.

We will assess formal Anglican pronouncements on Islam later in this study but it would seem important to note here the wealth of the theological resources offered in the earliest Christian encounters with Islam. In the tragedy of the isolation of the Eastern Churches in this period is a challenge to the ecumenical commitment of the Church of England: the possibility that the familial spiritual ties of the worldwide Church can overcome barriers of culture, state and tradition in reciprocal theological resourcing.

Islam's own self-identity as *umma*, superseding all other human loyalties, suggests a particular need for Christians to be especially cognizant of learning from other places and traditions, supporting and encouraging fellow Christians struggling as communities under Islamic rule. This knowledge may equally highlight both the freedoms and protection afforded by Muslim rulers to Christians, and the negative experiences of disempowerment or persecution under Islam.

As Islamic communities grow in confidence, supported by settled institutions that affirm Islamic ideals (mosques, halal butchers, madrasas), is there an inevitable and inexorable process that pushes Muslims away from reliance on and mixing with non-Muslims? Reflecting on the theological trajectory towards religious uniformity in Islam that Friedmann notes, one wonders whether Bishop Michael Nazir-Ali's contemporary concerns about Muslim-dominated inner-city areas becoming 'no-go areas'[111] are prescient. As Khaled Abou El Fadl notes, 'Because of the historical experience of the Prophet in Medina, a degree of territorial insularity became an integral part of Islamic ideology.'[112] That question will not be answered by this study, though it remains a vital arena of research for Islamic political science, generating creative discussion.[113]

The challenge of this inquiry is to draw on resources that inform an appropriate political theology for the organization of relations with Muslims by the Church of England. Before the hardening into respective animosities of both *dhimmitude* and religious imperialism, the earliest Christian encounters with Islam suggest possibilities for a rich vein of interrelating. These formative encounters, neighbourly, scholarly and political, demonstrate a keen appreciation of the respective *differences* between the faiths alongside a determination to adapt culture and language to explain and defend the Christian faith. It is a sympathetic encounter of unity in difference located in the primary Christian distinctive of the Church's participation in the life of the trinity that will be seen to be indicative of the ecclesial turn of contemporary Anglican Christian–Muslim relations. This ecclesial turn both confirms and is resourced by the retrieval of these formative Christian–Muslim encounters, which widens the canon of Anglican theologies of interreligious encounter.

Anecdotes from the field: do we worship the same God?

I am often asked by Christians whether Muslims worship the same God as we do, and while this is a question that goes to the heart of doctrinal debates that may seem abstractly theological, it also plays out in very practical ways. In Britain, Muslims will often use the word 'God' in conversation with Christians, rather than 'Allah'. Certainly, British Muslims presume that Christians and Muslims are talking about the same God. We might want to remember that Christians and Muslims agree that there is only one God and so to imply that Muslims might be worshipping 'another God' would be problematic. In the Middle East, Arab Christians use the word 'Allah' and Arabic Bibles also use this term, which is merely a coalescing of 'the God' in Arabic.

However, what Christians understand of God has clear differences from the Islamic tradition. The trinitarian revelation that is vital to Christian understanding of who God is marks a departure for Muslims, for whom Jesus could not be associated with the divine. Kenneth Cragg uses a linguistic device to allow for this distinction by suggesting that predicates about God may differ but the subject of differing predicates remains the same.

The debate is not entirely restricted to Christians because successive, religiously conservative Malaysian governments have sought to ban the use of the word Allah by minority Christians.

In communities like Sparkbrook, encounters with Muslims throw up continual reminders of the resonances between the faiths that echo similarities and debates in the formative engagements. Beyond the surface, the differences also begin to become apparent. So, for example, in my role leading collective worship in a church school with many Muslims, when I talk about 'God', the Muslim children are making connections between the Bible stories and lessons that I share, and their own faith. At the same time, there are points of potential confusion and contradiction to which I need to be sensitive. When I talk of a 'Father God' the controversies and debates of early Christian–Muslim encounters are readily awakened: do I mean to suggest that God had intercourse with Mary and is a literal father of Jesus? The practical realities of encounter are charged with possibilities and resonance from shared stories but also fraught with the potential for misunderstanding because of some fundamental differences between the faiths.

What is clear, though, is that a definitive rejection of *any* confluence between Christian and Muslim understandings of the divine inhibits dialogue that can result in the mutually enriching spiritual and public life, and curtails an exchange of witness that can ground evangelism.

2

Catholic Encounters with Islam

The Catholic Church and Islam: inheriting the Western Christian tradition

Pre-Vatican II

With the hardening of Christian–Muslim encounters symbolized by *dhimmitude* and religious imperialism there is a very modern tendency to summarize the Catholic Church's formative tradition of encounter with Islam as alternately caricatured by acquisitive, Crusader violence or spiritual, Franciscan peacemaking.[114] When the actual complexity of Christian Crusader relations with Muslims is recognized, the genuine spiritualities interwoven in the Crusader enterprise are more readily apparent. As Jonathan Riley-Smith argues so persuasively, the aggressive violence of conquest occasioned by the Crusades was dependent on a political theology of holy war: of seeking the kingdom of God, as opposed to a definitive hatred of Muslims.[115] Without glossing a period that has overshadowed so much subsequent Christian–Muslim suspicion in the last two centuries,[116] there is evidently a need to recognize the Crusader world view, with all its Christian motivation, in order both to acknowledge the wrongs and understand the good. By doing this, we are perhaps better able to set the contribution of Francis of Assisi (1182–1226) in a more realistic perspective.

Francis offered peacemaking and a priority for the poor, a tradition that Scott M. Thomas believes is integral to Vatican II and the Catholic Church's engagement with the issues of the world today.[117] Though St Francis may be a palatable model for modern sensibilities, the mythology must not be allowed to obscure what Thomas sees as his belief that shared citizenship is based on a 'genuine encounter of "thick", not "thin", religious practices and traditions'.[118] Catholic movements of mission that rejected violence and coercion but nevertheless strove to provide an apologetic for the Christian faith and engaged with the challenges of Islam were providing an alternative to the enmity of territorial conquest. One such influential missionary movement focused on the religious community of Cluny. Pope Gregory VII (1030–85) had been a monk at Cluny and expressed his concern for the 'conversion of the Moors'.[119] This evangelistic objective managed to find expression within a papacy 'synonymous with medieval triumphalist, imperialist, and juridical ecclesiology'.[120] Yet even with this triumphalism and evident evangelistic zeal, he was moved to write to the Muslim King of Mauritania: 'we believe and confess one God' and 'He is our peace who has made us both one.'[121] Anastasius of Cluny (d. 1085) responded to a missionary vocation to Muslims by developing a practice of polemics, highlighting the love and freedom of the Christian faith over and against the compulsion and violence of Islam.[122] Hugh of Cluny (1049–1119) wrote of Islam as having satanic inspiration and that it had 'deceived the children of Ishmael'.[123] There was, then, the recognition of similarity and even familial resemblance but the clear sense of error in Islam that required Christian proclamation and correction.

Peter the Venerable (1092–1156) oversaw the first Latin translation of the Qur'an, which enabled, despite its inaccuracies and omissions,[124] a fuller acquaintance by Western Christians with the realities of Muslim belief. Parallel to the trajectories of hostility, then, there existed an impetus towards enquiry and curiosity about Islam. Peter the Venerable, with clear evangelistic intent, advocated for discussions and debate with Muslims rather than coercion.[125] Peter Abelard (1079–1142) was remarkable for engaging in rational apologetics with Muslims on the subjects of the incarnation and the trinity, 'disdaining to a great extent the appeal to authority to establish his argument'.[126] Avoiding authority as a trump card in debate, Abelard countered the resort to power that characterized much of Christian–Muslim relations during the Crusades but, like Raymond Lull (b. 1235), who used similar methods, he met with little success.[127]

There was thus a stream of evangelistic, irenic Latin Christian encounters with Islam that included theological apologetics, rational disputation and polemics. Nicholas of Cusa (1401–64) is a noteworthy example in this tradition. Nicholas was conscious of the failures of many of the Christian evangelists to Muslims and rather sought to build good relations by concentrating on the commonalities between the faiths. The Protestant pluralist John Hick is fond of quoting Nicholas of Cusa's dictum that 'there is only one religion in the variety of rites.'[128] His *De cribratione alchorani*, commissioned by Pope Pius II, asserted that the essential fissure between Christianity and Islam was a result of Muhammad's mistaken acceptance of a heretical Eastern Christology.[129] This is a charge that the famed polemicist Ricoldo of Montecroce, missionary to the Tartars of Baghdad in the late 1200s–early 1300s, similarly makes. This suggests that Nicholas of Cusa was far from being a proto-pluralist, as Hick would like to see him, but rather just genuinely concerned for peaceful shared citizenship in the manner of St Francis.[130] Justin Martyr (*c*.100–*c*.165), though, might be considered to frame a more pluralist conception of Islam through his Platonic understanding of the *logos*: 'Christ is the *logos* of whom the whole human race partakes, and those who live according to reason are Christians even though they were considered to be atheists.'[131]

The towering influence of Thomas Aquinas (1225–74) on Catholic theology and identity is especially notable for the purposes of this study for his pronouncements on Islam. Thomas's Aristotelian scholasticism affirms the rights of unbelievers within God's providence such that the common good is available to all within the 'law of grace'.[132] For Michael Fitzgerald and John Borelli, there is accordingly the suggestion that Aquinas regarded Islam as a 'natural religion': a primitive response to the general revelation of God in the world.[133] However, in his *Summa Contra Gentiles* (I,6,4),

Aquinas states that 'Muhammad forced others to become his followers by the violence of his arms' and 'no wise man, men trained in things divine and human, believed in [Muhammad] from the beginning. Those who believed in him were brutal men and desert wanderers.'[134] It is worth highlighting, then, that a coherent political theology that is able to accommodate religious diversity is by no means dependent on a sympathetic understanding of Islam. The moderately Hildebrandine assertion of civil subjection to ecclesial rule that Aquinas suggests in his advocacy of papal supremacy in the civil realm is another aspect of his political theology that would be far more contentious for contemporary plurality. What we have at the heart of Aquinas's theology, though, is the liberty afforded by the search for truth, such that 'truth was where one found it'.[135] Thus, Aquinas could fashion a coherent theology of ethics having interacted with the Aristotelian thoughts of Muslim and Jewish philosophers. This enables David Burrell to observe that 'the received doctrine of God in the West was already an intercultural, interfaith achievement',[136] even if Aquinas's defence against challenges posed by Islam eschews a more recognizably contemporary, interfaith treatment of Islamic religion per se.

The *Council of Florence* in 1442 formally affirmed the doctrine of *extra ecclesiam nulla salus* ('outside the church there is no salvation')[137] that had held sway since the fifth century, consolidating the supremacy of the Church in spiritual terms, even while those outside the Church may share temporal rights. Even with a church-centred perspective on Muslims, there was a growing discipline of inquiry into Islamic belief.[138] In the midst of the polemics of Crusade encounters, reasoned Christian discourse on the interaction with Islam was being developed. Though the Christian faith was still seen as superior, Muslims were being respected as deserving of rational and cogent apologetics.[139] There are mere suggestions of Catholic perspectives with a pluralist hue in Nicholas of Cusa and Justin Martyr, but the dominant tradition is exclusivist and evangelistic after the Crusades. Muslims still often fulfil a role as archetypes of violence and sensuality, a role played out mutually and with good grounds by both Muslims and

Christians,[140] but there is a burgeoning corpus of Christian literature engaging with the realities of Muslim belief. In the Christian literature on Islam, it is Muhammad who frequently becomes the object of scorn.

It must be noted that the intellectual traffic between the faiths, supremely exhibited by Thomas Aquinas in this period, has made a huge contribution to the civilization of Western Europe.[141] The Thomist political theology of the Catholic Church lays the foundations for unity in diversity, a principle that is key to Hooker's Anglican ecclesiology,[142] while being a reminder that such political theologies are not dependent on doctrinal sympathies with Islam. Indeed, the principles of Thomism that welcomed the grace in nature from within non-Christian religions have suggested to Jan Van Wiele that the Vatican II affirmation of an inclusivist theology of religions owes its origins to Aquinas.[143] This is perhaps a reminder of the danger of superimposing contemporary debates and schema on historic issues. The Council of Florence sought to unite the fragmented parts of the global Church, and thus the doctrine of *extra ecclesiam nulla salus* acts as a powerful incentive to catholicity. It may be argued, then, that it is not, nor was it intended to be, a definitive statement about the salvific worth of other religions. Thus, Aquinas's significance in offering a constructive theology of God's grace provides a foundational theological resource through the Council of Florence in continuity with Vatican II.

Post-Vatican II

Thus far, the Catholic Church's appraisal of Islam has been largely drawn from a period where the West was identified with the Christian faith. The dominance of the Church in European civilization was in contrast to the experience of Catholic missionaries in Asia from which theologies of religion began to draw inspiration. Jules Monchanin (1895–1957), Henri Le Saux (1910–73) and Bede

Griffiths (1906–93) were three Catholic missionaries to India who had indirect influence on the seminal Vatican II ecclesial documents.[144] Following the pattern of the Jesuit missionary to India, Roberto de Nobili (1577–1656), they immersed themselves in the local cultures and sought a thorough grounding in the religious traditions they encountered. Influenced in turn by the Catholic theologian Henri de Lubac and Catholic Orientalist scholar and then Melkite priest Louis Massignon, their engagement with other religions was characterized by an appreciation of the mystical aspect of faith: the encounter with God that was available to all in the freedom of the Holy Spirit. This did not detract from their missionary vocation or sense of orthodoxy,[145] though de Lubac's advice to Monchanin included the encouragement to risk the disapproval of church authorities in the process of making home for the gospel in an alien culture.[146]

The theology of these three Catholic missionaries reveals a subtle but significant shift towards an approach that 'involved finding Christ even more than preaching him'[147] and was to be characteristic of the sensibility of Vatican II. This was evident in the theology of Jean Daniélou, who elucidated a 'fulfilment theory' of religions, such that in the manifestations of other traditions, there were 'seeds of the Word',[148] or *semina Verbi*, for which Christ was the full realization. The appropriate posture of Christian engagement with Islam, then, would be searching for those 'seeds of grace or truth' in honest and sympathetic enquiry, ready to express and proclaim that which required the completion of gospel revelation. Henri de Lubac's Christian mysticism reaffirmed this trajectory, making a vital distinction between God's natural revelation in the religions and the salvific revelation in the Church.[149]

Within this outlook, Islam is cast as a human response to the divine, allowing for some spiritual and doctrinal convergence but only incompletely and not effectual in salvation. This resonates with Jacques Jomier's vision of Islam as a 'natural religion'. For Jomier, Islam is 'an attempt at reforming Judaism and Christianity'[150] in the face of human accretions to the fully complete revelation in Christ.

The fulfilment theory of religions and doctrine of 'seeds of the Word' are explicitly and implicitly adopted by Vatican II. In *Ad gentes* (1965) 9, there is the affirmation that:

> Whatever truth and grace are to be found among the nations, as a sort of secret presence of God, this activity frees from all taint of evil and restores to Christ its maker, who overthrows the devil's domain and wards off manifold malice of vice. And so, whatever good is found to be sown in the hearts and minds of men, or in the rites and cultures peculiar to various peoples, is not lost. More than that, it is healed, ennobled, and perfected for the glory of God, the shame of the demon, and the bliss of men. Thus, missionary activity tends towards the fulfilment which will come at the end of time.[151]

The 'secret presence of God'[152] that may be apparent within another faith breaks with the condemnation of other religions that was evident in so many earlier judgements. This development is mirrored in *Nostra aetate* (1965), in the assertion that 'other religions to be found everywhere strive variously to answer the restless searchings of the human heart.'[153] Remarkably, 'The Catholic Church rejects nothing which is true and holy in these religions.'[154] Jacques Dupuis recognizes elements of continuity in Vatican II pronouncements on other religions with the earlier doctrine of 'baptism of desire' in *The Council of Trent* of 1547.[155] This hinted at the possibility of salvation for individuals outside the Church that Vatican II demonstrably, and radically, affirmed for the first time. As Gavin D'Costa states, 'There is widespread consensus that Vatican II was silent about the theological status of these religions, neither denying nor affirming that they can be viewed as "salvific means".'[156]

In *Lumen gentium* (1964) 16, the discontinuity with earlier negative verdicts on Islam is explicit:

> But the plan of salvation also includes those who acknowledge the Creator. In the first place among these there are the Moslems,

who, professing to hold the faith of Abraham, along with us adore the one and merciful God, who on the last day will judge mankind.[157]

While acknowledging Vatican II as a 'paradigm shift' in Catholic assessments of other religions, Andrew Unsworth also perceives there to be some continuity with the pre-Vatican II position; a view supported in the earlier Thomist tradition by Van Wiele, as we have noted already. In Pius XII's *Fidei donum* (1957), for example, there is a reference to Muslims as those who 'profess' the worship of 'the one true God'.[158] The paradigm shift was actually the formalization of a responsibility towards Muslims that made interreligious dialogue an indispensable practice of the Catholic Church. Vatican II made consequent allowance for dialogue in the establishment of the Secretariat for Non-Christians in 1964[159] and the encyclical on dialogue, *Ecclesiam suam*, in the same year.

As Robert Caspar states, 'We [Catholics] cannot ever say again that we do not adore the same God, even if we call Him by different names.'[160] The inclusive cast of Vatican II theology seems to be incontrovertible, though there is sufficient ambiguity in the encyclicals and decrees to hold a range of interpretations of that inclusivism. Jacques Dupuis has sought to defend a theology of religions through the Conciliar documents that does not merely permit salvation for the non-Christian but allows for other religions being purposive of God in their own right. This blurs the distinction between the specific revelation given to the Church and the general revelation apparent in other religions that a traditional fulfilment theory affords.[161] Dupuis strains to reaffirm the unique role of Christ and the specific role of the Church but permits a measure of 'participated mediations'[162] of Christ in the prophets and Scriptures of other religions.[163] The contrary position notes the unequivocal coupling of dialogue with mission in Vatican II[164] and the admission that Vatican II 'has yet to be fully "received" by Catholics'.[165] For theologians such as Jacques Dupuis, a number of subsequent pronouncements suggest some 'unravelling' of the progress, as he sees it, towards a full sympathy with other religions.[166]

An appreciation of the paramount significance of ecclesial self-consciousness in a world of plurality seems vital to an understanding of Vatican II.[167] It would seem, then, that Dupuis is overinvesting the fulfilment theory with a weight beyond that which Vatican II can appropriately bear. The Church, as an outflow of the Holy Spirit, is the gift of God and is the sacramental presence of the divine for the whole world, as *Lumen gentium* describes it. Fulfilment theory in Vatican II arises out of the prior grace of God to which Israel and subsequently the Church testifies, not through the initiatory human act of 'arms outstretched to heaven'. It would seem to be utterly consonant with Vatican II, then, that evangelism is explored doctrinally without having to articulate a theology of dialogue. It would be much more difficult, rather, to justify a theology of dialogue without reference to the Church's mandate to present Christ to the world. A hermeneutical perspective on Vatican II that properly orders the priority of the 'Dogmatic Constitutions' (*Lumen gentium*, and *Dei verbum* on the nature of revelation) over the Pastoral Constitutions (such as *Nostra aetate*) is affirmed by Gavin D'Costa and a reminder that isolated Vatican II statements should not be assumed to present definitively clear pronouncements without at least considering the relative conciliar context.[168]

The ambiguity surrounding a qualitative assessment of Islam is largely due to the pastoral nature of the respective encyclicals and decrees. Doctrinal statements on other faiths were not the primary intention of the documents; rather, a renewed engagement by Catholics with members of other traditions. It is important to note that Vatican II 'spoke about Muslims but not about Islam'.[169] Additionally, the original motivation for speaking specifically about another faith in Vatican II was to correct the historical breach between the Catholic Church and Jews that, post-Holocaust, demanded humble conciliation from the Church. Church leaders in the Middle East were anxious that any positive assessment of Jews would be problematic in a region traumatized by the establishment of the state of Israel and troubled by the Arab–Israeli conflict. They therefore advocated a parallel assessment of Muslims.[170] This is a reminder that Christian theology is never a timeless abstraction but rooted in the encounters and experiences of history.

The resultant inclusion of Muslims and Jews within a schema of monotheistic faiths owes much to the influence of Louis Massignon: 'In speaking of Moslems and of Jews, the Council stresses our common father in faith, Abraham. This is where Louis Massignon, one of the great pioneers in Moslem dialogue, told us to begin.'[171] Youakim Moubarac had posited the idea that Abraham was the 'father of all believers' as progenitor, through his faith, of natural religion and, through his seed, of Jews and Muslims.[172] Vatican II stops short of this verdict, remaining silent on the genetic link between Muslims and Ishmael.[173] Indeed, for the Christian, 'physical descent is unimportant; it is faith that counts.'[174] Louis Massignon had himself recommended an earlier wording of *Nostra aetate* that was not accepted: 'The sons of Ishmael, who recognize Abraham as their father and believe in the God of Abraham, are not unconnected with the Revelation made to the Patriarchs.'[175] Instead, there is a more qualified association between Christians and Muslims in the shared example of Abraham:

The Church regards with esteem also the Moslems. They adore the one God, living and subsisting in Himself; merciful and all-powerful, the Creator of heaven and earth, who has spoken to men; they take pains to submit wholeheartedly to even His inscrutable decrees, just as Abraham, with whom the faith of Islam takes pleasure in linking itself, submitted to God. Though they do not acknowledge Jesus as God, they revere Him as a prophet. They also honor Mary, His virgin Mother; at times they even call on her with devotion. In addition, they await the day of judgment when God will render their deserts to all those who have been raised up from the dead. Finally, they value the moral life and worship God especially through prayer, almsgiving and fasting. Since in the course of centuries not a few quarrels and hostilities have arisen between Christians and Moslems, this sacred synod urges all to forget the past and to work sincerely for mutual understanding and to preserve as well as to promote together for the benefit of all mankind social justice and moral welfare, as well as peace and freedom.[176]

Erik Borgman notes that this section of *Nostra aetate* is structured according to Q 3: 64–65, in reverse order, providing an Islamized Christian theology affirming certain commonalities and differences between Muslims and Christians under an overarching Abrahamic motif.[177] One is reminded by this contextual presentation of Christian orthodoxy in relation to Islam of some of the Eastern Church's formative apologetics. No doctrinal judgement in *Nostra aetate* is made beyond the assertion of the identity of the God worshipped by both faiths. Thus, the contentious status of the Qur'an and the prophethood of Muhammad are neatly sidestepped.[178] The diplomatic evasion of any salvific evaluation of Islam and Muhammad in particular suggests that Daniel Madigan's belief that the conversation between Christians and Muslims still circles around the themes evident in the eighth-century dialogue between Patriarch Timothy 1 and the Abbasid Caliph, al-Mahdi is an accurate assessment.[179] Madigan, in affirming *Nostra aetate*, points out that the parallels with this dialogue from the historic Eastern Christian milieu underpin the reality that 'Timothy goes probably as far as a Christian can go ... in the estimation of Muhammad.'[180]

While *Nostra aetate* asserts the shared object of worship for both Christians and Muslims as the God of Abraham, there still remain questions about the nature of the God who is worshipped. For François Jourdan, his Catholic tradition does not require a literal slavishness to a synthesis of Christian and Muslim conceptions of God: '*C'est lui ET ce n'est pas lui.*'[181] As David Burrell observes, the statement that 'God is one' is effectively 'shorthand' suggestive of deeper understandings from within the respective traditions that do not always converge.[182]

Louis Massignon came to his appreciation of the shared roots of the Christian and Muslim faiths through his personal experiences originally in the Ottoman Empire and then in a sustained commitment and presence in the Arab world.[183] It was in the idioms and cultures of Islamic lands that Massignon regained his Christian faith and grew to develop a spirituality that converged with the mysticism of local prayer cells (*badaliyya*)[184] around common points of pilgrimage.[185] With the radical departure that Vatican II presupposes from the influence of Louis Massignon, it is interesting to note Massignon's own respect for church authority and his repeated submission of proposals and ideas to theologians as an accountable scholar subject to a tradition higher than himself.[186]

Nevertheless, the Abrahamic faith 'theologoumenon' remains a motif not without controversy and demands further analysis. Sydney Griffith sources the concept in Q 4:125 as the 'true religion of Abraham the faithful Gentile'.[187] Unsworth sees Vatican II as establishing the orthodoxy of this theologoumenon and it certainly seems justifiable to recognize the Council's 'assertion that Christians and Muslims worship/adore the same God'[188] as at least founding a significant bond between Christians and Muslims. It is another thing, however, to see the Council as having affirmed the Abrahamic theologoumenon as proposed by Massignon. Within this concept is a recognition that Islam is in some senses an awakened natural religion in the pattern of Abraham; what O'Mahony calls 'a resurgence from the time of the Patriarchs; an "almost" Abrahamic schism preceding the Decalogue and Pentecost'.[189] Karl-Josef Kuschel has argued for the development of the Abrahamic faiths motif in his proposal for an 'Abrahamic ecumene'.[190] Kuschel sees in Massignon's characterization of Judaism as 'rooted in hope', Christianity 'dedicated to love' and Islam 'centred on faith' a complementary and converging witness to the world in peaceful dialogue.[191]

Such an analysis is not without its problems, though. For Islam, there remain questions about the status of Muhammad and the Qur'an that for a Muslim are definitive to their faith but for a Christian or a Jew undermine what they profess. Massignon sought to address this conundrum by advocating for the 'conditional authority' of the Qur'an and 'partial recognition' of Muhammad as prophet.[192] For a Jew, Abraham is not the progenitor of a natural religion but the friend of God who was bound in covenant with a promise of a land to his descendants through Isaac. For Gentile Christians, Abraham is the father of faith through the decisive death of Jesus on the cross. Both these understandings are rejected by Islam. To see Abraham as the shared hub of the respective faiths is to overlook the distinctives of each. As Roger Arnaldez says:

> There is no way of reducing it to a common core so long as we situate ourselves within one of the three religious families. One must be Jewish, Christian, or Muslim, adhering to a faith that excludes the other two ... To put it most forcefully, we would have to neglect the particularities of their messages, ignore the characteristics of each, and repress the very notion of a Messenger.[193]

The Israeli scholar Alon Goshen-Gottstein has commented on the tendency of the Abrahamic faiths motif to work most effectively for Christians and Muslims, 'while the Jews tend to watch from the margins'.[194] Abraham as the 'man of faith' is a tenable concept in Pauline theology but it works to negate the fullness of covenant obligation in Judaism. Michael Knowles points to the necessarily high Christology needed for grounding any understanding of Abraham's faith beyond the covenant with the Jewish people. For Knowles, the 'Abrahamic religions' concept negates the Christology of the Pauline account of Abraham's faith making it captive to an Islamic vision.[195] In the later analysis of the Church of England's assessment of Islam we shall see how the Abrahamic motif has the potential to work counter to the broader vocation of the Church of England's interfaith relations.

A thoroughgoing analysis of the Abrahamic texts suggests a story that contains considerable ambiguity for the respective faiths. An airing of the misogyny of Abraham or the exclusion of Hagar could act as sobering counters to any self-sufficient introversion in the Abrahamic faiths.[196] As Mary Mills notes, the only truly free actor in the story is the God who speaks,[197] arguably positing the Abrahamic ecumene in a mystical as opposed to theological frame.

The transcendent encounter with God was the source of Massignon's theologoumenon and we ought to bear in mind Robert Caspar's warning not to build a theology out of the work of an Orientalist.[198] This is not to denigrate the significance of the commonalities between Christianity and Islam represented by Abraham, or to diminish Massignon's significant influence on Vatican II, but to guard against investing too much in a static framework of Abrahamic faiths.

Additionally, Christianity and Judaism are built on layers of consecutive, historical revelation that keeps the respective integrities of Scripture and covenant. Islam, however, distorts the integrities of Christian and Jewish revelations in invoking the completeness and sufficiency of the Qur'an, revealing what David Burrell calls its 'chronological asymmetry'.[199] A full concession to Islam of the Abrahamic faith ideal thus threatens the theological significance of the Christ-event for Christians, and the Abrahamic covenant for Jews as well as the integrities of their mutual inter-relating. As Neal Robinson asserts:

> neither *Lumen Gentium* nor *Nostra Aetate* explicitly brackets Islam with Judaism as an Abrahamic religion different from other non-Christian religions. The most one can argue is that they do not close the door to future explorations which might show that it is one.[200]

In opening up the possibility of Islam being a natural religion after Abraham, the extent to which Islam itself can properly respond with a fuller recognition of the status of Christ and the authority of the biblical canon should follow. The issue of reciprocity, then, which has become a recurrent theme in the post-Vatican II scene, addresses the extent to which a Christian extension of friendship and partnership is followed by a similar Muslim response. As Jacques Waardenburg says, 'What seems to be needed for Muslim–Christian relations nowadays is reciprocity, action and reaction, speech and response. Reciprocity may be the key term in these relations, as well as in the study of them.'[201] Reciprocity was a significant theme of John Paul II's papacy, his groundbreaking visit to Casablanca in 1985 being an occasion to speak out specifically about the needs for religious freedom in Muslim countries. Building on the foundations of the Declaration on Religious Freedom, *Dignitatis humanae* (1965), in Vatican II John Paul II stated that: 'respect and dialogue require reciprocity in all spheres, especially in that which concerns basic freedoms, more particularly religious freedom.'[202] Robert Spencer has suggested that John Paul II was *too* irenic towards Islam but the forthrightness of the Casablanca speech was not an isolated episode and was at one with his intention of extending grace while being prepared to offer challenge to Muslims.[203] The symbolic gestures towards Christian–Muslim dialogue characterized by Pope John Paul II demonstrated a post-Vatican II temper towards empathy and good relations. However, these good relations were not achieved at the expense of asserting the ongoing mission of the Church to proclamation or by neglecting the advocacy for the religious freedoms of Christian minorities in Muslim countries.

The Catholic Church and Islam: summary

Vatican II marked a clear and explicit intent on behalf of the Catholic Church to work for peaceful relations and dialogue with Muslims. The historical similarities between Christianity, Islam and Judaism have been significant in affirming the resources for collaboration, notably in the admission that Christians and Muslims have a common responsibility to the one God, albeit in highlighting key differences. Reciprocity has been a strong theme in Catholic pronouncements on Islam in recent years, helped by the conciliatory effects of John Paul II's many visits to Muslim countries and willingness to enter into mosques in symbolic statements of interdependence.[204]

There remain, though, a variety of Catholic interpretations of Vatican II pronouncements on Islam. Hans Küng, for example, has notably caused controversy by advocating for the recognition of the prophethood of Muhammad by the Catholic Church. Küng proposes that the 'three Semitic religions of revelation' 'have the same basis'.[205] Significantly, he consequently qualifies and reinterprets the doctrine of the trinity in order to accommodate the 'common core'[206] of the three faiths. Küng's ideas do not reflect Catholic doctrine on the trinity but they do highlight the ambiguities that persist with regard to the conciliar documents. Benedict XVI's robust aversion to any dilution of Chalcedonian Christology underlines the unorthodox status of Küng's propositions.[207]

Daniel Madigan prefers to see behind the insistence of Muhammad's prophethood the concern of Muslims to be treated seriously and to present in turn a vulnerable Christian presence that is able to learn about and from the other without needing to agree on matters of belief. The purpose of Christian–Muslim dialogue, then, for Madigan, is not the goal of a 'common denominator'.[208]

The seminal status of Vatican II for Christian–Muslim relations lies in its pastoral assertion of the worship of the one God that is common to both faiths and the clear intention to disavow earlier polemical discourses. The documents of Vatican II can be located in continuity with a historic trajectory of Catholic engagement that is able to hold together the parallel tracks of dialogue and proclamation, supremely exemplified in St Francis and Thomas Aquinas. Throughout the history of Catholic relations with Islam, there is recognition of the doctrine of the trinity as an orthodox creed that is a crucial point of irreconcilable difference. Thus, Vatican II's empathetic cast does not extend to asserting the prophethood of Muhammad or the revelatory status of the Qur'an. A silent verdict on both these questions protects the continuity of the Church's self-understood ecclesiology as God's sacramental community in the world.

The account of religions in Vatican II, built on a theology of *semina Verbi* and fulfilment, reflects the influence of the missionary theologies of the likes of Jules Monchain, Henri Le Saux and Bede Griffiths. These theologies, consonant with a Thomistic economy of graced nature, underlined the prevenient presence of Christ such that the interfaith encounter could be as much about *finding* Christ as proclaiming him.[209]

The ecclesial global consciousness ventured by Vatican II has been increasingly demonstrated by the symbolic potential of the papacy as a focus for consolidating positive Christian–Muslim relations. This role has also embodied an advocacy for the status of persecuted Christians under Islam, acknowledging the interdependence of global Catholicism.

When exploring Anglican relations with Islam, it will become apparent that there are a number of resonances from the Catholic tradition that offer resources to the Church of England. The need for the Church of England to sustain both evangelism *and* dialogue and to be attentive to a global ecclesial identity will be evidenced in the development of Anglican documents on other faiths. Indeed, the doctrine of the trinity and the self-identity of the *ekklesia* will be shown to be recovered priorities for Anglicanism's relations with Islam that find confirmation in the Catholic Church's magisterium. Furthermore, the missionary theologies of fulfilment that evoke the *presence* of Christ in other faiths will be seen to have their parallel equivalent within Anglicanism.

Anecdotes from the field: can we do dialogue and evangelism?

When I first moved to Birmingham I took a group of prospective Church Mission Society mission partners to a local mosque to learn something about Islam and its tradition. A number of them were planning to move to Muslim countries such as Bangladesh, Sudan and Pakistan and were asked to share something of their calling with the mosque leadership. I was a little uncomfortable, not knowing quite what they would say and conscious that these mission partners were keen to witness to their faith and accompany their practical service with a desire to see the conversion of Muslims. I facilitated some of the sharing and the Muslim leaders heard stories of doctors and nurses, leaving flourishing careers in the UK to serve disadvantaged communities; and the stories included very clear presentations of what Christ meant to them in reaching out in the Muslim world. To my astonishment, the oldest member of the mosque community pointed at each of the mission partners and said, 'We need you in *this* country! Your faith is an example to us all.'

Throughout my time in Birmingham, I have been repeatedly reminded that evangelism can and ought to coexist with dialogue, and that transparent and ethical considerations of proclamation are actually conducive to rather than inhibitive of good relations. I am priest-in-charge of a parish that has a new church centre, and when we opened the building some years ago we were approached by some members of the local community concerned that we were just focused on evangelism. In conversation, as we outlined our commitment to the common good and social justice, and our clear sense of ethical boundaries so that the ministry among the marginalized or young was never exploitative, we affirmed that we still wanted to share what was precious in our faith with others. Our neighbours have recognized this, holding a parallel desire that we might convert to Islam. In many ways, the problems seem to be most apparent when there are seen to be ulterior motives, secrecy and exploitation. I think of a local mosque that I visit, where I count the leaders as friends, who are bold in the tracts they distribute to visiting Christians. Dialogue is not compromised by evangelism, but rather by dishonesty and an engagement that refuses to see the wider needs of people and communities. Where permission is given to the acknowledgement of difference, it seems that space is freed for Christians, and Muslims, to be present together more fully.

3

Christian–Muslim Encounters in the Wider Tradition

Post-Reformation Churches and Islam

The Catholic Church's antecedent relation to the Church of England means that its engagement with Islam is necessarily instructive for a Church that remains 'catholic' in identity. However, the break with Rome that presaged the birth of Anglicanism was also part of a wider fragmentation across Christian Europe that realized the nation state as the locus of ecclesial authority for Reformed Churches. The Church of England therefore also finds itself alongside Christian traditions that reject the unitary authority of the pope and responsible to territorial districts demarcated by temporal government. To what extent do such traditions speak of Islam and the Church's consequent engagement and how might they inform the Church of England's own vocation to the nation as it seeks space for Islam in its midst?

The significance of Martin Luther for the Christian history of Europe is given extra freight for the contemporary context by his explicit pronouncements on Islam. In the charged setting of Ottoman imperial expansion to the borders of European Christendom, the role of the 'Turk' in the ferment of churches seeking to return to their sources and roots – a distinctive feature of Protestant thought – became a significant theme for Luther.[210] He had access to an early Latin translation of the Qur'an in 1542 and concluded that it was 'evil' and that access to the essentials of the Muslim faith would confirm in Christians its error as a religion.[211] His fellow Reformer Theodor Bibliander published his translation of the Qur'an in 1543 and Luther wrote a foreword that revealed much of his attitude to Islam. The agenda of the Reformers to reaffirm a gospel of grace, not works, is evident in Martin Luther's juxtaposition of what he saw as the futile efforts to please God in the religion of the 'Turks', with the free forgiveness emanating from God in a true Christian faith. Luther regards Islamic beliefs as 'pernicious',[212] equating the rites of Islam with the papal errors he is exercised to oppose: 'For the gospel teaches that the Christian religion is by far something other and more sublime than showy ceremonies, tonsures, hoods, pale countenances, fasts, feasts, canonical hours, and that entire show of the Roman church throughout the world.'[213]

Luther accuses the Catholic Church of only highlighting the evils of Islam, and thus distinguishing falsely what is similarly deviant from the gospel within the Church itself. Thus, for Luther, 'The Turks were for Europe what the Babylonians were for Israel – a "schoolmaster" to discipline and to teach fear of God and prayer.'[214] Luther's vision of the human origins of Islam did not stop him from recognizing the good within Islam; the faithfulness and dedication he observed in 'the Turks are by far superior'[215] to those of the Christians. While essentially human in origin, false and dangerous, Islam needed to be seen in its completeness, which necessitated an appreciation of the good. This process demanded a consequent dependence on the original truth of the gospel, without extraneous rite and human effort. Bibliander was in accord with Luther in stressing the need for a thorough knowledge of Islam, a knowledge that was to be supplemented by anti-Islamic polemical literature given its dangerous error.[216]

Heinrich Bullinger followed this pattern of paralleling the works-driven faith of the Catholic Church with the beliefs of Islam, regarding it as a Christian heresy[217] much as the earlier Medieval Church had done. For Bullinger, Bibliander, Luther and also Zwingli, the growing strength of the Ottoman Empire was to be seen in the light of God's providential judgement on a corrupt and heretical Catholic Church.[218] The role of Islam as a tool of God's judgement was often overlaid with the apocalyptic gloss that

Muhammad was the 'Antichrist' or the 'devil incarnate'.[219]

At the level of doctrine, we might observe in Luther and his fellow European Reformers a clear dialectic that condemns Islam as a human construct, in contrast to the Christian gospel. Islam thus needs to be understood and engaged with critically as a means of bolstering the true Christian faith in the minds of the faithful. The implications for wider Christian–Muslim relations are that the Church is compelled to demonstrate curiosity and enquiry into the faith of Islam as a means of both successful proclamation and self-purification. This inquiry, then, would be motivated by two energies: the external goal of evangelism and the internal goal of Christian discipleship.

Much has been written about Martin Luther's political theology in general terms,[220] and for the purposes of the present study it seems useful to attempt to bridge these thoughts with his perspectives on Islam. The 'two kingdoms' that he emphasized echoes the dialectic that he applied to his analysis of Islam. The 'kingdom of God' is in total distinction from the 'kingdom of the world'. These *zwei Regimente* both serve the kingdom of Christ but there is a strict separateness between the jurisdictions.[221] The strict separation meant that Christians were obligated to almost complete obedience to civil rule, as much as civil rulers were barred from interference in spiritual matters.[222] This has led to the accusation that Luther's political theology advocates a Christian 'quietism' that exacerbates individual piety at the expense of corporate justice.[223] For Christians to interfere in the realm of politics, and vice versa, is redolent of the work of the devil who 'never ceases cooking and brewing up the two kingdoms together'.[224] This reminds us of the task of delineating truth and error that was important for Luther in the encounter with Islamic belief.

In the contemporary setting of a settled European Islamic presence, it seems appropriate to suggest that a 'Lutheran' sensibility might judge the decline of 'Christian' Europe on the failures of a decadent Church. Islam may be seen to have a providential role in returning the Church to its true vocation and tradition. However, today's context of European multiculturalism is very different from the issues that would have encouraged a political 'quietism' in Luther in the sixteenth century. Indeed, the challenges of totalitarianism in the 1930s famously produced, in Dietrich Bonhoeffer, a Lutheran political theology that argued for the 'visibility' of the Church over and against the state.[225] And the symbolisms of territory, religion and culture that Luther reflected on, bearing in mind the controversy occasioned by Pope Benedict XVI's Regensburg Address in 2006, illustrate the resilience of this consistent thread of Christian response to Islam. How the Church of England sees its national vocation in the light of this trajectory is a significant question to which we will return.

In 1990, the United Evangelical Lutheran Church of Germany published an evaluation of Islam that affirmed the need for dialogue with Muslims in parallel with proclamation. No statement was made about the constitutive nature of Islam with respect to salvation but the document 'leaves no doubt that Jews and Christians stand in "the same tradition of faith" and have much in common',[226] an affinity from which Muslims are implicitly and noticeably excluded. The Porvoo Communion of Churches, which includes a significant number of European Lutheran and Reformed Churches in an ecumenical venture with European Anglican Churches, published 'guidelines for inter faith encounter' in 2003.[227] There is a clear trinitarian foundation to the statement, which acknowledges the plurality of much of Europe and calls for discernment in interpreting 'God's purposes in our religiously plural societies'[228] in contrast to the ideal of a 'Christian Europe'. Admitting the diverse theologies and traditions of the Communion, there is, yet, a sustained commitment to dialogue that allows for proclamation and conversion; freedom to change one's religion being asserted as a mutual gift. Interestingly, the guidelines 'emphasize the importance of maintaining a vigorous and engaged Christian presence at a local level in multi-faith areas', while recognizing the 'need to be aware of the ethnic and religious discrimination in our societies'.[229] The Churches, here, seem to be conceding to the diversity of their respective nations while reserving the freedom to present the Christian tradition to other faiths in a manner that is just and respectful. The status of other faiths is again circumnavigated, but the centrality of Christ as the fullness of God affirmed.

As with the Catholic Church, there seems to be a contemporary reluctance to avoid pronouncements that are clearly exclusivist in tone, yet there is a commitment to dialogue and collaboration that does not detract from the vocation of proclamation. As regards the implications for political theology, the Porvoo guidelines assume a robust engagement with society at the level of interfaith relations but fall short of advocating for a vocation to guard the Christian heritage of Europe as a unitary, binding value system.

The dialecticism evident in Martin Luther's theology became a defining characteristic of the twentieth century's towering theologian, Karl Barth. Jacques Dupuis summarizes Barth's understanding of other religions as 'nothing but idolatrous human attempts at self-justification',[230] akin to what John Bunyan described as 'only a think-so'.[231] In the light of recent equations between Islam and fascism,[232] Barth, in the 1930s, was paralleling the ideology of Nazism with Islam. Where Nazism meets with opposition, it resorts to 'the might and right that belongs to Divinity': 'Islam of old as we know proceeded in this way'.[233] For Barth, then, Hitler was 'Allah's Prophet' of his day. Where Nazism absolutizes the state, arrogating to itself 'religious' claims to ultimacy, Islam absolutizes the oneness of God in a false objectivity that inherently violates all other claims and betrays the mystery of God's ineffability in the process.[234] An alternative interpretation of Barth by Glenn Chestnutt would suggest that there is some potential to view Islam under a covenant of grace – much as he viewed Judaism as retaining a covenant – by virtue of Muslims' identity in Ishmael: 'the God of Israel is also the God of Ishmael.' Chestnutt would then see Barth offering an ontological link between the Church and Islam; Muslims akin to 'paganized Jews', however much he elsewhere argues for the distinction between the Christian God and the God of Islam and of Judaism.[235]

George Lindbeck builds on this assumption of exclusivist revelation, drawing on Barth's conception of the 'all-inclusive or all-absorbing character of the "Strange New World of the Bible".[236] Other traditions are thus inherently 'untranslatable' to the Christian faith.[237] For Barth, though, the dialectic was not between the Church and other faiths, nor Christian tradition and other faiths, but between God and humanity. It is in the very revelation from God, embodied in Jesus, that 'true religion' is manifest. Thus, he could say that 'Religion is never true in itself and as such', and 'No religion is true. It can only become true.'[238]

One of the political implications of this theology is that 'the task of the Church was not to shore up Christendom.'[239] The organic nature of true faith means that the revelation of Jesus Christ needs to be known and presented anew for each context. The guarding and protecting of historic influence is in utter contradiction to the Christian vocation because 'We do not speak about God by speaking about humanity in a loud voice.'[240] The exclusivist dialectics of Barth thus produce a more nuanced political theology that is arguably more liberal in its impact on the role of the Church in plural societies than approaches that seek to return to the roots of Christian Europe emanating from an inclusivist theology of religions. Thus, the Lutheran and Reformed traditions that had identified with the respective territorial jurisdictions post-Westphalia are able to ground a vital critique of *all* political regimes.[241] Even while separating ecclesial and state jurisdiction, the Church has a responsibility to identify the provisional nature of human authority.

An interpretation of Barth that founds a sympathetic theology of religions is supported by Tom Greggs, who recognizes that a rejection of 'religion' per se 'means that the Christian religion stands in solidarity with other religions'.[242] The surprising resourcefulness of Barth to constructive interreligious relations is confirmed by Glenn Chestnutt along similar lines.[243] The specific polemic aimed at Islam and Muhammad by Barth is less than convincingly circumnavigated by these two authors in the admittedly positive opportunities for encounter with other religions they see in Barth in general.

By questioning the foundational presumptions of prevailing

cultures, Barth's project, as Paul Brazier notes, can be seen to find more resonance within Roman Catholicism. Even allowing for Barth's challenges to the Catholic Church, there is a shared determination to frame the discussion of church, culture and religions from an understanding of God and salvation history:

> the focus is, therefore, as we see in Barth's mature work, on the Word of God (the *Deus dixit*) as an event and person beyond ecclesial structure and authority, but to which all ecclesial structures should (for Barth – *müssen*, must!) bear witness.[244]

What Barth was rejecting was a public theology that was subservient to history and anthropology, not a theology that could account for God's providence beyond the Church. Furthermore, Barth's dialectical approach to other religions opens up space for the mystical and ethical work of God in the world. A theology emphasizing the freedom of God and the futility of human grasping at revelation must in turn acknowledge the possibility of God's providence in another religion and not be constrained to evaluate other religions on the basis of a salvation question specific to the Christian faith. This approach has led the American Dominican theologian J. A. DiNoia to avoid the straitjacket of the threefold typology[245] in assessing other religions and to foster a theology of religions that is inherently dialogical. It is in the process of dialogue and encounter that the discernment of God's freedom can be made.[246] In similar terms, Jürgen Moltmann has stated that we should not be assessing the paths of salvation in other religions or identifying 'anonymous Christians',[247] but 'looking for *life* in other religions'.[248] The search for 'life' in other religions has echoes of Aquinas's embrace of 'truth' wherever it is encountered. An engagement with Islam that moves beyond the traditional exclusivist–pluralist spectrum, that retains the subjective truths of the Christian faith while treating the other with integrity, not superimposing Christian patterns on to Islam, thus seems possible.

In 1948, the World Council of Churches (WCC) became the

main international ecumenical forum for Protestant Churches. In 1971, the WCC initiated the 'Program for Dialogue with People of Living Faiths and Ideologies', but it was only in 1979 that sufficient consensus on the tensions between dialogue and mission was reached to be able to publish 'Guidelines on Dialogue'.[249] These guidelines focus on the ethical practice of dialogue rather than offer a theological evaluation of other faiths.

The WCC aims to serve a broad spectrum of theological tradition and thus the more pluralist positions advocated by the likes of Wesley Ariarajah and Stanley Samartha have attained a legitimacy within the WCC ecumenical discourse.[250] Interestingly, despite such theological diversity in the WCC, their 1992 document *Issues in Christian–Muslim Relations: Ecumenical Considerations*, robustly recognized points of contention for many Churches as they engaged with Islam. Among the issues noted were political governance and the search for the common good as opposed to sectarian interests, Shari'a law, freedom of worship and equal citizenship for Christians in Muslim contexts and mutual practices of evangelism or *da'wah*.[251] The ecumenical and global reach of the WCC seems to have permitted an honest appraisal of concerns from a determination to develop dialogue with Muslims. The concluding section, entitled 'Living and working together',[252] underlines again the significance of political theology and the common good in Christian–Muslim relations.

Douglas Pratt's summary analysis of the WCC's reflections on dialogue with Muslims confirms the consistent breadth of theologies and engagements, reaffirming the need for cooperation and collaboration between Christians and Muslims in the midst of their respective universal trajectories. A growing concern for the WCC, highlighted originally at the fractious conference on Christian and Muslim mission at Chambésy, Switzerland, in 1976, and manifest in a series of regional consultations, is that of religious freedom.[253] A conference held in May 2006, including Muslims, concluded that meaningful interreligious dialogue 'should not exclude any topic, however controversial or sensitive, if that topic is a matter of concern'. It acknowledged differences, disagreements and even the lack of an agreed understanding of 'conversion'.[254] For all the efforts of pluralist theologies within the WCC to establish a rapprochement between the two faiths, the prevailing concerns are to establish codes of conduct and efforts towards society-building in recognition of the vital *differences* between Islam and Christianity.

The determination of the WCC to found dialogue and good relations on a robust appreciation of mutual integrities and differences is confirmed by the 2011 document 'Christian Witness in a Multi-Religious World: Recommendations for Conduct', produced in conjunction with the Pontifical Council for Interreligious Dialogue and the World Evangelical Alliance.[255] The document addresses issues of ethics and treatment of converts, presuming that evangelism is a normative practice of Churches. Collaboration between faiths and a responsible public presence is not attained by eliding the distinctive vocation of Churches to proclamation:

> Mission belongs to the very being of the church. Proclaiming the word of God and witnessing to the world is essential for every Christian. At the same time, it is necessary to do so according to gospel principles, with full respect and love for all human beings.[256]

The breadth of signatories of this document suggests that a genuinely ecumenical perspective on relations with other faiths cannot afford to neglect the issues of evangelism and conversion, albeit within appropriately ethical frameworks.

John Hick is perhaps the most celebrated of the pluralist theologians, and it was in the seminal *The Myth of Christian Uniqueness* that he argued for a Copernican revolution in the theology of religions.[257] Instead of an *ecclesio*centric theology of religions (exclusivist), or a *christo*centric theology (inclusivist), a *theo*centric theology is more appropriate to contemporary diversity. A theo-centric theology recognized all faiths as circling the more properly termed 'Real'; who is only known in part in the diversity of the manifestations of faith. For Hick, then, the doctrine of the trinity, as classically understood, is an unnecessary obstacle to good relations with Muslims: 'we should not insist that Jesus was literally God incarnate, but should see him as a human being who was so startlingly open and responsive to God's presence that God was working through him for the salvation of many.'[258]

We have noted already that Nicholas of Cusa is called upon by Hick to justify pluralism as a more long-standing theology in the Christian tradition.[259] One might also see in the writings of Clement of Alexandria the traces of a pluralist theology in the way he abstracts God from the specific revelations within religions.[260] Meister Eckhart's writings are explicitly referred to by Hick; Eckhart's distinction between God and the godhead 'opens the door to the distinction between the Real and the plurality of its manifestations'.[261]

Despite questions that may be brought about how representative these thinkers are of mainstream Christian tradition, or the interpretation that Hick applies to them, there are other persuasive contemporary voices that seek to conceive of a more pluralist theology of religions. The noted Christian Islamicist and Canadian Presbyterian Wilfred Cantwell Smith has suggested a world theology of religions that seeks to unify the religious impulse in every faith.[262] In blurring the distinction between the religious and the religion, Cantwell Smith reduces the significance of the Christ-event, the elevation of which he calls 'the big-bang theory of Christian origins'.[263] One of Cantwell Smith's most important contributions was his critique of theologies of religion that assess the nature and practice of religions from an outside vantage point in contradiction to the perspective of the adherents. He famously said that 'Islam is (will be) what Muslims say it is.'[264] This helpfully guards against a sterile, forensic approach to religions but is a hostage to fortune when the central tenet of Christ's incarnation is disparaged as a 'big-bang theory', thus denying for Christianity a freedom conceded to Islam. Kenneth Cragg notes the inner contradictions of the worldwide theology of religions that Cantwell Smith proposed in so far as it relates to his conception of Islam. Cantwell Smith's efforts to qualify objective truths and revelation as they appear in Islam, for Cragg, are unpalatable to most Muslims: "'The truth that transcends" has been Islamically defined and with it the response it requires from the humanity it unifies.'[265] In Cragg's inimitable logic, there is the essential quandary of the pluralist project: how can irreconcilable beliefs be brought into one schema?[266] If a unitary theological schema across the faiths is properly elusive, then the theological rationale for a unitary political schema that affirms peaceable relations in diversity becomes ever more pressing. It seems that the task facing the Church is not one of diluting the claims of the Christian and Muslim faiths. Rather, it is so rooting the Christian encounter with Islam firmly within its tradition that the trinitarian stream of self-giving love and unity in diversity is exemplified.

There are considerable problems for a pluralist theology conceptually and in terms of integrity in the Christian tradition. Our earlier study of the formative encounters with Islam established the centrality of the trinity and incarnation of Christ as distinguishing theologies.[267] Indeed, we might agree with George Lindbeck that the trinity is the 'grammar of Christian discourse'.[268] This trajectory is eloquently articulated by David Burrell in his preface to Roger Arnaldez's *Three Messengers for One God*: 'Rather than reach for commonality, we are invited to expand our horizons in the face of diversity. The goal is not an expanded scheme, but an enriched inquirer: discovery of one's own faith in encountering the faith of another.'[269]

Protestant Churches, then, exhibit a wide range of responses to Islam that span a spectrum from the polemical condemnation of Islam as a totalizing religion of violence, through to pluralist theologies of religion. Even though the WCC has generated theological perspectives that include the pluralist position, in formal accounts of Islam, an orthodox trinitarian position has been upheld that has embraced both dialogue and evangelism. When the WCC has considered the lived reality of Christian–Muslim relations at a global level, the challenges of persecution, conversion and Shari'a law seem to have produced theologies that are akin to those expressed in Vatican II by the Catholic Church. The ability of

Churches to found good relations with Muslims that are able to affirm difference rather than bypass it seems to be reflective of the mainstream of Protestant interreligious considerations. As with the work of Thomas Aquinas, even robust judgements on Islam such as those documented by Barth have the potential to resource a theology that is conducive to confirmation of the prevenient grace of God in the faith other.

It remains to be seen, as we explore more fully the political theologies at the disposal of the Church of England, how a high view of the Church might be able to provide theological space for Islam in its midst. The challenge would seem to be then to develop a corresponding political theology that can reckon with evangelism and dialogue among Muslims and resource the pursuit of the common good.

Eastern Orthodoxy and Islam

There is a notable Anglican indebtedness to Eastern Orthodox sensibilities, exemplified by the influence of the twentieth-century Russian Orthodox émigré movement on Anglican theology and ecclesiology. There has also been a long-standing fascination among Anglicans with the Eastern Church of the Middle East, often due to the shared rejection of papal authority, episcopal hierarchies, and common theologies of priesthood and eucharistic sacrament, as well as their historic commitment to territory.[270] The territorial commitment of Orthodoxy, therefore, may offer resources for the encounter of the Church of England with Islam in its vocation to the nation.

In recent years the 'Caesaro-papism'[271] of the Russian Orthodox Church, which suffered persecution and suppression during the Communist era, has been reawakened and harnessed to foster a new religiosity as a rejection of the previous secularism.[272] The identification of Russian Orthodoxy with a 'canonical territory',[273] which Basil Cousins sees as akin to the Islamic *umma*,[274] has led to a shoring up of exclusive Orthodox Christian presence in Russia. Other Christian traditions have been rejected and the ecumenical project has stalled within Russia. That there is a significant Islamic presence within Russia itself suggests that there may be potential resources for the Church of England in the experience of the Russian Orthodox Church.[275] The outlying former Soviet states have been neglected by the Russian Orthodox Church, with the result that Islam has grown unabated in the region.[276] The continuing concept of canonical territory seems, therefore, to inhibit a political theology that supports ecumenical relations and religious plurality. Instead, it seems to hasten the fragmentation that is in danger of being rewarded with the religious extremism it would otherwise seek to avoid.[277] Jacques Waardenburg observes that when Europeans see the need to exert power in their association with Islam 'as power', then 'their discourse about Islam has to do with power rather than with faith or religion'.[278] The contemporary Russian context suggests that this observation may also be true for the Church in its understanding of its fellow Christian traditions and underlines the ecumenical implications of the Christian encounter with Islam.

In many countries around the world, one of the most pressing concerns is the freedom and level of citizenship given to Christian communities in Islamic regimes. The Russian Orthodox Church's advocacy of canonical territory such that Christian 'states' develop in parallel with Muslim 'states' is a model that ill serves Christians in other countries. Thus, in Egypt, Coptic Christians have had to adapt to the constraints of political and cultural structures that are prejudicial to the full expression of their faith and civic freedoms and responsibilities.[279] The Coptic Orthodox Church has been at pains to be seen as a loyal community in Egypt and has been co-opted into previous governments' programmes for national unity. The realities of Egyptian citizenship for ordinary Coptic Christians seem to be some way removed from the rhetoric of national unity, Christian–Muslim relations are still largely charged by 'ignorance and suspicion' and loyalty to the state has 'not brought tangible rewards' for most.[280]

Adriano Garuti's study of canonical territory in Russia highlights the ecclesial sensibility of the Orthodox tradition around geography in contrast to the Catholic Church's emphasis on the personal dimension of the papacy.[281] This disjunction of identities has created much of the controversy between the two Churches when the Catholic Church has sought to extend its presence into Orthodox canonical territories. Essential to Garuti's analysis is an understanding of the Catholic Church's mission as universal and a rejection of any conceptualizing of the pope as the 'Patriarch of the West'. Anthony O'Mahony's reflections on the Eastern Christian presence in the Italian Peninsula reveal that there is a complex reality that *precedes* the hardening of nation-state jurisdictions, offering the potential for greater conviviality between the two traditions. Here, the Catholic Church and Orthodox Church can draw on a historical pattern of ecumenism that is not beholden to unitary ecclesial, geographical authorities.[282] Indeed, the trinitarian emphasis of Orthodoxy demands a vision extending beyond the individual and the local to 'that great human family whose vocation is to discover its Trinitarian identity by means of the Church'.[283]

Adrian Hastings uses the case study of the break-up of the former Yugoslavia to warn against the dangers of too close an identification with canonical territory. Here, Serbian Orthodox mythologies about Muslims were mobilized in the service of a 'narrowly ethno-religious construction' and 'huge territorial ambition' to perpetrate atrocities on minority Muslim communities in the 1990s.[284] Hastings contrasts the Caesaro-papism of the Serbian Orthodox Church with the Church of England by admitting the dualism inherent in the Western Christian tradition. Reformed Churches, and supremely the Church of England, hold together a conflicting agenda of both nation-forming and universalism.[285] Canonical territory is ultimately an alien concept to the Church of England, because while rooted in and defined by the political roots of the United Kingdom, it retains the universal scope of its own Catholic roots. The Church of England's ability to take root in different forms, both confluent with and divergent from nation states across the Anglican Communion, would seem to support this contention. This would provide additional support to the approach of this study, which would assess the Church of England's Christian–Muslim relations, and its political theology in response to Islam, in the context of the global Anglican Communion and wider ecumenical resources.

The contemporary reality of Eastern Orthodoxy is that there exist similar tensions between territoriality and globality to those within the Anglican Communion. The perceived threat of globalization has provided momentum to a 're-territorialized' religiosity – an aspect of the modern synthesis of Orthodoxy with the nation state – against the grain of the globalist Ecumenical Patriarchate of Constantinople.[286] The dilemma facing the Ecumenical Patriarchate provides some resonance with the Church of England: 'working within the context of a Turkish Republic locked in a struggle between Islamic revivalism and secular political values; but a church ever seeking to find ecclesial jurisdiction based upon authority for a global Orthodox Church.'[287] This assessment has more than a little in common with the Church of England's own engagement with the parallel challenges of Islam and secularism in the public square. All this takes place in the context of a global communion looking to the Archbishop of Canterbury to steer it through potential fragmentation. How the Ecumenical Patriarchate conceives of its relations with Islam, then, offers a productive line of enquiry for the Church of England.

Andrew Sharp has studied recent formal dialogues between Orthodoxy and Islam, to which the Ecumenical Patriarchate have contributed, as evidence of what he believes to be a clear 'position' on Christian–Muslim relations. Sharp concludes that there is a tradition-centred encouragement to good relations with Muslims. He considers that a trinitarian economy, setting a high Christology with the Holy Spirit active beyond the confines of the Church, is the basis for a contemporary Orthodox 'position' on Islam. Importantly, the renewed formal efforts towards dialogue between Orthodox and Muslims are being set in a historical context. Though the doctrine of the trinity has often been problematic for Muslims, the earliest fruitful encounters with Islam of the Eastern Church are being drawn upon: the trinity is intrinsic to the recognition of God's grace in the faith other. The theological resources most called upon by Orthodox participants in formal dialogue with Muslims are the Russian émigré theologians of the twentieth-century 'neo-patristic synthesis'. Sharp's thesis is apparently echoed by Metropolitan Georges Khodr of the Church of Antioch, who, drawing from Vladimir Lossky, talks of the 'economy of the Spirit' that displays the life of the creator in non-Christian religions. The 'seeds of the Word', according to Khodr, compel the Church to 'awaken the Christ who is sleeping in the night of religions'.[288]

This trinitarian theology of religions is already very apparent in the understanding of the Eastern Orthodox Church, whose doctrine of the *perichoresis* of the godhead suggests that mission is not primarily about 'the propagation or transmission of intellectual convictions, doctrines, moral commands', 'but rather about the inclusion of all creation in God's overflowing, superabundant life of communion'.[289] In this economy, God is a God of mission and dialogue, revealing a deep accord between Vatican II and the Orthodox tradition.[290]

Post-Reformation Churches, Eastern Orthodoxy and Islam: summary

The wider post-Reformation traditions reveal a broad range of responses to Islam, yet there remains a persistent need to ground relations between the two faiths from within Christian orthodoxy, despite repeated calls for a revised schema of religions. As they are for the Catholic Church, evangelism and the issues of conversion across the Christian and Muslim faiths hold significant places in interreligious dialogue. That the post-Westphalian scene has led to the increasing territorialization of ecclesial responsibilities has merely sharpened the challenge that Christian orthodoxy should be equipped to respond constructively to Islamic shared citizenship. The tensions inherent in the ecclesial task of nation-forming and universalism arguably explain the diversity within the Western

Christian tradition towards Islam as Churches negotiate the wider context of plurality.

In Europe, the parallel traits of nation-forming and universalism, as Jørgen Nielsen notes, exist within Catholic and Protestant denominations and have been subject to repeated renegotiations. Nielsen's contention is that just such renewed negotiations are necessary for a continent recently forgetful of its religiously informed political heritage of freedom.[291] As Nielsen elsewhere states, the presence of Muslims in Europe has resulted in a 're-opening of the issue of national identity'.[292] For the Church of England as the formally established state Church, Anglicanism's contemporary relationship to national culture, the state and law is thus a vital arena of study for the shaping of a political theology responsive to Islam.

An overview of the post-Reformation tradition would suggest the possibilities for an inclusivist understanding of God's sovereignty within Islam that is yet attentive to totalizing elements and the vulnerability of Christians in minority situations.

The Russian Orthodox Church and the Egyptian Coptic Church illustrate the persistence of concepts of territorial responsibility in ecclesial identities yet highlight the need for these to be understood in more ecumenical and universal terms. It is evident that, across these traditions, a *hard* conception of canonical territory is an ambiguous gift to the Church in its prophetic witness to the state.

The Orthodox Church has sought to recover the neo-patristic synthesis of the Russian émigré movement in its engagement with Islam, such that a participatory, trinitarian vision can give space for the discovery of Christ in the religious other. The recent steps forward in international dialogue between Orthodox Christians and Muslims thus stands in the tradition of Vatican II, recalling as it does the Church Fathers and a eucharistic ecclesiology.

Conclusion

The shift in global church numbers from the 'north' to the 'south'[293] is likely to exacerbate the urgency of constructive Christian–Muslim relations. The greatest growth has been in churches that are 'far more traditional, morally conservative, evangelical, and apocalyptic than their northern counterparts'.[294] It is to be expected that the examples of Christian relations with Muslims in countries such as Nigeria will become increasingly important on the global stage. The airing of theologies of interreligious encounter that can accommodate the missionary impulses within Islam and Christianity is thus to be welcomed as being reflective of the realities of so much of the respective traditions.[295] As David Marshall says, 'it makes little sense to attempt to construct a formula for Christian–Muslim relations which includes the demand that Christians give up all idea of proclaiming the Gospel of Christ to Muslims (or, indeed, vice versa)'.[296] The pragmatic realities, at least, suggest the fallacy of expecting the universalizing trajectories of both faiths to be denied.

In many of the encounters between Christians and Muslims around the world, the issue of territory is significant. The historic, political and doctrinal mutual histories of Islam and Christianity infuse the interreligious encounter with the potential for deep conflict around issues of territorial dominance and sacred space. Such conflicts underline, again, the frequent primacy of political theologies of coexistence and shared citizenship for shaping Christian–Muslim relations. There exists, though, the potential for local, territory-specific encounters to inform those relations for good, highlighted by the effectiveness of Pope John Paul II's visits to Muslim countries.

The Abrahamic narratives within Christianity and Islam point to the consonance of truths and stories but also long-standing conflicts. Framing the interreligious encounter within the Abrahamic fold continues to be a useful tool for many but arguably does not do enough justice to *either* tradition to be a defining motif. Furthermore, the Christian–Muslim relationship cannot be taken in isolation from other groups in society, and thus a cementing between Christians, Muslims and Jews in the Abrahamic covenant is in danger of undermining the Christian responsibility to the whole of society. So while there continue to be reminders in the Abrahamic motif of so much shared story between Christians and Muslims, and there continue to be pluralist conceptions of religions, the prevailing Christian tradition would point to the essential 'otherness' of Islam.

A trinitarian understanding of God is a common theological distinctive in the engagement with Islam, shaped around the revelation of the Christ-event and energized by the life of the Holy Spirit in the world, affirming an encounter of both dialogue and proclamation. The trinitarian aspect to this theology affirms the possibility of God at work within Islam; a more inclusive evaluation of other religions predominating. The influence of a corresponding eucharistic ecclesiology and a participatory ontology of the godhead redolent of the Church Fathers and the earliest encounters with Islam provide resources for Orthodoxy's encounter with Islam and, indeed, for the seminal documents of Vatican II for the Catholic Church. Subsequent chapters will confirm this development within Anglican interreligious documents.

A range of theologies of territorial responsibility seems to flow from the doctrinal position on Islam. It is by no means the case that an inclusive or pluralist position determines a more liberal understanding of societal relations. Conversely, exclusivist theologies have the potential to produce more liberal, tolerant political theologies. Conclusions of political theology cannot, it seems, be predetermined by the prior doctrinal determination of Islam. The task of interreligious dialogue, though, seems to be grounded in recognition of the truths that *do* exist within Islam.

A transparent and authentic presentation of the respective traditions and belief systems that does not evade difference seems to offer the most encouraging modes of encounter. Such encounters are most possible when there is a shared vision of the common good; of equally responsible citizenship. There remains, though, a keen awareness of centuries of mutual animosity and stereotyping as well as examples of hope and progress. In essence, then, the pursuit of a political theology for the Christian engagement with Islam is arguably the most pressing task for the Church in its relations with Islam and Muslims today. If, as seems apparent, the Church of England is to be increasingly conscious of both difference from and similarity to Islam, then the foremost challenge may be towards, as Kenneth Cragg puts it, 'Living mutually and yet belonging sincerely'.[297]

Anecdotes from the field: Christian–Muslim encounters and the trinity

One of the joys of living in and ministering among a largely Muslim population is that faith conversations are normalized: God-talk is not something that has to be shoehorned into conversations. It does mean that sooner or later the subject of the incarnation will come up, often occasioning the sort of bemusement that we read of in the early exchanges between Christians and Muslims. In Sparkbrook, there are a number of people from other faiths who are exploring with us as a church community, praying with us and even worshipping with us, while not having made a decisive step of conversion. One such Muslim man was with us as we were singing carols in the run-in to Christmas and, after singing 'O Come all ye Faithful', he brought us up short: 'I've just read those words, "Very God begotten not created, O Come let us adore him Christ the Lord". Do you seriously believe that Jesus is the same as God?'

I recall a conversation in Tunis with a local friend who was astonished that I could believe that Jesus would have been crucified because, surely, if Jesus is God's prophet, would not God have rescued him? For all the many resonances and confluences between the faiths, there are these breaches that separate Christian faith from Islamic faith, supremely in the Christian understanding of who Jesus is and the nature of the godhead in trinity. It has not been my experience that apologetic exchanges on these matters can somehow *persuade* a Muslim of the sense or rightness of Christian doctrine, though rational and thoughtful theological exchanges are important. In dialogue with Muslims, it would seem odd and disingenuous to avoid those truths that are central to the Christian faith, however awkward they may seem. When I first began to be involved in formal dialogue events, I occasionally was encouraged to 'leave my convictions at the door' so as to engage more fully with the other. That such a move is philosophically impossible merely adds to my conviction that dialogical integrity is about bringing all that is important to me in vital exchange with the other.

Moreover, the 'trinity' is not merely some abstract notion in dialogue. Taken seriously, a Christian understanding of a God who sustains this world, is the source of all that is good and true and beautiful, makes dialogue an imperative. In the dialogue with a Muslim, I should not be surprised to encounter gifts of grace that reveal the goodness of God to me; to experience love and holiness in the hospitality of the other. The measure of that truth and goodness can only be Christ Jesus, but the Holy Spirit of God can be speaking and challenging me in unforeseen ways.

Reflecting on some of the historical trajectories of Christian–Muslim encounters, then, I would want to affirm that stream of Christian tradition that would seek to bring the Chalcedon tradition in robust engagement with Islam, but in a way that models the curiosity and wonder that is at the heart of the trinitarian mystery. I think of Javed in Sparkbrook, a Muslim community leader known for his wisdom, faith and peaceableness. When the far-right English Defence League was distributing anti-Muslim leaflets in front of a local supermarket during Ramadan, they attracted a crowd of angry teenage Muslims who were ready for confrontation. Javed was called by the local police and he arrived to calm the situation. Turning to one of the teenage boys who was swearing at the police, Javed accused him of breaking his fast because he was not acting in a godly manner. The boys quickly dispersed and the heated protest was diffused. Javed was drawing from his own faith to model respect and grace in the midst of a provocative situation. I cannot judge his faith, or his relationship to God, but I can witness to the goodness and righteousness that come from God that I see in his life. He and I have regular conversations, agree to disagree about many things, and I am grateful for the gift of God that he is to me.

4

Contemporary Issues in Christian–Muslim Encounter

Religious freedom

Before assessing Anglican encounters with Islam, it is important to situate the contemporary scene with an analysis of factors sharpening the context of Christian–Muslim relations. In recent years the subject of religious freedom has grown so visible that it has become a priority foreign-affairs issue for many governments, dominating news media and generating official legislation.[298] The implication of resurgent faith communities to international foreign-policy makers is underlined by Scott Thomas, for whom the particular fault lines of Christian–Muslim interaction raise the spectre of religious persecution.[299]

The concept of religious freedom challenges the capability of *both* faiths to embrace plurality with integrity. J. Leon Hooper, assessing the seminal work of John Courtney Murray in the elaboration of a Catholic rationale for religious freedom, acknowledges that 'the church's endorsement of religious freedom was an act of humility on the part of the church, since the church had done little to develop the institution.'[300] Any Christian appraisal of the issues of religious freedom in Christian–Muslim encounter then needs to proceed with humility. For Murray it was of vital importance that a rigorous apologia for religious freedom be rooted in the Catholic tradition. Though Murray was instrumental in such advances, Hooper notes his dissatisfaction with the theology supporting *Dignitatis humanae*, the seminal encyclical of Vatican

II. Murray grounds his advocacy of religious freedom[301] on a rights theory of the law of nature, or reason, manifest to humanity, binding on all governments and not dependent on the assent of the Catholic Church, though fully rooted in that tradition. Murray's search for a religious rights theory that was authentically 'Catholic' poses questions in turn to Muslims engaged in their own theological explorations of identity in the midst of plurality: to what extent are revised ideas of Islamic minority status, equal rights and freedom to convert from Islam genuinely rooted in the faith tradition? As a recent study on religious persecution has highlighted, 'more than seven in ten Muslim-majority countries harass Muslims compared with Muslims being harassed in only three in ten Christian-majority countries', a fact exacerbated by the renewed cogency of Shari'a law in Islamic contexts.[302] An inescapable backdrop to Christian–Muslim relations, then, is the reality of the oppression of Christians in many Muslim countries.

One of the consequences of this lack of religious freedom is that questions are being asked by contemporary commentators who accuse Islam of being inherently totalitarian.[303] The neologism 'Islamo-fascism' has been coined to suggest the totalizing tendencies of Islam. Atheist commentators, political scientists and novelists, such as Christopher Hitchens, Francis Fukuyama, Martin Amis and Ian McEwan, all voice their disquiet about a perceived repressive drive in Islam.[304] As Scott Thomas reminds us, such a reading of Islam draws from earlier analyses that suggest that totalizing political ideologies are themselves religious in character. There is thus a thread being drawn between these *religio*-political ideologies and fundamentalist religions.[305] For Thomas, 'there is a connection between the religious nature of fascism and what is "fascist" or "totalitarian" about certain forms of religion.'[306]

Ahmed Ibrahim Abushouk admits the challenge facing Muslims in responding to these charges of totalitarianism and calls for a campaign, 'first and foremost, among Muslims themselves' and then in the West in general to convince people of the peaceful roots of Islam: that 'Islam has no "fault lines of war" with other civilizations'.[307] It is interesting to note that the historian Arnold

Toynbee, writing in the 1940s, expressed something akin to Samuel Huntington's 'clash of civilizations' thesis[308] in this vein. Referring to the 'discordant panmixia set up by the Western conquest of the world', he wonders that:

A panmixia may end in a synthesis, but it may equally well end in an explosion; and in that disaster, Islam might have quite a different part to play as the active ingredient in some violent reaction of the cosmopolitan underworld against its Western masters.[309]

Toynbee's assessment is explained in his perception of Muhammad's 'counter-transfiguration' at the heart of the *hijra*. For Toynbee, Muhammad's moral trajectory collapses into the temptation of political power and makes force definitive to faith.[310] In the divine pathos of the crucifixion lies the 'higher religion' that permits human freedom as a foundation to civilization.[311]

Olivier Roy recognizes totalizing tendencies in Islamist strains of the religion but cannot equate these with 'fascist' ideologies. Islamism, for Roy, prohibits any social space, any conviviality, outside of the unit of the family. If the family unit, via men, the mosque and the state are the three units for Islamization, there exists no other legitimate social structure. In purely pragmatic and historical terms, this is a denial of any notion of Muslim civilization and leads to an inevitable 'social conformity' and 'schizophrenia'.[312] With this logic, human sociability has and always will undermine the attainment of a properly Islamist society. Additionally, it must be noted that the manifestation of Islamist extremism that has arguably engendered the fear of 'Islamo-fascism', 9/11, is generally regarded as resulting from a peculiarly Westernized, privatized, reframing of Islam. In Kippenberg and Seidensticker's analysis of the religious rationale for the 9/11 atrocities, the *9/11 Handbook*, the authors identify a conflation of Islamic motifs with contemporary, radical liberalism. The ideology of the *9/11 Handbook* owes as much to the personalized religiosity of the West as it does to traditional Islam.[313] If Islamism is intellectually self-defeating, as Roy suggests, then it should be no surprise that the very ideologies and tools of modernity are employed in its cause. It may then be that the idea of a 'pure' Islam in political terms is as elusive as the 'pure' peaceable Islam that Abushouk seeks to reclaim. Perhaps the most fruitful path for Christian interrelating with Islam, then, is an engagement that is equal to what *is* rather than what *purports to be*, whether inherently irenic or totalizing.

It is the backdrop of concerns about the perceived oppressiveness of Islam and the fragility of the heritage of European Christian civilization that suggests that the Catholic Church is embarking on a 'new realism about Islam',[314] culminating in Pope Benedict XVI's Regensburg Address in 2006. Combined with his repositioning of the Pontifical Council for Interreligious Dialogue as a freestanding agency of the Holy See, and the transfer of the experienced Archbishop Michael Fitzgerald from the PCID in 2006, it may seem that Benedict's papacy took a fresh trajectory with regard to other faiths.[315] Though the controversial element of Benedict's Regensburg Address was the quotation from the Byzantine Emperor Manuel II Paleologus that asserted the violence of the prophet Muhammad,[316] the political theology exhibited by the substance of the speech is arguably more contentious, expressing as it does his personal perspective on a properly Christian Europe. Pope Benedict's assessment of the 'convergence' of biblical faith and Greek philosophical enquiry as the 'decisive character in Europe' and as what 'remains the foundation of what can rightly be called Europe'[317] superimposes the role of host on to the Church, Muslims being guests in or strangers to the wider culture. This is a recurrent theme for Benedict, his earlier work, *Truth and Tolerance*, arguing that Christianity was the 'synthesis of faith and reason'[318] and thus at home in the culture of Christian Europe. He seems to be conscious of a creeping relativism and secularism that is undermining the civilization of Europe and in danger of leading to despotism and sectarian violence. This is characterized for him by what he sees as a 'peculiar Western self-hatred'[319] that seeks to sever the roots of European civilization in the progressive self-forgetting of Christian institutions. This is not a significant departure from Pope John Paul II's description of European relativism as a 'culture of death'[320] and suggests a continuous papal concern for the guarding of Christian culture in Europe.[321]

Anthony O'Mahony observes a long-standing papal burden for Europe in the very origins of the continent's identity. For O'Mahony, the '"idea of Europe" is an extension and achievement of the ecumenical goal of Christianity'.[322] As this 'idea' extends eastwards, the ecclesial diversity becomes apparent and a necessary ecumenical horizon encompassing Western and Eastern Churches becomes visible.[323] That Islam should be a significant presence in the newly configured Europe underlines a papal determination that the cultural inheritance of Christianity should not become victim to a collective amnesia. For Michael Kirwan, talk of a return to the Christian roots of Europe is more redolent of political 'mythology' than theology, rightly conceived, though he concedes grounds for the fear of fragmentation and totalitarianism that exercised Pope John Paul II.[324]

How the Church should negotiate its public proclamation across this shifting and diverse collective we call Europe without seeming to revert to a mythic conception of Christianity's cultural legacy strikes at the heart of the political theology question. It is worth noting that this European debate is just a larger equivalent of the question faced by the Church of England: how does the Church contribute to a British (or English) civilization of evident religious diversity from an increasingly marginal position? As the established Church in England, the notion of a 'Christian nation' might serve to exclude the cultural presence of Islam if that presence is deemed to undermine presumed liberties. How can the Church itself be regarded as conducive to liberty in this account? If the Church of England's political theology is to underwrite a more pluralist conception of the public square, how does it articulate its rejection of oppressive strains of Islamic politics?

The 'double jeopardy' for Middle Eastern Christians of being a marginal branch of an already marginalized region provides another context to the challenge of religious freedom. This double jeopardy is given a 'hermeneutical key' by George Sabra's alternate designation of 'Arab Christian' or 'Eastern Christian'. For the former, the primary identity is seen in ethnic terms, such that Western ecclesial and political overtures are viewed with suspicion and in imperialistic terms. For the latter, their marginal status as minorities under increasingly oppressive Islamic regimes generates a search for liberation from the resources of the West.[325] Both lenses have been undermined by political events in recent years, and both hold elements of truth that need to be taken seriously by the Church in the West.

Illustrative of these 'two ways of being a Christian' in the Muslim Middle East are the Western interventions in Iraq. The influence of broader political tensions and the conflation of 'West' with 'Christian' have had a disastrous effect on the fortunes of the Christian communities in Iraq following the two Gulf Wars.[326] This has had far-reaching implications for the predominantly Chaldean Christian Church community which, despite the post-Saddam Hussein regime, has found its freedoms increasingly circumscribed and its numbers decimated by emigration and persecution from the ISIS movement. This creates an ambiguity for the world Church: pursuing advocacy for suffering Christians in marginal situations while trying to avoid the repetition of perceived colonizing interference that may exacerbate the insecurity of Iraqi Christians.[327]

In Nigeria it seems that religion has been 'mobilized' in the pursuit of social and economic advantage.[328] Interestingly, Stanislaw Grodz believes that a reawakened shared sense of *Africanness* is a fruitful discourse for West African Christians and Muslims.[329] In the common experiences of a historic African culture that has often been suppressed by each faith, there are perhaps resources for a shared citizenship that can overcome religious difference. By enculturating the respective religious experiences in the African milieu, the charged 'clash of civilizations' script is avoided and an appeal to the civic needs of everyone made possible. Peaceful coexistence between Christians and Muslims, it is suggested, cannot be a mere matter of heightened religiosity but has to draw on each community's conception of social and political structures. Thus, with regard to the controversial implementation of Shari'a law in northern Nigeria, a response that argues for the privatization of religion is wholly inadequate to the context. What is required is a shared understanding of citizenship and a full responsibility in the public realm that provides a forum for the negotiation of the genuinely different and sometimes conflicting religious belief systems.[330] Rabiatu Ammah similarly calls for a sense of shared citizenship among Nigerian Christians and Muslims, recognizing the increasingly radicalized traditions that are holding sway.[331] Josiah Idowu-Fearon reiterates the need for a Christian civic engagement *with* Muslims specifically for the Anglican Church in Nigeria but stresses the importance of support for this within the broader Anglican Communion.[332] The reframing of the respective exclusivist beliefs is not likely to be as successful in averting conflict as developing public theologies for Christians and Muslims that affirm the common good.[333] Indeed, the very collaboration of missionary Muslims and Christians for the good of African society is already being articulated in local theologies and offering the potential for a model for Christian–Muslim relations globally.[334]

In the only Asian country that has a majority-Christian population, the Philippines, there has been the sense of a 'special vocation' to 'bear witness to the Gospel in the heart of Asia' that underscores the vulnerability felt by Muslims towards Christians.[335] For Rocco Viviano, the primary challenge facing the Catholic Church in the Philippines is the appropriate handling of the tension between dialogue and proclamation:

> how to maintain the cosmic dimension of the church's mission while allowing that religions may have a purpose in God's plan; how to integrate faithfulness to the missionary mandate ('go, proclaim, baptise'), while learning from other religions (i.e. how can 'Tradition' be enriched by 'traditions'?).[336]

Once again, the mutual enrichment of traditions is played out in the 'socio-political dimension' with a problematic overarching narrative of colonialism, Islamic extremism and the quest for autonomy by specific ethnic groupings in the Philippines.[337]

In Malaysia, the Christian minority carries the weight of following a faith that is perceived as 'foreign',[338] another example of the broader socio-political history prejudicing mutual, shared citizenship. For Peter Riddell, this is expressed in the aspiration of a 'liberal and tolerant society based on a common vision which is both articulated and owned by all faith communities'.[339] In India too, the colonial and missionary past informs a profound suspicion of the Christian minorities among Hindu and Muslim neighbours.[340] The legacy of the 'two-nations theory' that resulted in the foundation of Pakistan as a Muslim state informs Muslim attitudes to plurality in India such that it has been argued that the core question facing Muslims is 'the idea of citizenship'.[341] Can Muslims engage fully in the plural realities of modern-day India for the good of all?

To many Christians in Britain, the negative portrayal of the experiences of the Christian minority in Pakistan by campaigning groups such as the Barnabas Fund suggests the inability of Muslim-majority regimes to robustly entertain plurality.[342] Even at the level of academic dialogical exchanges, Islamic majority status has been noted as creating inertia in the task of mutual interrelating. One Muslim scholar is quoted as saying of the openness of Christian–Muslim dialogue in Britain in contrast to his home country of Pakistan: 'we need you there, we do not need you here'.[343] For all the evidence of need for explorations of citizenship, of efforts for the common good among Christians and Muslims, churches have to reckon with the realities of persecution in many Muslim-majority contexts.

The significance of local statements and symbolic actions impacting Christian–Muslim relations on a global scale was evidenced by the violence inflicted on Christians in some Muslim cities consequent upon the Regensburg Address. Similarly, the publication of cartoons of the prophet Muhammad in a Danish newspaper in 2005 had repercussions for Christian–Muslim relations elsewhere.[344] The articulation of a political theology for the Church of England in relation to Islam, then, must reckon with the realities of Christian–Muslim relations worldwide, which include the negative experience of religious persecution.

Islam, Judaism, the state of Israel and Christian–Muslim relations

One of the concerning manifestations of totalizing elements within Islam has been in attitudes to Jews. This has led a number of scholars to reflect on whether the primary and original other that is totalized in Islam is the Jew. As Camilla Adang notes, 'Islamic polemics against Judaism and its adherents is a phenomenon as old as Islam itself, and the Qur'an is its very first source.'[345] The medieval Islamic polemics towards Judaism that Adang observes express an aversion to the particularity of Judaism: there is no universal aspiration that emboldens it beyond its ethnic confines. Judaism 'wielded no power, and worldly power and military victories are among the signs of God's grace'.[346] This seems to support the reserve found by Arnold Toynbee about a civilization that seems unable to concede ground to the other; in Islam, the formative other being Jewish.

Gudrun Kramer recognizes the existence of anti-Semitism in Islamic history and among contemporary commentators. However, for her the primary sources do not eventuate in Islamic totalizing of Jews. The Qur'an also offers a sympathetic portrayal of Jews, and Jews are merely part of a wider canvas of non-Muslims that, post Medina, are then seen more polemically.[347] Kramer's assessment posits the charge of Islam's inherent anti-Semitism as an element of the trade in mutual polemics and invective: a 'grey zone'[348] that is by no means inevitable within the respective religions and communities. The critique of Islamo-fascism is just one more contemporary expression of that same dynamic of mutual polemics, for Kramer, that is directed at Islam.[349]

However, the ambivalence of Islamic relations with Judaism is given added freight by the scholarly investigations of Gerald Hawting into the qur'anic context of monotheism. His controversial thesis would suggest that the traditional interpretation of the Qur'an's call away from idol worship is not supported by the realities of seventh-century Arabian monotheism; indeed, that the Qur'an is rather advocating a 'pure monotheism' around food and purity regulations. The traditional interpretation then is driven by the need to establish the veracity of the Abrahamic connection (the formative history in Jewish revelation) rather than by a substantive correction of idol-worshippers (*mushrikūn*).[350] It is beyond the scope of this study to take this line of argument further but what it raises are some of the genuine questions that exist around assumptions of Islam's Abrahamic roots. Hawting's analysis would posit Islam as responding to and adapting Judaism[351] and Christianity rather than reverting to a natural religion prophetically exercised by Arabian idol worship, further undermining the Abrahamic faiths motif.

By contrast, Fred Donner's thesis would observe the unifying tendencies of Muhammad's prophetic vocation, which is rather characterized as a 'monotheistic reform movement' that embraced both Christians and Jews in the Medinan milieu.[352] It was only later, after Muhammad's death, that relations between Muslims, Christians and, in particular, Jews solidified into sharp distinctions. For Donner, Muhammad's Islamic mission was to constitute a community of monotheistic 'believers' that *included* Jews, albeit reformed according to the qur'anic revelation.

Timothy Winter supports the traditional Islamic abrogationist view that Islam corrects the waywardness of later Judaism and Christianity, but reconfigures this sympathetically in suggesting a relative intercessory role within each of the Abrahamic faiths by their respective prophets. Thus Moses will intercede for Jews, Jesus for Christians, to God who has revealed his purposes to Muhammad, the primary intercessor. Winter is thus able to assert the particularity of Islam in its universal aspiration while allowing for concession to revelation in Judaism and Christianity, though no explicit Islamic tradition or text is used to support such a reading.[353] Muhammad is the vehicle of this 'mercy' to Christians and Jews. But there remains the nagging sense that the integrities of those faiths have been manipulated and distorted to ground a purported Islamic inclusivity. In his agreement with Samuel Goitein's phrase that in Islam there is a 'creative symbiosis' with Judaism,[354] it is difficult to see how Winter's analysis avoids contradicting his advocacy elsewhere that Abrahamic religions 'be about allowing them to bear witness to themselves'.[355] There is no mention of what Islam offers Judaism in this bilateral relationship beyond its correction. Winter's inclusive Islam *still* sees Judaism as believed and practised as errant, and Christianity as founded on the false premise of Christ's crucifixion. There remains a challenge to Islam to present an understanding of itself that can give an account of Judaism that allows Judaism to exist with full integrity.

For Douglas Pratt, whatever the theological bases for destructive perspectives, the pursuit of positive Islamic paradigms of inter-relationships with Judaism is an urgent task in the contemporary context.[356] Jacques Waardenburg similarly notes the persistence of entrenched accounts of mutual animosity between Christians, Jews and Muslims and recommends an attention to the diversity of *all three faiths* that is belied often by static pronouncements from religious leaders and inadequate frameworks that perpetuate religious rivalries.[357] Once more, an emphasis on the *lived reality* of faiths in all their diversity seems to be a priority for relations between the religions.

In the context of global geopolitics, Israel remains a focus for much tension in Christian–Muslim relations. In Israel the very viability of a sustainable Christian presence in the Holy Land is in doubt.[358] With respect to Palestinian Christians, there is the double jeopardy of being a marginal presence within an already disenfranchised Arab community in Israel. Their plight is often subsumed under a wider political conflict that takes a more complex hue than the simplistic shorthand of 'the West and Islam'.[359] That the power blocks are not as clearly delineated as might appear does not deny the 'apocalyptic'[360] potential of the situation. The particularly visceral nature of religious struggle in the Holy Land, a tension that is also manifest *within* Christian communities[361] as well as between the faiths of Judaism, Islam and Christianity, points to the ineluctable connections between the traditions. We may wish to hold some reserve about the helpfulness of the Abrahamic faiths motif, yet there remains a sense in which Abraham both affirms commonality and becomes the 'focal point for claims of exclusivity'.[362] There is little doubt that the fact that place and prophethood are so deeply intertwined for Christians, Jews and Muslims in Israel, and supremely in Jerusalem, raises the temperature of relations between and within these three faiths in the Middle East. Anthony O'Mahony summarizes this judgement for Christian–Muslim relations with his observation that:

> There is an intimacy to the Christian–Muslim encounter, which offers a familiarity, but allows for little theological commonality due to difference. Thus throughout the centuries since the rise of Islam, Muslim–Christian relations have revolved around this double axis of familiar, biblical appeal and strenuous, religious critique.[363]

The sharpness of the respective religious histories that are displayed so acutely in the Middle East is one of the reasons why the Catholic Church has put such a priority on the support and continuance of a Christian presence in the Holy Land. Only by returning to an essential belief in the one God worshipped by Jews, Christians and Muslims in neighbourly interreligious dialogue and peacemaking, it is argued, can catastrophe be averted.[364]

The significance of the Holy Land to Pope Benedict XVI for Christian–Muslim relations globally was confirmed by his invitation in February 2009 to a special Synod of the Middle East taking place in October 2010. This Synod's 'crucial issue' was seen to be 'the presence of Christian communities in regions of strong Islamic supremacy'. Though the self-preservation of the Christian witness is clearly in mind,[365] for the Holy See there is a far-reaching potency in the ongoing vitality of the Church in the Middle East. The presence of Christians in the Middle East represents a richness for the whole of society and a guarantee of social, cultural and religious development. In Anthony O'Mahony's words, 'Christianity in the Middle East has a witness beyond itself'.[366]

For Robert M. Johnson, the Church has a role as a 'mediator between the two antagonists' of Judaism and Islam in the Holy Land, akin to that advocated by Louis Massignon.[367] That the

Church could be a broker within the charged rivalries over holy sites is largely, for Johnson, to do with the incidental nature of place within the Christian narrative in contrast to Judaism and Islam, for which land is, respectively, gift and vindication from God. It is in a negotiation of a 'theology of land' with Muslims and Jews that honours the significance of place yet prioritizes the exigencies of cooperative citizenship that the Church's gift rests.

The ongoing presence of a Christian community in the Holy Land likewise acts as a guarantor of the ability of Islam to take plurality seriously. This is implicit in the 'Memorandum of their Beatitudes the Patriarchs and of the Heads of the Christian communities in Jerusalem on the Significance of Jerusalem for Christians':

> Jerusalem is a holy city for the people of the three monotheistic religions: Judaism, Christianity and Islam. Its unique nature of sanctity endows it with a special vocation: calling for reconciliation and harmony among people, whether citizens, pilgrims or visitors. And because of its symbolic and emotive value, Jerusalem has been a rallying cry for different revived nationalistic and fundamentalist stirrings in the region and elsewhere.[368]

This ecumenical commitment to the religious diversity of Jerusalem and the consequent inclusivist political theology is reiterated in the writings of the Anglican Islamicist Kenneth Cragg. Cragg argues that Jerusalem 'by irreducible historical factors – has to have a plural, that is a triple, "ownership" of love and may not properly be unilaterally annexed'.[369] The argument for an inclusive cast to the site of the Holy Land for the three faiths is yet envisaged with a full appreciation of the tragedy of Zionism for the Arab peoples. For Cragg, the establishment of the modern state of Israel through a militant movement under the British Mandate paradoxically realized the 'Palestinian politics of statehood'. Zionism's apotheosis was Arabism's nadir: 'From that consummation of fulfilment and of frustration proceeds the incompatible defence of the one and redress of the other.'[370] Bishop Michael Nazir-Ali likewise affirms 'an open and inclusive city' as reflected in the Lambeth Conference of 1998, and notes the ecumenical and international responsibilities to protect religious and civic freedoms within the state.[371]

Such statements of Anglican goodwill cannot but be tarnished by British implication in the political roots that furnished the 'competitively loved'[372] land, though. The iniquities, in Cragg's view, of the 1917 Balfour Declaration's wilful neglect of the vast majority of Palestinian presence in the Holy Land, and the political opportunism of the British government's betrayal of earlier commitments to the Arab peoples, undermined the integrity of the Anglican presence in the Middle East. This earlier injustice paralysed the subsequent Mandate, such that Jewish yearnings for a homeland under the shadow of the Holocaust were then subject to similar prevarications. This has given an 'Anglican unease in Zion',[373] according to Cragg, that 'can mean hope as well as reproach'.[374] Bearing the humbling associations with the British government's role in the contemporary political nexus that is Israel, the Anglican Church has the potential to articulate a future that is not 'power-ensured'. This repeated characterization by Cragg of the will-to-power that inhibits true faith is best challenged by a self-giving presence that undermines the idolatries at the heart of the monism inherent in both Zionism and Islamism, as idealized in the *hijra*.[375] This is a difficult tension for the Church to hold: to engage robustly in the public life of the Holy Land in a manner that does not grasp power or hide from its own past mistakes and associations. Yet this is a temper that seems relevant to our primary research for the Church of England too.

It is the Anglican 'unease' in Jerusalem that brought urgency to Kenneth Cragg's project, as Assistant Bishop in Jerusalem from 1970, to Arabicize the bishopric and create a truly local ecclesial, Anglican presence. This gave public reality to a community that had itself suffered under the establishment of the state of Israel and thus could more authentically witness to shared citizenship among the three monotheisms.[376] It is in the spirit of a rejection of all that is 'power-ensured' that the Anglican episcopate is known as the Bishop *in* Jerusalem rather than *of* Jerusalem, simultaneously deferring to the primacy of the Greek Orthodox patriarch[377] and, it would seem, knowingly conscious of 'Anglican' colonial pretensions. It has, according to Michael Marten, enabled the Anglican Church to punch above its weight by acting as a broker across the ecumenical divide. Considering the Church of England's own challenge of diversity, it is worth comparing John Sentamu, as Archbishop of York, and his preference in his previous role to be called the Bishop *for* Birmingham as opposed to the Bishop *of* Birmingham.[378] One wonders if there is something patterned for the Church of England in the fact of the *Arabic* Anglican Church in Jerusalem and a *Ugandan* Archbishop of York modelling a political theology that gives away to become a more potent public presence. The wilful loss of the *possessive* provides a means for the Anglican Church to retain a public presence, albeit in a similarly plural and minority situation, and points forward to the likely shape of a political theology for the Church of England in encounter with Islam.

Recalling the impetus for the inclusion in Vatican II of statements on Islam, there seems to be an unavoidable link between Christian and Muslim relations and international political relations, especially as regards Western foreign policy. If, as Douglas Pratt asserts, 'the founding of the State of Israel is to some degree the legacy of the relationship of Judaism to Christianity',[379] then contemporary Christian–Muslim relations cannot be considered without reference to the Church's engagement with Judaism and the concrete reality of the state of Israel. So while ecclesial histories have to be reckoned with, the Church's theological understanding of Judaism and 'the land' also comes under the inevitable scrutiny of the other monotheisms.

The movement of Christian Zionism complicates the scene for Palestinian Christians suffering the double jeopardy of marginalization. A movement that gives Christian justification to the establishment of the state of Israel as an outworking of biblical prophecy, and views Middle Eastern politics through the lens of pre-millennial eschatology, inevitably isolates Palestinian Christians. If God holds a preference for the entitlement to the land of Jews over Palestinians, and the culmination of the flowering of Israel is to be the conversion of all Jews, then aspirations to shared citizenship and inclusivity are illusory. Indeed, within this world view it is not clear what it can mean, in any real sense, to be a *Palestinian Christian*.[380]

The Anglican Church has associations with Zionism that date back to the work of the Anglican missionary society, the London Society for Promoting Christianity among the Jews.[381] This society had seen the Anglican Church presence in the Holy Land purely as a focus for work with Jews and resisted the Arabicization of the bishopric. Part of the contemporary Anglican presence in Jerusalem is a Christian-Zionist congregation in the former cathedral church at Christ Church in the old city.[382] There is a formal commitment from the Christian communities in Jerusalem, including the Anglican Church, to a vision of shared citizenship.[383] Signed in 1994, a memorandum agreed by heads of the various Christian communities affirms that no one can appropriate Jerusalem 'in exclusivist ways'. However, formal and informal links with Christian Zionism cannot but underline the 'unease' of the Anglican presence. While asserting the religious freedoms of the Christian community, the formal ecumenical commitment also holds open the possibility for the inclusive citizenship that Kenneth Cragg called for, and rebuffs trajectories among Jews and Palestinians that would seek to monopolize power in the Holy Land. This is an important statement in the context of global Christian–Muslim relations because of the high profile Israel has in Islamic communities.

The impact of perceived injustice against Palestinians on the attitudes of British Muslims to their sense of citizenship and loyalty in Britain and the potential for this alienation to take religious form is well documented.[384] The dangers of a conflation of 'West' with 'Christian' are all too evident around the competing animosities of the Holy Land when Churches are seen to underwrite Christian Zionism. Muzaffar Iqbal's commentary on Islam's relations with and in the West is a particularly revealing example of how Christianity can so easily be held responsible for a culture and a politics it would otherwise disdain. Iqbal presents a continuity from the Crusades with a contemporary stand-off between Islam 'and the West' over the sovereignty of Jerusalem.[385] This immediately Christianizes the Zionism that he would oppose while invoking the violence and persecution of the Crusades as present realities. All that is colonial, secular and militaristic is then perceived as a legacy of the Church. Thus, Iqbal concludes: 'it is a contradiction of the modern West that while apparently it maintains an irreligious posture, it remains deeply rooted in the rituals of a Christianity which has hardly anything to do with the noble Messenger of God.'[386] It would be disingenuous for the Church to deny *any* responsibility for the actions of Western governments.[387] However, a lazy conflation of Western political institutions and Christianity needs to be challenged if only because of its ignorance of the significant Middle Eastern Christian communities that the Latin Church, ecumenically, is committed to support.

In order to assert the specific, cultural identity of Palestinian Christians, there has been a growing self-consciousness around liberation theologies that support a just solution to the Palestine question. As Laura Robson notes, this movement works in two directions: to communicate to Western Christians the plight of the Palestinian Church, and to alert Middle Eastern Muslims to a Christian rationale for Palestinian liberation.[388] The 1987 Anglican Consultative Council meeting in Singapore acknowledged the existence of the state of Israel but rejected 'the interpretation of holy Scripture which affirms a special place for the present state of Israel and in the light of biblical prophecy, finds it detrimental to peace and justice, and damaging to Jews, Christians and Muslims.'[389] Here the Anglican Communion seems to be rejecting Christian Zionism and appreciating how this doctrine can impact negatively on relations across the three monotheisms. However, there is an apparent risk to relations with Jews from too much identification with the Palestinian cause.

The sensitivity of this issue is noted by two long-standing Anglican exponents of Christian–Jewish relations, Marcus Braybrooke and Bishop Richard Harries.[390] Can Anglican Christians advocate justice for Palestinians in the Holy Land without alienating Jews? And what might an acknowledgement of the inheritance and legacy of Judaism to the Christian faith mean for relations with Muslims?

Answers to these two questions are beyond the scope of this study, but it is important to recognize the interdependence of the theological and political issues that converge at the meeting points of the three monotheisms. The issue of conversion of Jews is indicative of a theological dilemma that cannot but bring to the fore the histories of anti-Semitism as well as probing questions about covenant, Christology and salvation. While the 'relationship between Christianity and the Jewish other remains fragile',[391] the Anglican Church has made a priority of the 'Anglican Jewish Commission of the Archbishop of Canterbury and the Chief Rabbinate of Israel', such that, since 2006, there are now annual meetings between the respective religious leaders alternately in Lambeth and Jerusalem.

The Anglican Jewish Commission meeting in Israel in July 2008 witnessed a statement that acknowledged the diversity of Anglican perspectives on covenant, salvation and the Holy Land but reaffirmed the position of the 2001 publication *Sharing One Hope?*[392] that replacement theology was utterly repudiated by the Church of England.[393] *Sharing One Hope?* supports the continuing validity of God's election of the Jews as a vital area of Christian consensus.[394] To regard the Church as having fully superseded all of God's plans for the Jewish people is believed to lead to the 'teaching of contempt' indicative of the anti-Semitism that the Church is seeking to reject. Yet at the same time the document still opens the possibility for mission among Jews, expressing a range of approaches within the Church.[395] The Church of England's position seems agonizingly delicate. It is, perhaps appropriately, Rowan Williams who summarizes the inner contradictions in a way that provides some clarity about what the Church is *not* saying:

The important thing is to recognize that Judaism and Christianity are now separate religions, both claiming legitimate descent from the religion of biblical Israel. This at least saves us from the implicit or explicit claim that Judaism has no post-biblical history, from the ignorant assimilation of contemporary Judaism to the polemical targets of the New Testament rhetoric, and from the unbroken reading of Jewish experience in exhaustively alien categories determined by Christian needs and interests.[396]

Williams' statement allows for the assertion of difference such that the debts to Judaism do not become totalized and subsumed in an occlusion of the other. What is particularly striking about this more agonized approach to Judaism is the implication for Christian–Muslim relations. If the Church is to be self-conscious of the dangers of supersessionism with respect to Jews, then there is arguably a similar challenge to Muslims to give space to the integrities of Christianity and Judaism in their post-biblical reading of revelation. It obligates the Church to bring an appropriate space for a living Judaism into the mutual understandings of Christians and Muslims and implicitly demands that Islam respect the integrities of the New Testament that Christians present. This is no easy and tidy resolution to the historical antipathies of the three monotheisms but confirmation of a theological 'unease'.

Conscious of the fragility of Christian–Jewish relations, any reflection by the Church of England on Islam has at least to be aware of the implications for consequent relations with Jews within the inextricable histories of these three monotheisms. Such reflections would, it is argued, be capable of bridging rather than submerging differences between the respective faiths.

Conclusion

The contemporary context of Christian–Muslim relations underlines the global consciousness in which any statements and actions of the Church of England are situated. Growing awareness of the difficulties facing many Christian communities in Muslim countries demands that any political theology in response to Islam be able to undergird religious liberties for other faiths and challenge religious persecution. The Church of England's own responsibilities as part of a global Anglican Communion suggest the need for it to advocate for and be especially cognizant of the full diversity of Anglican experiences of Christian–Muslim relations.

Relations with Judaism and the problematic status of Israel for contemporary Christian–Muslim relations remind the Church of the failures of both religious communities towards Jews and the inextricable connections between the three faiths. That political agendas in the Middle East and beyond can have such significant effects on Christian–Muslim relations elsewhere highlights the need for the Church of England to develop its theologies in global and political cross reference.

It is apparent that in many situations around the world, Christian–Muslim relations have a decisive effect on the peace and well-being of the wider community. Those relations are frequently charged by socio-political factors, though the religious roots of the respective traditions are integral to the encounters. For Christians, issues of religious freedom among Muslims and fair treatment as minorities are very present challenges to Islam. In many contexts, the prevailing Islamic trajectory seems to mitigate plurality. For Muslims, the association of Christians with the 'West' remains problematic and challenges churches to a more authentically contextual presence and a willingness to resist a discourse of power in response to Islam. However, the importance of ecumenical and international support for and in contexts of Christian vulnerability cannot be overestimated.

Anglican reflections on Islam will need to be attentive to the interactions of the local with the global, noting the new vista opened by the *A Common Word* initiative of Muslim–Christian dialogue from international Muslim scholars and leaders.[397] Additionally, the inextricable role of Judaism for Christian–Muslim relations cannot be avoided, and rather draws attention to the priority of the politico-theological question posed by the controversies over the state of Israel.

These reflections will be seen to be confirmed in the development of recent theologies of interreligious relations in the Church of England and Anglican Communion, and provide a foundation for the much-needed political theologies suggested by the delicate interaction of the local and the global for Christians and Muslims.

Anecdotes from the field: the inescapability of our world context

One of the most tangible examples of the global interconnectedness for Christian–Muslim encounters is in the current refugee crisis. In many of our cities there are scores of refugees from countries such as Iraq and Afghanistan that continue to source Christian–Muslim encounters across urban communities that are informed by events elsewhere. In many UK cities, including Birmingham, a notable feature of this immigration has been in the influx of Iranian Muslim refugees who are coming into churches and seeking baptism. While there are some that may be seeking baptism in order to gain political asylum, there are many examples of genuine spiritual searching from Iranians coming to church and consequent growth in Christian communities across a range of different ecclesial traditions.[398]

The stories of many of these Iranian refugees include the struggles of the Christian minority. In gatherings with local imams in Birmingham, I will mention the situation of converts from Islam in Pakistan or Iran, when appropriate, as they all feature as backdrops to our local relationships. Sometimes there is ignorance of their plight and statements can be made that are opportunities to build good foundations of religious freedom. At the international level, in 2016 a coalition of Muslim leaders published the 'Marrakech Declaration' affirming the rights of minority religions in Muslim countries.[399] Airing the realities of destructive relating as well as constructive coexistence moves the Christian–Muslim encounter away from essentialist readings across our faiths. Our stories are a mixed bag that includes the Church's own implication in persecution and racism. In a climate where it is easy to slip into respective victimhood status, the complexities and diversities of encounter and the experience of the global Church and its historical traditions are all vital. It must be remembered too, under the headlines of religious violence associated with the likes of ISIS, that it is Muslim minorities who are often the most numerous casualties.

Both Christian and Muslim communities have the potential to speak for the good of the other community at local, national and international levels. When I was working in the Springfield area of Birmingham and the parish church I was attached to was seeking permission to convert its community project into a Children's Centre, a Muslim politician objected to state funding going to a church project in a largely Islamic community. Permission was eventually granted following a letter written by the leadership of the local mosque, who encouraged the venture because they saw how much their neighbourhood was being served. The local Muslim community were advocating for the church in this instance. Arguably, a mark of mature relationship across faiths will be a mutually rigorous speaking out for the good of the other, even it proves costly to our own community.

PART 2

ANGLICAN ENCOUNTERS

5

Anglican Encounters with Islam
Pre-1998

The Church of England and Islam: a history of relations

Anglican assessments of Islam can be traced back to the origins of
the English Reformation. The Church of England Prayer Books of
1549, 1552 and 1662 all contain, in the rite for Good Friday, the
prayer: 'Have mercy on all Jews, Turks, infidels, and heretics.'[400] In
the context of the broader Reformation across Europe, the 'Turks'
were a peculiar class of infidel representing a goad to Christendom
to avert God's judgement poised against a corrupt and errant
Catholic Church.[401] The reality for Muslims in Reformation England
was that they had no status as citizens under the Crown, their
description alternately 'Turk' if Ottoman or 'Moor' if North African
and essentially alien by virtue of their religion. As G. K. Hunter
points out, for the Elizabethan imagination there 'seem, in fact, to
be Moors everywhere, but only everywhere in that outer circuit of
non-Christian lands.'[402]

Probably the earliest British mention of Islam, though, is by that
most English of ecclesial commentators, the Venerable Bede in his
Ecclesiastical History of the English Nation in 735: 'At that season,
the most grievous pest, the Saracens, wasted and destroyed the
realm of Gaul with grievous and miserable carnage; but they soon
after received and suffered the due punishment of their perfidy.'[403]
For Bede, the relative success or failure of a civilization rested with
the truth and potency of the faith it held. This association of the
merits of cultures as they reflected religion was to be a persistent

view of many Anglican Christians.

It was during the reign of Elizabeth I that English Christians began to have first-hand experience of encounters with Muslims due to her policy of encouraging trade with North Africans and Ottomans. Alongside the sometimes mythic image of marauding Muslims, enhanced by the uncomfortable proximity of North African pirates off the south coast of England, there were the more prosaic relations of the marketplace and diplomacy.[404]

What is noteworthy for contemporary reflection is that some of the Elizabethan experiences of Christian–Muslim interaction reveal ways the respective religions do not seem to problematize relations unduly. Indeed, there is evidence that Elizabethan merchants were becoming aware that Christians attained greater freedoms under Islam than Muslims in Christian countries. It was noted in a number of accounts that Muslims did not force conversion and that there was a vibrant Eastern Christian community that had adapted to the realities of Islamic civic and religious rule in the Middle East.[405] Even where the encounters involved imprisonment, slavery and release of Muslim pirates, contemporary accounts suggest that Muslims were treated fairly by their British captors and without any additional hostility occasioned by the issue of faith. Thus, Matar can state that in this period before British colonialism and Orientalism, 'the interaction between Britons and Turks was cordial, open and devoid of "domination" and construction.'[406]

Matar's studies on the earliest Anglican Christian–Muslim encounters highlight the surprise that Elizabethans experienced when Muslims, hearing about the Christian faith, did not convert. Moreover, the numerous examples of Christian conversions to Islam, whether under societal pressure or not, undermined the self-assured tenor of Christendom. As Matar notes, 'So common was conversion to Islam that by the end of the seventeenth century, Englishmen had to admit that it was as widespread as conversion to Christianity from Islam was rare.'[407] The extent of conversions to Islam necessitated Archbishop Laud's presenting a bill before Parliament in 1637 entitled 'A Form of Penance and Reconciliation of a Renegado or

Apostate from the Christian Religion to Turcism'.[408] The penitential rite was used extensively and establishes the clear theological disjuncture for seventeenth-century Anglicans between Christianity and Islam. What the description 'renegado' does is to reveal the sense of national betrayal in an English citizen becoming Muslim. An English Muslim was effectively a renegade, a 'fifth column'. This role would continue to be the defining position for British Muslims as settled citizenship from emigration within the British Empire began in the nineteenth century: the 'infidel within'.[409]

The contribution of John Locke (1632–1704) to liberal political science provides an illustration of the beginnings of attempts to make space for Islam in the Anglican polity.[410] This was done in the context of the advocacy of religious freedoms for Jews, Dissenters and pagan Native Americans in England. Ostensibly, Locke was arguing for the freedom of worship for Dissenters and used the case of Muslims, who at this stage were still not permanently resident in England, to do this. Reflecting on the status of Christians in Muslim countries, Locke was to highlight the inconsistency of prohibiting the practice of Calvinist and Arminian Christians in England when these would be acceptable in Muslim Constantinople.[411] Interestingly, Locke's argument was not theological: he regarded Islam as a false and deficient religion. Yet in advocating for Muslim religious freedom, he does 'demonstrate his willingness to treat Muslims and Christians as sincere seekers of God'.[412] It was not the business of the state to enforce 'right religion'. In Chapter 8 we shall be exploring more fully the Anglican political theologies that give an appropriately full space to Islam in the contemporary context. What is important to note here, though, is the importance of the wider discourse of religious plurality to Christian–Muslim relations, both internationally and ecumenically. In Locke's case, the political role of Islam is instrumentalized to justify freedom of religion to Dissenters. Matar's studies on Anglican Restorationist theologies[413] show how support for the return of Jews to Israel could be instrumentalized by Anglican Christians fearful of Islamic and Catholic empires.[414]

Alongside the indictments on and clear discontinuity with Islam expressed in the Book of Common Prayer, there is another more sympathetic approach that is evocative of fascination and curiosity. Within Anglicanism there is evidence of a persistent stream of inquiry into Islam and the Orient, including Christian Arabs and the Eastern Church, typified in the early initiatives by Archbishop William Laud to establish a chair in Arabic Studies at Oxford University. Through Laud's personal commitment to knowledge of Islam and the Islamic world, Edward Pococke (1604–91), chaplain at Aleppo, was appointed the founding lecturer in Arabic at Oxford University, translated the Book of Common Prayer into Arabic (1672) and wrote a history of the Arab world, *Specimen Historiae Arabum* (1650), which remained the authoritative text for 150 years or more.[415] It will become apparent that the sympathetic stream of inquiry and engagement of early Anglicanism may be seen to be given continuity within the more contemporary accounts of Kenneth Cragg and Rowan Williams in their reflections on Christianity in the Middle East.

Shereen Khairallah observes three stages in the growth of Arabic studies in England, which are important indicators of the political and cultural contexts of those epochs.[416] The first stage is the 'apologetic and polemic era' that we see in the meeting of the two civilizations in the earliest encounters and through into the Crusader era. This would be characterized by missionary zeal and evident in the writings of John of Damascus and Peter the Venerable. Into the sixteenth and seventeenth centuries, the 'biblical epoch' emphasizes attention to respective texts and sees the expansion of Arabic studies as a tool for better exegesis of biblical Hebrew. In this era, Muhammad remained a 'pseudo-prophet, and Islam a heresy'.[417] Alexander Ross (1580–1660), who produced an English translation of the French *du Ryer Qur'an* for King Charles 1, concluded typically that:

> there was no harm in reading the Qur'an as long as the reader bore in mind that he was first and foremost a Christian; he would not perjure his soul, but on the contrary, would learn what real heresy was.[418]

The crucial break in this period was that Arabic culture and Islamic religion were receiving attention in their own right rather than as vehicles for other knowledge, whether within the natural sciences or biblical languages.[419] Third, there is the 'modern era', which is symbolically marked by Napoleon's campaign in Egypt (1798–1801) and consequent arrival of French scientists to make objective observations of Islamic society. This epitomizes the beginnings of the encounter of the Enlightenment West with Islam.[420] This forensic encounter with Islam, exemplified by British Orientalists such as E. W. Lane (1801–76), Sir Richard Burton (1821–90) and Sir William Muir (1819–1905), tied Anglican encounters with Islam to the colonial project.

These respective eras indicate trends that continue to flow through formative Anglican reflections on Islam rather than being self-contained, evolutionary stages. Thus, the 'apologetic and polemic era' continues into the seventeenth century in Humphrey Prideaux, Dean of Norwich, and his publication *The True Nature of Imposture Fully Displayed in the Life of Mahomet*, which amounts to a 'violent attack on Islam and the person of the prophet'.[421] Indeed, the colonial character of the Enlightenment era's scientific appraisal of Islam and Arabic culture is evident in an earlier era in the instrumental role of the Levant Company's appropriation of Arabic documents at the request originally of Archbishop Ussher in 1624, and his successor William Laud.[422] Each approach to Islam and Arabic culture contains elements that are both sympathetic to and condemnatory of Islam. In Kenneth Cragg's view, the seventeenth- and eighteenth-century Anglican Orientalists are 'erudite and their observations tireless, even when their impressions are somewhat naïve. They are the eighteenth-century form of the fascination of the Bible, territorial, enthusiastic, but not yet missionary'.[423] For many commentators, the Western Christian assessment of Islam, typified by British Anglican Arabicists up to the turn of the nineteenth century, was 'a blend of patronizing disdain and romanticization of the Orient and the Levant'.[424]

The Anglican clergyman Charles Forster (1787–1871) continued in the vein of an open inquiry into the nature of Islam, offering a more irenic counterpoint to Muir's characterization of Islam as inherently destructive to civilization. His *Mahometanism Unveiled* (1829) caused considerable controversy by questioning the widely held presumption of Islam's violence, recognizing that 'Islam is a spiritual religion' and 'distortion and prejudice obscured facts in common understanding of Islam'.[425] W. R. W. Stephens, Prebendary of Chichester Cathedral in the 1870s, wrote a commentary on the Qur'an during this era of colonial fascination with the Orient. Critical of Bosworth Smith's account that had referred to Islam as a 'form of Christianity', he advocates friendship and respect but is clear that the Church should not 'dilute Christian doctrine'.[426] Whether the responses to Islam were positive or sympathetic, it was clear that Anglican Christians were fascinated by the Arab world and its religion, and determined to study it.

As the Church of England embarked on a more substantive encounter with Islam into the missionary era of the nineteenth century, the role of the Turk as 'enemy' was recast into the drama of British imperialism. Thus, the Anglican apologist and colonial civil servant William Muir could write in his bestselling account of the faith of Islam, *The Life of Mahomet* (1858–61): 'the sword of Mahomet, and the Coran are the most fatal enemies of Civilization, Liberty and the Truth which the world has yet known'.[427] For Muir, who was a prominent supporter of Anglican missionary endeavours in the Muslim world and whose writings following the Indian Mutiny of 1857 had a huge influence on British perceptions of Islam: 'Islam was a false religion which kept Muslims "in a backward and in some respects barbarous state"'.[428] The existence of thousands of Muslim 'lascars' living and working in several British port cities during the Victorian era allowed the foreign missionary endeavour to become a domestic objective for Anglican Christians. The 'backward' nature of Islam meant that this evangelism was ostensibly a beneficent act of condescension that combined with a vocation to 'civilize' what were seen as depraved 'Muhammadans'.[429]

Islam was essentially still 'over there' in terms of the perception of the Church of England until the second half of the twentieth century. However, the example of several notable Anglican missionaries in the Middle East and North Africa are worth mentioning at this stage, in terms of their impact on domestic responses to Islam. Henry Martyn (1781–1812) was an Anglican priest and missionary to India, 'the first of the modern missionaries to the Islamic world'.[430] What Martyn lacked in the achievement of converts he compensated for in raising of the profile of Islam among British Anglicans as a vast body of humanity requiring the attentions of evangelicals in prayer and missionary support.

As part of the consequent wave of nineteenth-century mission to Islam, Karl Gottlieb Pfander (1803–65), a German missionary to Egypt with the Anglican Church Missionary Society, is notable for his emphasis on polemics in public debating with Muslim leaders as an evangelistic tool. He offers a significant counterpoint to his partner in Anglican missionary work in Egypt, Temple Gairdner (1873–1928).[431] Gairdner's approach was very different from Pfander's. As Michael Shelley's study of Gairdner notes, he had a very fluid attitude to Islam, changing his perception of and becoming sympathetic to the genuine spirituality at the heart of the faith, while never losing his evangelical passion. Importantly, too, Gairdner advocated for a response to Islam that united all strands of Christendom and was a vital ecumenical endeavour.[432] These features can equally be ascribed to Constance Padwick, another Anglican missionary to Muslims in Egypt and collaborator and biographer of Gairdner. Padwick's *Muslim Devotions* remains an unprecedented labour of evangelical devotion to the compilation of an anthology of Islamic spiritual writings, and displays a remarkable sympathy with the Islamic spirit.[433]

It is important to recognize the existence of the two strains of the polemical and the irenic – symbolized by Pfander and Gairdner – in the Anglican missionary movement. We shall see how Gairdner and Padwick in particular shaped the work of Bishop Kenneth Cragg and influenced in turn the formal documents of the Anglican Communion and Church of England on Islam as the lived reality of a substantive, contemporary British Islam came into being.

Lambeth Conferences and Islam

Pre-1988 Lambeth Conferences

In exploring the Church of England's understanding of Islam I am seeking a theology of interreligious relations that seems to be authoritative for the context of Christian–Muslim relations in England while drawing from the Anglican tradition as a whole. In doing so, there is recognition of the inclusive nature of Anglican theology. This inclusivity is part of an Anglican process that can hold a range of positions outside the core beliefs of the creed: the *adiaphora* characteristic of the roots of Anglican self-identity supremely articulated by Richard Hooker in the *Laws of Ecclesiastical Polity*. Joan Lockwood O'Donovan summarizes Hooker's contribution, the 'theological architect of the Church of England' as 'a masterly account of the interaction of such judgements of divinely revealed truths and commands, rational principles of right, justice and equity, the universal and local traditions of the church, and particular exigencies of time and place'.[434] Thus, Scripture, reason and tradition[435] need to be brought to bear in expressing the Church of England's understanding of Islam, an understanding that will be especially attentive to context while sensitive to the global identities of a Communion of Anglicanism that is itself in encounter with a faith of universal aspiration. As Michael Ipgrave points out in his description of Anglican approaches to interfaith relations, Lambeth Conferences are significant expressions of church thinking for the Anglican Communion globally while lacking the definitive status of, say, Roman Catholic conciliar decrees.[436] For my purposes, then, I will be analysing a number of Lambeth Conference resolutions alongside statements and initiatives local to the Church of England to suggest an overall trajectory in Anglican theologies of relations with Islam.

The Lambeth Conference of 1897 published an Encyclical Letter that sought to settle a policy for interfaith relations, and provides an early positing of the priority of the triumvirate of Christian–Jewish–Muslim relations:

In preaching His Gospel to the world we have to deal with one great religious body, which holds the truth in part not in its fullness, the Jews; with another which holds fragments of the truth embedded in a mass of falsehood, the Mohammedans; and with various races which hold inherited beliefs ranging down to the merest fetichism.[437]

In this short statement one sees the framing of interreligious relations in the context of mission ('His Gospel') and an evident tension in seeking out that which is truthful in other religious traditions while holding fast to the gospel, 'lest that good, such as it is' become a 'substitute for the Gospel'. At a time when the bulk of Anglican encounters with Muslims would be in the context of parishes and bishoprics established from missionary stations, the prior motive of evangelism seems to be paramount, tempered by the commitment to truth in the affirmation of what is consonant in other traditions. Within this schema, Islam offers something more than 'merest fetichism', but is seen as embodying elements of truth, obscured by lies: Judaism as incomplete truths.

It is over 70 years before Islam is addressed again during a Lambeth Conference. In that intervening period, two world wars and the steady dismantling of the British Empire witness a growing attention to ecumenical endeavours. The first World Missionary Conference in Edinburgh in 1910 marked what David Bosch sees as the 'all-time highwater mark in Western missionary enthusiasm, the zenith of the optimistic and pragmatist approach to missions'.[438] Bosch notes the harnessing of Enlightenment progress thinking to the resources available to world evangelization, as described in Edinburgh, which provided a symbiosis between Christian missionary endeavours and the colonial project.[439] The carnage of two world wars and, for the British, a steady dismantling of empire began to undermine the optimism in the fruits of 'secular science' so evident at Edinburgh 1910.[440] Importantly for the Church of England, though, Temple Gairdner, Church Missionary Society missionary and Arabicist, was entrusted with presenting to Edinburgh 1910 on the nature of Islam and reporting back to the

Church on the proceedings.[441] For all the naïve optimism and combative overtones replete in the language of Edinburgh 1910, there are some remarkable statements that anticipate the work of Kenneth Cragg and inform so much of subsequent Anglican thinking. Islam was deemed a 'living faith' and 'it was this living faith, intense, more intimate and more comprehensive than sight'.[442] From the heart of the missionary enterprise, and exemplified by Temple Gairdner, then, is an assessment of Islam that strives to see beyond the polemical, to encounter Islam in its genuine otherness, but with sympathy and affection.

The burgeoning concern for ecumenical unity, particularly within Protestantism and between the Church of England and Eastern Orthodoxy, is evident in the Encyclical Letters of the Lambeth Conference of 1930, which talk of 'that great human family of which God is the Father'.[443] The parallel tracks of mission and unity that become embodied in the World Council of Churches are evident too in the call for ecumenical relations on the basis that 'Every extension of this circle of visible fellowship would increase the power of the Church to witness to its Lord by its unity'.[444] Already apparent, then, is that trajectory that became epitomized by Vatican II: the Church's encounter with the world becoming fuel for a reflection of its self-understanding; mission demanding a deeper ecclesiology.

It is in the Lambeth Conference of 1968 that the language and imperative of dialogue becomes first apparent. In a decade exercised by the applied ecclesiology modelled in Vatican II, interreligious dialogue is seen not in the context of a theology of religions but in the reality of plural life, which includes atheism and Marxism.[445] Thus, Resolution 11 encourages 'positive relationship to the different religions of men (sic)', such as will 'call Christians not only to study other faiths in their own seriousness, but also to study unbelief in its real quality'. Resolution 12 further recommends 'a renewed and vigorous implementation of the task of interreligious dialogue already set in hand' and 'commends similar assistance for dialogue with Marxists and those who profess no religious faith'.[446] Michael Ipgrave assesses this shift to situate the religions within a wider diversity of belief systems as expressing the priority of dialogue with diversity rather than of an attention to a theological assessment of the realities of that diversity.[447]

In the Lambeth Conference of 1978, Resolution 37, there is a return to the framing of interreligious relations within the 'Gospel', but this is opened out to include 'the obligation to open exchange of thought and experience with people of other faiths'. There is no mention of atheistic ideologies this time, suggesting perhaps the previous 1968 Conference's own preoccupations with the ferment of the Cold War, student protests and the burgeoning social liberalism of that era. There is recognition of the 'vocation' by churches in, again, a broader mission of 'theological interpretation, community involvement, social responsibility, and evangelization' where specific other religions predominate (Hinduism, Buddhism, Taosim, Confucianism and Islam). No theological assessment of these faiths is attempted. However, there is a very specific mention of the need to 'seek opportunities for dialogue with Judaism', hinting at the especial obligation to remedy of Christian–Jewish relations post-Holocaust that had so charged the climate of Vatican II.

Lambeth Conference 1988: 'The Way of Dialogue'

It is with the Lambeth Conference of 1988 that a more systematic attempt was made to order Anglican interreligious relations and to provide a theological rationale for the encounter with Judaism and Islam in particular. The key text in this regard proposed to the Conference in Resolution 21 is 'Jews, Christians and Muslims: The Way of Dialogue'. The significant starting point for 'The Way of Dialogue' is in the statement that 'we recognise a special relationship between Christianity, Judaism and Islam'.[448] For 'The Way of Dialogue', 'All three of these religions see themselves in a common relationship to Abraham, the father of the faithful, the friend of God'.[449] Michael Ipgrave analyses the particular indebtedness of this document to Vatican II's *Nostra aetate*, the seminal account of the Roman Catholic Church's interreligious relations.[450] As Adrian Hastings observes, 'in speaking of Moslems and Jews, the Council stresses our common father in faith, Abraham.'[451] As with Vatican II, the political realities of churches in majority-Muslim contexts beyond Europe influenced the conception of 'The Way of Dialogue' as a document that was instigated to explicate Christian–Jewish relations but necessarily evolved into an articulation of relations between the three faiths.[452]

While faiths outside of any perceived Abrahamic heritage, in contrast to *Nostra aetate*, are excluded from 'The Way of Dialogue', the Lambeth Conference seems to continue the pattern of privileging the understanding and consonance of revelations in Judaism and Islam. *Nostra aetate* famously shuns an assessment of the status of the Qur'an or Muhammad. Similarly, 'The Way of Dialogue' prefers to hold up the Abrahamic schema as an apologia for the significance of good relations and dialogue between Christians and Muslims without making a judgement on the prophethood of Muhammad, for example. However, in some ways the Anglican proposal goes further than Vatican II. In *Nostra aetate*, Muslims are described as those who 'submit wholeheartedly … just as did Abraham, with whom the Islamic faith is pleased to associate itself'.[453] *Lumen gentium* admits 'the plan of salvation', which 'includes those who acknowledge the creator. In the first place among these there are the Moslems, who, professing to hold the faith of Abraham, along with us adore the one and merciful God.'[454] Where 'The Way of Dialogue' accedes to a 'common relationship to Abraham', Vatican II merely notes that Muslims *profess* to hold the faith of Abraham and are pleased to *associate* their faith with the submission modelled by Abraham. There is thus a further theological step that the Anglican account of Islam is prepared to make, beyond *Nostra aetate*. While clearly being inspired by and indebted to Vatican II, 'The Way of Dialogue' seems to misunderstand the nuanced intent of the conciliar document.

Following Vatican II, the theological rationale underlying the concept of the Abrahamic faiths has been the subject of extensive discussion that suggests that the premise of the Lambeth

Conference document of 1988 may be anachronistic. It seems clear that both Vatican II[455] and 'The Way of Dialogue' admit that Muslims and Christians worship the same God. It is rather less clear whether Vatican II goes as far as accepting the Abrahamic theologoumenon as proposed by Massignon, who had such an influence on the conciliar documents. The 'father of the faithful', as described in 'The Way of Dialogue', need not be merely the literal progenitor of Jews and Muslims, even though there are serious scholarly objections to the assumption of Islamic lineage traced back to Ishmael.[456] Taking a Pauline understanding for Christians of Abraham as the model of faith in the one God, Muslims might be seen to relate as heirs of Abraham 'by faith'. Thus Paul, in Romans 9, includes Gentiles in the promises of YHWH despite their lack of genetic lineage to Abraham. Their qualification is merely that of 'faith', the very qualification of the first Jew, Abraham the patriarch, who was compelled to leave the land of Ur in simple obedience. In a parallel fashion, it could be argued that Muslims 'by faith' inherit from God, explicitly drawing, as they do, from the originating monotheism of Abraham.[457] As noted in Chapter 2, however, a high Christology, which is lacking in Islam, is required to ground an Abrahamic vision of faith by grace in the book of Galatians.[458]

We have already seen how the Abrahamic motif can sideline Jews in the practice of interreligious dialogue. For the English context, and the Church of England's self-understood vocation to *all* people, this is a particularly pertinent observation, noting the dangers of an exclusive Christian–Muslim dialogue forum that seems to work at the expense of other religious groups.[459] This was highlighted in 2007 with the publication of a document by the Hindu Council UK that criticized the privilege given to Abrahamic faiths within interreligious discussions. A more accommodating outlook was argued for by the author, Anil Bhanot, that was genuinely 'respectful of the other' according to the Hindu principles of *Dharma*.[460] The potential for the Abrahamic fold to be an interfaith clique is evident in Anil Bhanot's submission but his line of reasoning betrays the essential problematic of finding an all-embracing religious theme that has integrity beyond the source community. *Dharma* has no more weight as an understanding of right religion to a Christian than Abraham does to a Hindu. It is worth noting from this particular debate that the theological rationale of the Abrahamic schema produces implications that go beyond Christian–Muslim relations.

'The Way of Dialogue' thus follows the lead of Vatican II in stressing the particular confluences between the Abrahamic faiths, but is suggestive of a rather more controversial and questionable synchronicity that is avoided in the conciliar documents.[461] It is noteworthy that the considerable controversy generated by 'The Way of Dialogue',[462] especially among bishops from Asia and Africa, is focused more on the interpretation of historical precedence, Islamic theology and the practical application to interreligious relations than on the underlying theological schema itself.

Taking this Abrahamic foundation, three theological principles are then used to inform the content of 'The Way of Dialogue': understanding, affirmation and sharing. Michael Ipgrave identifies the influence of Max Warren, a former general secretary of the Anglican Church Mission Society (CMS), and his concept of 'Christian Presence' in the outworking of interfaith understanding as 'affective entry into the world of the other'.[463] Max Warren, another advocate of Christian Presence and former general secretary of CMS, and John V. Taylor, Bishop of Winchester, brought a missionary sensibility to this incarnational approach to interreligious encounter. Graham Kings identifies Temple Gairdner of Cairo[464] and Kenneth Cragg as two key influences on Warren and Taylor[465] and the idea of Christian Presence. Both these towering figures of Anglican engagement with Islam have clearly continued a legacy that has informed the encounter with Islam and a general theology of religions back in the British context.

'The Way of Dialogue' sets relations with Islam in a historical perspective, noting the historic enmity evinced in the Crusades but also the positive cultural contributions from Islamic to Christian civilizations.[466] The principle of *understanding* is embodied by offering correctives to stereotypes of Islam such that the burden is on redressing negative Christian patterns towards Muslims and challenging stereotypes of, for example, Shari'a law treatment of women,[467] *jihad*[468] and traditional Islamic understandings of the crucifixion.[469] Lucinda Mosher's analysis of the 1988 Conference discussions notes Bishop Michael Nazir-Ali's particular dissatisfaction with the emphasis of these correctives.[470]

Allied to the perceived 'glossing' of Islamic theology, concerns were also voiced at the insufficient treatment of the evangelistic mandate of the Church.[471] Evangelism, or proclamation in the language of Vatican II and subsequent Roman Catholic encyclicals, is only mentioned incidentally in 'The Way of Dialogue':

> if we are truly to share our faith we must not only affirm what we can but share our own deep convictions, even when these appear irreconcilably opposed to our partner's faith and practice. In the case of *Islam* particularly, Christians must first understand Islam if this witness is to be effective.[472]

The conditional 'if' posits evangelism as an optional practice subservient to the wider thrust of dialogue, even if the respective integrities of traditions are affirmed robustly within 'The Way of Dialogue'. It is notable in it, however, that issues of human rights in Muslim societies, the doctrine of apostasy as it affects minority-Christian communities and the challenge to Muslims to correct distorted images of Christians and Jews provide elements of reciprocal obligation.

The feeling, especially among evangelicals, that too much was being given away and presumed positively of Islam, can be traced back in some of the preparatory documents to Lambeth 1988. *Towards a Theology for Inter-Faith Dialogue* (hereafter *TTID*)[473] was published in 1984 as a report to the General Synod of the Church of England by the Inter-Faith Consultative Group of the Board for Mission and Unity. This report was circulated as advance reading for Lambeth 1988 and introduces the contemporary experience of British plurality as an opportunity to explore a renewed understanding of the theology of religions, seen through the prism of the 'threefold typology' of religions.[474] Within *TTID*, pluralism is regarded as a developing, innovative response to the challenge of religious diversity. It is presented on a par, in terms of theological legitimacy, with inclusivism, while exclusivism is viewed as an inhibition to the affirmation of spiritual truths in other faiths.[475] Additionally, the *Filioque* clause in the Nicene Creed is offered as a potential limitation on fruitful resources for a theology of religions. An Eastern Orthodox understanding of the Spirit speaking and acting 'in other religious cultures'[476] flowing from the Father-creator is tentatively noted as providing a doctrinal foundation that can embrace trinitarianism, a corresponding high Christology and the grace of God beyond the Church.[477] It will become apparent that this initially tentative retrieval of Orthodox trinitarianism as a potential resource becomes a major grounding for later Anglican reflections on relations with other faiths. The subsequent development of Anglican resources would suggest that this early mention of Eastern Orthodoxy is a landmark of what will come to be regarded as a more substantive resource than the theologies of pluralism.

TTID provoked a response by Bishop Michael Nazir-Ali, included in the 1986 edition,[478] redolent of his objections to 'The Way of Dialogue'. Paying particular attention to the Christian–Muslim milieu, Nazir-Ali corrects the sense of novelty that he sees in the exploration of interreligious relations in *TTID*, reminding readers of the long-standing traditions of dialogue, coexistence and mission in non-Western Anglican contexts. Again, Nazir-Ali criticizes the seeming compromise of the 'scandal of particularity'[479] of the gospel in the service of dialogue. The ignorance of the global precedents of interreligious relations and the overarching narrative of salvation for Christians in *TTID* makes, for Nazir-Ali, a 'fleeing of history'. This abnegation renders the work of the Holy Spirit (described in *TTID* as 'unpredictable, culturally and historically indeterminate'[480]) somehow less than biblical.[481]

The emphasis on the Church's need to rethink its attitudes, actions and theology in *TTID* informs Christopher Wright's robust critique in an *Anvil* journal edition of 1984. There is an important distinction to be made between the challenge to the individual Christian contained in the encounter with truth within another tradition, and a challenge to Christian revelation itself. For Wright, this distinction is blurred in the text of *TTID*,[482] which also offers an unbiblical qualifying of the Great Commission in the service of interfaith dialogue.[483] It is interesting to note Christopher Lamb, one of the authors of *TTID*, responding to Wright's critique by expressing his admission that 'Though we wanted to see people moving in a certain direction we had no illusions that we were producing a definitive report.'[484] The impression is given of a discussion document that is deliberately tipped towards dialogue as a provisional redress of balance for a Church of England insufficiently open to interreligious encounter.

This impression is supported by the feedback given to *TTID* by the Anglican Consultative Council meeting in Nigeria in 1984 and published in their report *Bonds of Affection*. In their view:

> the book needed a greater emphasis on the doctrine of redemption, and we questioned some of its biblical exegesis, as well as the selectivity of biblical texts. People from non-Western societies especially found the approach too academic and cerebral, and thus it was classified as largely irrelevant to them.[485]

There are efforts at practical application in *TTID* but they all, revealingly, denote the responsibility of Christians as the holders of power and privilege to change and adapt to the new economy of diversity. Thus:

> It is no longer with someone out there, at a distance, that we engage in conversation, but with those with whom we share in a way quite other than any previous generation. Nevertheless, we ought not to minimize the fact that numerically those of other faiths are few compared with the number of practising Christians in Britain. The relative size of communities has a profound effect on our self-understanding, and conditions the way we relate to others. Adherents of different faiths seldom

meet as equals, and isolation and cultural dominance are hard to overcome.[486]

Perhaps the 'irrelevance' observed by Anglicans outside of Europe is in the language of cultural dominance assigned to the Christian faith and reflected on from experiences of long-standing diversity or even Islamic cultural dominance. The presumption of both 'The Way of Dialogue' and *TTID* is that the Church is in a prior position of host to those of other faiths. For *TTID*, and subsequently 'The Way of Dialogue', there is recognition of the importance of dialogue, especially with Muslims, but, for many, incomprehension of the language of host to guest and a discomfort at the relegation of evangelism.

Roger Hooker and Christopher Lamb combined to publish a significant resource for Church of England parishes in 1986, *Love the Stranger: Ministry in Multi-Faith Areas*.[487] *Love the Stranger* sought to encourage an irenic encounter with other faiths, providing stories and anecdotes and highlighting some of the theological challenges of dialogue and evangelism. It is redolent of the mood of 'The Way of Dialogue' and *TTID* in its provisional tone. There is a reluctance to define and assess evangelism or dialogue at a time of such rapid cultural and religious diversity: 'Are such incidents to be described as dialogue, witness, service, evangelism or what? The answer is that we do not yet know.'[488] A picture of transition is conveyed that posits the primary obligation on the Christian 'hosts' who 'bear the burden of our collective past. We bear the burden of present misunderstanding.'[489] The shadow of colonialism looms over the book's emphasis on the Church's need to reach out to the 'stranger', even allowing for the gospel imperative to service. Indeed, it is telling that a Church of England priest who may be regarded as a specialist in interreligious matters is likely to have 'served in India, Pakistan or Bangladesh, and has some knowledge of the background, religion, culture and language of a particular Asian group.'[490] It seems that for the Church of England in the 1980s, Islam may well have been 'over here', but 'here' was still Anglican and 'they' were still from elsewhere. What is particularly noticeable about the concluding chapter of *Love the Stranger*, though, is the beginnings of a discussion about an anticipated challenge from Islam to political theology, the nature of nationhood, politics and the common good.[491] It would seem, then, that *Love the Stranger* exemplifies some of the Anglican interfaith motifs of the time while also prefiguring more contemporary debates.

Anecdotes from the field: reckoning with the good and the bad of Anglican history

Alongside the tendency to caricature Islam as entirely good or entirely bad exists a parallel temptation to regard Anglican – and broader – Christian encounters with Islam as wholly noble or wholly ignoble. As with much of life, the truth contains a mix of these realities. The colonial legacy of Anglicanism and associated collusion between the Church and empire ventures of exploitation give good cause for Muslims to be suspicious of ulterior motives. Are we endeavouring to change their culture; do we really care for them or are we just using them to further the growth of the Church? These are questions that circle in the background when Muslims encounter Christians, and we would be wise to be alert to those fears.

At the same time there is often a profound sense of respect for the Church of England and a generous disposition to see the Church take a significant role of spiritual leadership in the nation. When the new church centre was completed in Sparkbrook, it was gratifying to hear the numbers of local Muslims delighted to see a revitalized Anglican Christian presence in the neighbourhood. I have had several conversations with local Muslims who recall fondly their education in church schools and the role of the parish church in fostering good relations across the community. A humble Christian presence that is cognizant of history needs to be able to build on the good and reject the bad. The exploitative histories highlighted by postcolonial readings are there to stir the Church into better action, not to paralyse Christians into inaction.

6

Anglican Encounters with Islam Post-1998

Lambeth Conference 1998: 'embassy, hospitality and dialogue'

The depth of the controversy occasioned by Lambeth 1988 was perhaps behind the extensive sharing of stories from around the Communion of encounters with Islam for the Lambeth Conference of 1998, as opposed to the pursuit of any theological investigation.[492] Gambia, Northern Nigeria, the Middle East, Pakistan and Bradford were all contexts providing stories of constructive Anglican–Muslim engagements, all notably Muslim-majority in complexion. The 'major issues' identified included dialogue, conversion, basic freedoms, working ecumenically and monitoring.[493] Pointedly, in 'monitoring', the Network for Inter-Faith Concerns is sanctioned with resources in 'monitoring Christian–Muslim relations as they affect the different provinces of the Anglican Communion', recognizing 'both the opportunities for interfaith encounter and the difficulties'.[494]

Of additional note for the 1998 Lambeth Conference is the address by Bishop Michael Nazir-Ali specifically on interfaith relations, providing perhaps his preferred approach where *Towards a Theology for Inter-Faith Dialogue* (*TTID*) and 'The Way of Dialogue' may have failed, in his view. Nazir-Ali provides a number of practical illustrations that flesh out the objections expressed to *TTID* and the apparent concerns over 'The Way of Dialogue'. He does this by way of affirming Kenneth Cragg's espousal of the missionary values of 'embassy' and 'hospitality'.[495] Hospitality may be demonstrated by Christians in the West opening up their homes to people of other faiths who have recently arrived in the country or making church halls available for social functions. However:

> The use of church buildings is a classic situation where Western Christians can learn from the history of Christianity elsewhere. In the early days of the expansion of Islam into the Christian countries of the Middle East, for example, the new rulers sometimes took over a part of a church for their worship, leaving the rest to the Christian community. In many cases, however, the whole building was eventually taken over.[496]

This illustration is elicited as an example of ill-considered and naïve hospitality that pays insufficient attention to that dimension of mission, *embassy*: 'going out to them and sharing the Gospel with them'.[497] In Nazir-Ali's view, it is the very history of privilege and dominance of the Western Church that has stymied the full expression of mission as embassy, but now 'The situation is changing'.[498] A more equitable balance of power between the faiths, and especially with Muslims, is being highlighted, one that needs to be cognizant of the breadth of encounters in history and across the Communion. It is noteworthy that in 1996, the Church of England produced a document on the use of its premises and other faiths, *Communities and Buildings*. A brief description is given of Islamic understandings of the mosque but no account of the potential symbolism of competitive power that Nazir-Ali alludes to as within Islamic tradition.[499] The issue for churches, according to *Communities and Buildings*, is largely a procedural one with respect to consecrated properties, which calls on local church leadership 'with a gift and a vocation for adventurous friendships'[500] that may admit expansive hosting of other faith communities. Chad Emmett's study of the siting of churches and mosques would seem to suggest that there is indeed a complex of mutual power-relations indicated by signs of location, conversion and prohibition that can reveal degrees of tolerance and perspectives on success and dominance that cannot be dismissed.[501]

'The Way of Dialogue' remains the most recent authoritative statement on the theology of interreligious concerns in relation to Islam for the Anglican Communion.[502] There is an evident indebtedness to Vatican II and in particular to *Nostra aetate* in the situating of relations with Islam in the context of the Abrahamic faiths. However, 'The Way of Dialogue' goes somewhat further than Vatican II in how the relationship between the Abrahamic faiths is framed, and one wonders how this may be appropriately applied to the Church of England's interreligious relations beyond Christianity and Judaism. Noting Gavin D'Costa's analysis of applying an appropriate hermeneutic to the documents of Vatican II,[503] 'The Way of Dialogue' arguably misinterprets the intent of *Nostra aetate* by overemphasizing the import of the Abrahamic motif.

One feature of the controversies over Anglican publications on other faiths in the 1980s is the apparent lack of coherence with other doctrinal publications and creedal statements. Where the Roman Catholic Church sought to present a comprehensive range of conciliar documents in the light of the Church's engagement with the world during the Vatican II process,[504] there is the suggestion of piecemeal and often self-contradictory progress from the Church of England and through the Anglican Communion. Thus, pluralist theologies could be presented as legitimate options for a theology of religions in *Towards a Theology for Inter-Faith Dialogue*, along with an encouragement to 'recognise and respond to all manifestations of the Logos' while still affirming the 'decisive revelation of God in Jesus'.[505] 'The Way of Dialogue' roots the community of the Church within an Abrahamic schema without attending to the implications for this for theologies of salvation or Christology, overlooking the challenge of any purported 'natural religion' to the universal significance of the Christ-event. Yet in 1995, the Church of England's Doctrine Commission could produce *The Mystery of Salvation* explicitly endorsing the creedal statements of the Church and the historic formularies by emphasizing the particularity of Christ as the second person of the trinity and the focus on Christ as judge and hope of the world.[506] Martin Davie's 2009 report for the Church of England entitled *A Church of England Approach to the Unique Significance of Jesus Christ* would seem to endorse the clarity of *The Mystery of Salvation*. It was able to reflect on the trinity as a doctrine that demanded an inclusive sense of God's work within other religions yet could uphold a high Christology that did not compromise on the particular claims of Jesus as Lord.[507]

A lesson for the Church of England would seem to be that any thoroughgoing analysis of interreligious theologies cannot afford to ignore the implications for soteriology, ecclesiology and Christology. The context to the 2010 Church of England report *Sharing the Gospel of Salvation* is indicative of this need for a coherent ecclesial self-understanding. This report was prompted by a Private Member's Motion at General Synod to declare the gospel imperative of evangelism to those of other faiths as an outflow of the unique revelation of God in Jesus Christ. There was evidently a perceived danger that the theologies that drove dialogue could be prised apart from those that impelled proclamation. As the Foreword to the report noted:

The stronger sense of difference and diversity – including religious diversity – in Britain today has challenged us to become a more generous culture. Sadly, it has also made many nervous of publicly espousing a vision of the common good for all people. Yet, if the Good News of God in Christ is good for us, how can we refrain from commending it as good for others too?[508]

If the Holy Spirit's work beyond the Church cannot be considered without reference to the Church's sacramental presence as Christ's body on earth, then, conversely, the unique claims of Christ as a basis for evangelism cannot be declared without acknowledging the breadth of God's mission in the sovereign grace of the trinity. Commending Martin Davie's report on the unique significance of Christ, *Sharing the Gospel of Salvation* admits that 'the only adequate response is to present the whole gamut of the Church's work in mission and evangelism.[509] Rowan Williams' introductory remark that 'Christ's saving work is not a commodity to be sold but a gift to be shared'[510] underlines this tension. The Church does not *possess* truth in exclusivist terms but *participates* in a life that has implications for relations with other faiths. The apparent shift from 'The Way of Dialogue' and its attempts to provide a schema for the theology of religions to a more ecclesially conscious position such as *Sharing the Gospel of Salvation* represents will become especially evident when we consider the important 2008 Anglican Communion report, *Generous Love: The Truth of the Gospel and the Call to Dialogue.*

For critics of 'The Way of Dialogue', the document is weak in not presenting the full particularity of the gospel and paying insufficient attention to the vocation of evangelism. It is perhaps ironic that the evident use of resources from a missionary tradition that includes Temple Gairdner, Kenneth Cragg, John V. Taylor and Max Warren in the articulation of its theology is seen in this light. It must be noted that the thrust of the document was *dialogue* and the overarching tone was one that sought to open up the Anglican Communion to constructive relations with Jewish and Muslim neighbours in dialogue and partnership. This emphasis on dialogue can be seen to be part of a continuity with the preparatory document *Towards a Theology for Inter-Faith Dialogue*, where the Church is seen as host and Muslims, and those of other faiths, as guests. For many evangelicals and Anglicans beyond Europe, both documents display an unrecognizably positive portrayal of the realities of Christian–Muslim coexistence and an exaggeration of the power of the Christian community.

Moving to Lambeth 1998, a clear effort to hear the stories of Christian–Muslim coexistence from beyond Europe was made and an appreciation of the diverse realities of interreligious engagement. This commitment to the lived reality of the interface between Christianity and Islam was institutionalized for the Communion in 1998 through the responsibilities given to the Network for Inter Faith Concerns (NIFCON), established in 1993, to disseminate such information and resources. Additionally, the recurring motifs of Christian Presence, hospitality and embassy that run through 'The Way of Dialogue' and originate in the missionary theologies of Kenneth Cragg and Max Warren among other, were presented anew to embrace both dialogue and evangelism.

Lambeth Conference 2008: *Generous Love*

The latest formal Anglican Communion document for inter-religious relations is the 2008 report, *Generous Love: The Truth of the Gospel and the Call to Dialogue*, issued by NIFCON, discussed at the Lambeth Conference 2008 and brought to and commended by the Church of England General Synod in January 2009.[511] While the document comes out of the Lambeth Communion, it was particularly attentive to the local stories of the *Presence and Engagement* report of the Church of England in 2005 and thus is an important account of Church of England theology in its Anglican global context.

Archbishop Rowan Williams comments in his Foreword on the strategic context of Vatican II for *Generous Love*, while noting that 'the situation has moved on, both in theology and in practical relations between communities'.[512] This makes the document an important indicator of Anglican theologies behind some of the changes we have observed since *TTID* and 'The Way of Dialogue'. For Michael Ipgrave, the principal author of *Generous Love*, the optimism apparent in *Nostra aetate* has been replaced by a markedly less sanguine approach to interfaith relations.[513] The religiously motivated violence supremely exemplified by 9/11 has influenced an approach that is decidedly pastoral in facing the diverse realities of Christian–Muslim experience in a more sober context. In terms of a theological shift, Catholic documents since Vatican II have certainly given a greater attention to the subject of proclamation,[514] while the 1990 collection of essays in *Christian Uniqueness Reconsidered: The Myth of a Pluralistic Theology of Religions* is emblematic of a broad front countering novel schemas of theologies of religions.[515] Within the Foreword and in the subtitle to *Generous Love* there is already an express commitment to both 'the truth of the Gospel and the call to dialogue'; 'that double conviction that we must regard dialogue as an imperative from Our Lord, yet must also witness consistently to the unique gift we have been given in Christ'.[516]

The document is explicitly theological rather than practical, seeking to present a Christian basis for relations with other faiths but not striving to formulate a scheme of theology of religions in the way that *TTID* sought to do in 1984. What is immediately apparent, though, is the trinitarian language of the theology. It 'begins with God' and the 'mystery of his being' that 'through the life, death and resurrection of Jesus of Nazareth the One God has made known his triune reality as Father, Son, and Holy Spirit.'[517] In echoes of the *perichoresis* theology of the Church Fathers and of Eastern Christianity, the work of God in the world and across cultures and religions is set in the 'boundless life and perfect love which abide forever in the heart of the Trinity' and 'are sent out into the world in a mission of renewal and restoration in which we are called to share.'[518] The 'beginning with God' uses phraseology from the *Guidelines for Interfaith Encounter in the Churches of the Porvoo Communion* with the Anglican Communion of 2003.[519] Ipgrave was keen to build on the pattern of the Porvoo guidelines in articulating theology out of a prior understanding of the nature of God rather than the customary Anglican pattern of a beginning in context. Interestingly, an important drive behind *Generous Love* was to present a document to the Conference of 2008 that affirmed the mission of the Church and that could command widespread assent, in contrast to the internal disagreements over sexuality.[520] As such, the significance of *Generous Love* is arguably deepened by the sense that it is not an attempt to break new ground but is a genuine consolidation of Anglican principles for interreligious relations. Where *TTID* was accused of using the Holy Spirit as an unbiblical, freewheeling motif for discerning truth in other religious traditions, *Generous Love* articulates a pneumatology that repeatedly references back to the Father God and the revelation of that fatherhood in Jesus, the Son of God.

It is revealing that Lucinda Mosher's analysis of the 1988 Lambeth Conference includes observations on reports written by Rowan Williams in parallel to but separate from the interfaith reports: 'Communion with God and the Life of the Christ' and 'Christ and Culture', together with an introduction to the concept of the report of the Communion as a whole. Mosher observes that his reports are 'replete' with 'Eastern Orthodox theological flavour' in talk of us being caught up into a 'great pattern of relation' in the trinitarian revelation.[521] This language finds resonance in section 8 of *Generous Love*, on 'sending and abiding', where it is affirmed that:

> our relationships with people of different faiths must be grounded theologically in our understanding of the reality of the God who is Trinity. Father, Son and Spirit abide in one another in a life which is 'a dynamic, eternal and unending movement of self-giving'.[522]

This latter reference is extracted from *The Church of the Triune God: The Cyprus Statement Agreed by the International Commission for Anglican–Orthodox Theological Dialogue*.[523] It seems more than coincidental that the 'characteristic idioms'[524] of Williams' patristic and Orthodox-infused trinitarianism observed at the Lambeth Conference of 1988 are apparent in this strategic statement of Anglican interreligious relations while he is Archbishop of Canterbury. We noted in the Introduction how Williams's Orthodox-infused Anglicanism was particularly influenced by the Russian émigré school. It is worth highlighting, here, that *Generous Love* borrows language from a dialogue with the *Greek* Orthodox tradition, and a document that Rowan Williams and the Greek Orthodox theologian John Zizioulas[525] had a major part in drafting.

Where the concept of the trinity is not even mentioned in 'The Way of Dialogue' and is a potential source for explaining the activities of God within other religious traditions in *TTID*, the trinity provides the whole shape for Christian relationship with the other and infuses all aspects of *Generous Love*. It seems characteristic of some of the weaknesses of Anglican ecclesiology noted in the Introduction that the doctrinal reports on Christology written by Williams for the Lambeth Conference of 1988 seem wholly divorced from and irrelevant to the interreligious documents pertaining to that same conference. In *Generous Love* there seems, rather, to be an effort to root relations with other faiths in the very identity of the Church as a sacrament within its understanding of the trinitarian godhead: an *ecclesial turn* in interfaith relations.

Generous Love offers a brief perspective on what is distinctively Anglican for a trinitarian theology of religions; recognizing the plurality in unity characteristic of the roots of Anglicanism. This understanding affirms God's work in the world but also a Christian unity that avoids sectarianism.[526] This makes for a commitment to local context and an attention to the particularities of time in the light of God's unfolding providence.[527] The significance of Scripture is reaffirmed as crucial to Anglican method, the practice of 'scriptural reasoning' particularly noted as an example in this regard[528] and the 'Building Bridges' programme of Christian–Muslim scriptural reflection implicitly endorsed as a necessary endeavour.[529] Though *Generous Love* articulates a theology of interreligious relations and makes no attempt to evaluate specific religious traditions, the specificity of Christian–Jewish relations is underlined, and 'The Way of Dialogue's reminder that we must 'reject any view of Judaism which sees it as a living fossil, simply superseded by Christianity'.[530]

The variety of Anglican experiences especially with Islam is mentioned, from the stories of Lambeth 1998 to NIFCON consultations on 'mission and dialogue' in Bangalore, India (2003) and on faith and citizenship in Kaduna, Nigeria (2007). There is no attempt to foreclose the nature of the Christian encounter with other faiths, and specifically with Islam, nor to give particular emphasis on one practice at the expense of the other, save to encourage a dynamic 'presence *and* engagement'. The 'two poles' of this presence and engagement utilize two of the most persistent themes for Anglican encounters with other faiths – embassy and hospitality – originating in the theology of the great missionary scholar of Islam, Bishop Kenneth Cragg, and reaffirmed as we have seen by Bishop Michael Nazir-Ali. The combined 'going out' and 'welcoming in' are seen from within the trinitarian dynamic around which the eucharist is both symbol and source of that self-giving love.[531] There seems to be a very clear break from the casting of the Church as host that is apparent in earlier documents and a recasting of the hospitality metaphor so that the Church actually has a responsibility as *both host and guest*. Thus, 'the giving and receiving of hospitality is a most powerful sign that those who were strangers are reconciled to one another as friends.'[532]

For *Generous Love*, the Church also has to learn to be a guest, understanding that the real host of our shared space is Christ the Lord. There are echoes here of the theology of religions articulated by the Jesuit scholar Michael Barnes, who espouses a *dialogical* theology, or comparative theology, that reflects from within tradition in the experience of the encounter with the other. Thus, Barnes can say, in the spirit of *Generous Love*, 'The mediation which Christians practise is motivated by the Spirit of love, in imitation of God's own action of welcome and hospitality towards all people … To put it another way, God is himself both host and guest.'[533] For Barnes, as with *Generous Love*, relations with the other are posited within the Church's understanding of God's relationality and not abstracted to an objective schema of religions.

Clare Amos[534] hints at this dual track of Christian hospitality in her reflections on *Generous Love*, *A Common Word* and Rowan Williams' Shari'a law speech. For her, the ongoing establishment of the Church of England presupposes at least some identification with the role of 'host', akin to Rabbi Jonathan Sacks' picture of the 'country house' model of religious diversity.[535] There are also times when the Church of England is called upon to act generously and give away privilege: the advocacy by Anglican bishops for seats in the House of Lords for other faith leaders, for example. Arguably this analysis still gives insufficient attention to the Church as a genuine 'guest', where the power and privilege may well be located elsewhere. In some very real senses, the Church too is residing in a country house and beholden to an 'other'. What *Generous Love* suggests is a Christian understanding of interreligious relations where the Church is simultaneously both host and guest. Within this dynamic, God is the only host,[536] as Barnes notes, and Kenneth Cragg's vision of Christian hospitality is recalled: a vision that encompasses the embassy of Christ, to 'decide by the Gospel as the people of the Gospel must'.[537]

In what must be a reference to some of the Christian experiences of Islamic majority, reciprocity in interfaith relations globally is asserted but generous love patterned in love for enemies that does not seek retaliation. A clear statement of identification with the suffering Church is offered too in the imperative to solidarity and support of 'Christians who have to witness to their faith in difficult circumstances'.[538] Alongside the theological retrieval of Eastern Christianity is a tangible affirmation of the interdependence of the Christian experience in contexts such as the Middle East.

Generous Love is a remarkable document that provides a trinitarian impulse in support of an ongoing shift in formal Anglican approaches to other faiths and to Islam in particular. There is an attempt to cast that in an Anglican distinctive way that embraces diversity in unity, is contextual, and rooted in Scripture. This diversity models an approach to other faiths based on embassy and hospitality, affirming the breadth of mission in dialogue and evangelism. The Church is both to be host and guest in this economy: receiving, learning and being challenged, as well as reaching out, proclaiming and challenging in turn. Where earlier Anglican documents suggested that the challenge of other faiths might provoke a new schema of theologies of religions, an 'external discourse' shaping the Church's vision, *Generous Love* begins with God and the consequent nature of the Church within the life of God. What this ecclesial turn demonstrates, then, is not a *new* innovation in theology but a recovery of inherited traditions: a genuine *ressourcement*.

The ecclesial turn is evidenced by the appeal to the Eastern Orthodox tradition evoked in *Generous Love*, and the inheritance of the Church Fathers and in that Anglican Church Father, Richard

Hooker, in their emphasis on the Church's participation in the godhead. The attentiveness to the lived reality of Christian–Muslim relations in all their complexity around the Anglican Communion contributed to this ecclesially conscious theology that has had to command credibility across Anglican diversity and be able to embrace a diversity of interreligious experience. *Generous Love* emphasizes the context of the worshipping community but defers to the self-identity of the patristic milieu that we identified as intrinsic to Anglican ecclesiology in the Introduction. *Generous Love*, then, arguably offers itself as an authoritative and authentic resource for Anglican Christians relating to Muslims.

Initiatives of the Church of England

For many years the Church of England was content to focus national initiatives on relations with Islam through ecumenical groupings, and in particular through the World Council of Churches.[539] However, from the early 1970s, at diocesan and city level, it had in many cases taken a lead in initiatives such as community relations, interfaith chaplaincies and local bilateral dialogue groups.[540] It must be noted too that the Church of England's parish system, legal obligations to non-adherents of the Christian faith and involvement in church schools provide long-standing forums for encounter with Muslims.[541]

The 1976 publication *A New Threshold: Guidelines for the Churches in their Relations with Muslim communities*[542] deserves mention as one such ecumenical initiative focused on Muslim–Christian relations. Written by Bishop David Brown of Guildford, incidentally another former Church Mission Society missionary, it embodied the work of the British Council of Churches and the Conference of Missionary Societies in Great Britain and Ireland. Until 'The Way of Dialogue', this would have been the only formal, institutional resource available to Anglicans in Britain in their understanding of the interface between Christianity and Islam.

Published in the same year as the Festival of Islam in London, *A New Threshold* seems to reflect something of the effort to reconcile Christians to the perceived new vista of religious pluralism in Britain. It is indicative that in the Preface to the document, the Community and Race Relations Unit of the Church of England are especially noted as having prior involvement in the document in addressing questions of religious and cultural identity now posed to 'our society which have grown out of our Christian heritage'.[543] At this juncture, race is regarded as equivalent to or even consonant with religion. Already, the sensibility of host/guest relations is evoked and the spectre of racism suggested as a backdrop to the need for the guidelines produced.

A New Threshold provides brief descriptions of Islam, its diversity and core theology and something of the history of Muslim–Christian relations. In the section 'Theological Issues', David Brown declines to present a 'theology of religions' and admits something of the provisional nature of the document, suggesting that the theological implications of religious diversity in Britain have yet to be worked out: 'It will take some years for the theologians and governing bodies of our Churches to adjust to the realities and perspectives of the pluralist society which Britain, in common with the rest of the world, is rapidly becoming.'[544] While admitting the tradition of religious plurality across the globe, no attempt is made to retrieve this in informing practice in Britain, an omission that, as we have seen, could be argued is characteristic of the era culminating in 'The Way of Dialogue'.

David Brown does not explicitly name Abraham but his rationale for what he terms 'spiritual kinship' clearly points to an obligation to 'share in mutual understanding with people who worship God' that draws from the pattern of Jewish revelation and our common 'spiritual heritage'.[545] This seems to anticipate 'The Way of Dialogue's establishment of Old Testament roots shaping the nature of Christian, Muslim and Jewish faiths through the Abrahamic motif. After affirming commonalities, David Brown then identifies 'factors which divide'.[546] First and foremost here are the 'social factors', which sometimes lead to racism and exclusion of Muslims, perhaps suggestive of one of the primary concerns behind the document being to foster sensitivity and welcome greater religious and cultural diversity among Christians.

Brown recognizes the incarnation (and consequently the trinity), sin (and the fact and necessity of the crucifixion) and Christian sectarianism and hierarchy as the three main points of Islamic theological contention with Christianity.[547] Interestingly, again, the emphasis here is on Islamic issues with Christian theology. Thus, no mention is made of Christian issues with regard to traditional Islamic notions of apostasy, religious governance of public affairs or the belief that the Bible is a corrupted text, for example.

The 'threshold' referred to in the title is what David Brown refers to as the 'modern Antioch' of Christian encounter with other faiths in contemporary Britain, revitalizing and reframing theology.[548] The 'purifying and enriching' process of interaction with Islam suggests three new insights for Brown: 'a new awareness of the universality of the divine love', 'a more modest assessment of the authority of ecclesiastical institutions' and 'a clearer grasp of what is unique in the Christian faith'.[549] Establishing some commonalities and differences, the tone of the document is decidedly provisional, qualifying 'present interim theologies'[550] in the light of the challenge and opportunity of interaction with Muslims.

The postscript 'Problems of Relationships' to chapter 2 of the document[551] does little to alter the perception that *A New Threshold* is speaking into an understanding of the Church's privilege and dominance, suggestive of the host/guest paradigm we have noted elsewhere. Thus, problems entitled 'Human Rights and Community Relations' are actually about the human rights of Muslims culturally and economically. 'The Sharing and Use of Buildings' and 'Recognition of Islamic Occasions by the Churches' all place an onus on the Church in its vocation of hospitality, and prefigure some of the later accounts that inspired the objections of Bishop Michael Nazir-Ali. 'Evangelism' is recognized as integral to both faiths but beyond the mention of this having 'political overtones' 'in the past' within Islam, it is merely noted that 'principal missionary societies are making a reappraisal of mission' in the light of mutual sensitivities.

In 1980, the Inter-Faith Consultative Group (IFCG) was established to help the Church of England coordinate and resource the encounter with other faiths and was behind the publication of *TTID*. In parallel with this, NIFCON (see above) was set up in 1993, tasked with a similar role across the Anglican Communion. Following the mandate we have noted in the Lambeth Conference of 1998, it is NIFCON that is charged with the sharing of stories and monitoring of Muslim–Christian relations for the Communion.

Archbishop George Carey instigated two projects of especial note that are both part of the wider picture of Anglican engagement with Islam. An agreement was established between the Archbishop of Canterbury, as representative of the Anglican Communion, and al-Azhar al-Sharif, Cairo, 'a leading locus of spiritual authority in the world of Sunni Islam'.[552] This agreement fosters dialogue and bilateral exchanges, making possible a connection between the Church of England and a major source of Islamic teaching and practice globally. It is worth noting, in anticipation of our political theology question, that this bilateral agreement is suggestive of a state-to-state role for the Church of England: acting as a national Church with a focus for national Islamic authority in Egypt. To what extent is this 'public' role connected to the Church of England's self-understanding of its mission nationally and internationally? George Carey also initiated the 'Building Bridges' series of seminars facilitating studied reflections on the Bible and the Qur'an by international scholars around specified themes. The first of these seminars was chaired by Carey in 2002; subsequent annual seminars have been chaired by his successor Rowan Williams up until 2012. The published outcomes of these scholarly exchanges provide a now substantial theological resource for the Church of England in its relationship to Islam.[553]

In 2005 the report *Presence and Engagement: The Churches' Task in a Multi Faith Society* was issued by the Mission and Public Affairs Council of the Church of England. The Presence and Engagement Task Group, supported by the Church of England's national Adviser on Inter Faith Relations, has superseded IFCG as the focus for resourcing of the Church of England's interfaith encounter, and this report is thus a significant indicator of the direction of more contemporary reflections. It is surely no coincidence that the motif of Christian Presence, so significant in the missionary theologies of Kenneth Cragg, John V. Taylor and Max Warren, is used in the title of this report, and understood in incarnational terms through the coupling with engagement, relevant to context and local realities.[554] The report is especially focused on the actual contexts of parishes facing a significant proportion of other faiths, reflecting on their understanding of that 'presence and engagement'. Utilizing 2001 census statistics, the first British census to ask questions about religion and thus to be able to assess properly the nature of contemporary religious diversity, an important picture is drawn of the opportunities and challenges of Church of England parish life in a post-9/11 world. A crucial observation from the report is that:

> the presence of significant other Faith communities is now one of the major contexts in the ministry of the Church. At the time of the 2001 census, some 900 parishes out of a total of 13,000 had more than 10 per cent of their population as people of other Faiths than Christian and this figure is now higher and growing.[555]

These 900 parishes represent 23 per cent of the total population of all English parishes, and 32 per cent of these parishes have over 25 per cent of their population as people of other faiths. What is clearly discernible is a shift from the perceived novelty of religious diversity in the 1970s and 1980s to the settled reality of differing faiths in English parishes, of which the Christian faith is frequently now in the minority.

The report draws attention to the fragility of many of these parishes with a significant faith other, reflected in often weak financial sustainability but also in the diversity and vigour of 'presence and engagement'. The range of encounters and approaches is interrogated and the sensitivity of 'conversion' particularly noted in relations with Muslims, a word that:

captures the worst fears and the highest hopes of many people whether of Faith secular. But it is not a word that can be banished, nor is the concept behind it one that can be removed from the place it occupies at the heart of Christianity and Islam.[556]

The guiding principles of the report process, 'identity', 'confidence' and 'sustainability', seem to have freed respondents in providing a snapshot of genuine complexity in the Church of England's local encounters with other faiths. The stories of celebration are there alongside the vulnerability and fear, and there is a huge spectrum of approach offered (dialogue, evangelism, community action), in a spirit of catholicity. The diversity of encounters with Islam across the Lambeth Communion that was asserted in response to 'The Way of Dialogue' seems to be a feature *within* the Church of England and not just a matter of Anglican experience globally. That identity, confidence and sustainability should constitute the guiding principles of presence and engagement also redresses something of the perceived imbalance of earlier approaches to interreligious relations that set the onus on the Church's need to change in the encounter with the faith other.

The *Presence and Engagement* project continues with the support of local initiatives in resourcing and modelling interfaith encounters, notably at the St Philip's Centre, Leicester and the Bradford Churches for Diversity and Dialogue (BCDD). An ongoing Presence and Engagement Task Group signposts materials for parishes and hosts web discussion boards, all part of an effort to network and support the Church of England's mission in a multifaith context.

Up until 2006 there was no formal network forging bilateral relations between Christians and Muslims in Britain, akin to the Council for Christians and Jews (CCJ). However, following over two years of 'listening' to Muslim leaders and representatives with a number of church leaders across denominations, initiated by the Archbishop of Canterbury, George Carey, the Christian Muslim Forum was established with Carey's successor, Rowan Williams, as Founding Patron. The Forum works towards collaborative projects and open discussions between Christian and Muslim leaders through a 'web of open, honest and committed personal relationships'.[557] It is noticeable that, though rooted in an initiative of the Archbishop of Canterbury, the representation of the Christian communities on the Forum is ecumenical and includes a representative of a black-majority Pentecostal tradition. This points to the changing realities of the British Christian scene and a welcome by the Church of England of the interdependencies of ecumenism for Christian–Muslim relations. Towards the end of 2006 a statement was issued by the Forum, jointly by the Christian and Muslim representatives, about the status of religious festivals. This groundbreaking public statement was made:

> As Christians and Muslims we are wholeheartedly committed to the specific religious recognition for Christian festivals. Christmas is a celebration of the birth of Jesus and we wish this significant part of the Christian heritage of this country to remain an acknowledged part of national life.[558]

This statement is remarkable for enjoining Christians *and* Muslims in a shared conviction about the place of religion in wider British society. That the Church is seen to be the vulnerable party in a need for advocacy over the status of a festival such as Christmas underlines the significance of secular liberalism as another factor in the outworking of contemporary religious diversity. Notorious efforts to reconfigure Christmas as a non-religious festival in the interests of diversity are clearly in the sights of the Forum.[559] The subversive nature of the statement rests on the bilateral nature of the appeal. The statement thus avoids pandering to the reactionary, folk nostalgia of some of the lurid headlines about the erosion of the Christian heritage, while properly stating the religious antecedents of the festival and *demonstrating* how different faith traditions can mutually support respective distinctives. Muslim representatives evidently believe that support for the cause of the Church, in this instance, best serves an appreciation of faith in public life.

On 22 June 2009 the Forum published a further statement, this time focusing on combined ethical guidelines for mission.[560] This seems to represent a genuine grasping of the nettle of evangelism and conversion, apostasy and conversion. Issues that are contentious for Christians and Muslims are openly addressed with efforts at an agreed ethic that essentially allows for the missionary impulses of the respective faiths. So coercion, financial inducements, ridicule and manipulation are among practices in the cause of mission that are rejected. Sensitivity to children, young people and vulnerable adults is called for and a fundamental respect for the decisions of individuals to make their own choice in responding to a call to conversion. The underlying tenor of the document is one that recognizes the differences of Islam and Christianity and how they might prompt mutual evangelistic appeal (or *da'wah*). The document acknowledges that it is not a theological treatise as such, and thus implicitly not assuming a unitary foundation for mission and ethics. But this is done with tangible sympathy and with an evident ability to prove the pursuit of the common good between the faiths.

It remains to be seen what future initiatives emanate from the Forum, but its initial activities are further supportive of a more mutual approach between the Church of England and Islam, as well as an embrace of the diversity of engagements through the ecumenism of its membership. That the Christian Muslim Forum should be demonstrably supportive of collaborative statements and ventures that can hold together difference and commonality confirms the ecclesial move of the Lambeth documents.

Conclusion

The Lambeth Conference 1988 endorsement of 'The Way of Dialogue' still provides the most formal Anglican pronouncement to the Christian faith on the nature of Islam. Following the lead of Vatican II, the Abrahamic roots of Christianity, Judaism and Islam are integral to a proper understanding of relations between the three faiths. However, the accompanying theological resource of 'The Way of Dialogue' seems to push the Anglican position further than Vatican II went in its emphasis on the shared possibilities with Islam and the relegation of proclamation. It must be noted that *Nostra aetate* was also accompanied in Vatican II by *Lumen gentium*, a statement about the unique status of the Church in the world, *Gaudium et Spes*, on the relationship of the Church to the world, and *Ad gentes*, on the mission of the Church to the world. Bearing in mind the strategic impact of Vatican II on interreligious dialogue globally, the controversy created by 'The Way of Dialogue' suggests the potential for doctrinal unity on interreligious issues when theological considerations of dialogue and proclamation are not splintered apart.[561]

A telling element of the processes and discussions of *TTID*, 'The Way of Dialogue' and subsequent Lambeth discussions of interfaith concern has been the contribution of the diversity of Anglican experience globally. This experience is informed by the stories of persecution of Christians in contexts of Islamic political dominance, and the Anglican Communion is not alone in ceasing to baulk at addressing this challenge to Muslim leaders. The Church of England has been obliged to listen to the realities of Christian–Muslim encounter elsewhere in addressing its consequent theology, and been encouraged to reflect on contexts of more long-standing precedent. It is perhaps beside the point whether the earlier emphasis on the need for dialogue and assumption of Christian majority in the British context ever reflected the reality or not. However, the *Presence and Engagement* report underlines the breadth of Anglican encounters with Islam within England now and their fragility and vulnerability in many instances. This is not to say that the efforts towards dialogue are to be relaxed or that the spectre of racism has disappeared. Rather, the nature of the encounter between Christians and Muslims seems to be recognizably more as equals; the 'great other', to both faiths, is the secular liberalism that would reduce the potency of religious discourse in public life. Illustrative of a move to acknowledge mutual challenge and therefore to assert a more equalizing relationship is Philip

Lewis's contention that British Muslims contain 'agency'. For Lewis, Muslim communities should not be regarded as monolithic, passive victims of prejudice, as there are some problematic and isolationist tendencies, and the Church of England will find itself challenging these within a breadth of Christian–Muslim encounter.[562] The developments of the Christian Muslim Forum and many of the activities of the *Presence and Engagement* project also suggest that the Church of England's growing sensitivity to global Anglican concerns are increasingly being informed by those from other Christian traditions too, in the fashioning of reflections on the Christian–Muslim encounter.

Generous Love seems to be a landmark in interreligious theology for the Church of England, recognizing the mutualities of relationship between faiths. It is unapologetically 'Christian' in its trinitarianism and does not endeavour to provide the new schema for interfaith relations that were hinted at in the provisionality of *TTID* and 'The Way of Dialogue'. I would argue that *Generous Love* marks a key milestone in an ecclesial turn to Anglican interreligious relations, arguably prompted by the particular challenges faced in the encounter with Islam. This ecclesial turn evokes the rich inheritance of the Eastern Christian tradition and the Church Fathers. The turn is evident in the retrieval exhibited at Vatican II and confirms the ecclesiological self-identity suggested in the Introduction. The influence of Archbishop Rowan Williams, 'Orthodox in Anglican form', is palpable in the trinitarian, participatory ontology permeating *Generous Love* and associated programmes for engagement with Islam.

Anecdotes from the field: being host and guest

The Church of England is used to acting as host. The establishment status, parish system and network of buildings, often with associated church halls for community activities, play into a role that frequently pushes churches into dynamics where the power relation is decidedly tipped in our direction. This is a mixed blessing because when the

Church always holds the strings, it is difficult to develop relationships of mutuality, and for the vulnerability that seems intrinsic to the Christian Presence model of mission to be made manifest. While I was chair of the Springfield Project in Birmingham, a church-based project serving the Muslim-majority parish, we talked of the need for 'the draught to go both ways': to envisage practices and behaviours that enabled the church both to reach out, influence and shape the community, and for the community to be shaping what happened within the project and the church. It is something that has become important to our church centre in Sparkbrook, enabling the local residents' association, led by a cluster of Muslim parents, to talk of Christ Church as 'our church' because of the sense of ownership they feel in what happens there. At the church's Ladies Day project during this last Ramadan, the usual shared lunch was followed by conversations about faith and prayer, led each week not just by the Christian volunteers but also by Muslims who attended; Muslims who are increasingly given responsibility and taking leadership alongside the 'hosts'. This movement is what Sam Wells has described as the shift in mission from working for, working with, being for, to being with. Each of these is valid but the ultimate reflection of God's priority within which we exist is the 'being with'.[563]

7

Anglican Encounters with Islam:
The Legacies of Kenneth Cragg and
Rowan Williams

The Legacy of Bishop Kenneth Cragg

In the analysis of Anglican responses to Islam, the name of Kenneth Cragg has figured prominently. The influence of his writings on formal documents of the Church of England suggests that Cragg's work deserves particular attention. Born in 1913, Kenneth Cragg was raised in an evangelical Anglican household and after serving a curacy in Merseyside left Britain to be Chaplain and adjunct professor of philosophy at the American University of Beirut.[564] On his return to Britain, he completed doctoral studies on comparative religions at Oxford University, prior to holding a professorship in Arabic and Islamic Studies at Hartford Seminary, Connecticut. Over many years, Cragg exchanged periods teaching in Britain with substantive roles for the Anglican Communion in the Middle East. In 1970 he was made Assistant Bishop in the Jerusalem Archdiocese, based in Cairo, and was instrumental in ensuring an Arab appointment to the Jerusalem Archbishopric.

The seminal works, *The Call of the Minaret* and *Sandals at the Mosque*, continue to dominate the landscape of Anglican Christian–Muslim relations over 40 years since publication.[565] Cragg has been called the 'Louis Massignon of Anglicanism'[566] and 'the Massignon of the Anglo-Saxon world',[567] echoing the towering influence of the French Orientalist on the interreligious relations of the Catholic Church. Cragg's own explicit retrieval of tradition is significant in helping to situate his thought in a line of Anglican missionary endeavour. Christopher Lamb has noted his indebtedness to the formative influences of Temple Gairdner and Constance Padwick,[568] missionary scholars who have prompted sympathetic and eloquent tributes from Cragg himself.[569] For Lamb, this missionary inheritance has given Cragg an abiding understanding of Christian *hospitality* towards Islam.[570]

This concept of 'hospitality' will be elucidated in more detail subsequently, but the precedence of Temple Gairdner helps to explain something of Cragg's own vocation. We have noted already that Temple Gairdner could speak of the 'living faith' that is Islam at the Edinburgh World Missionary Conference of 1910.[571] This living faith, according to Gairdner, needs to be recovered by the Church that its witness may authenticate the 'finger of God'.[572] In Gairdner we see the germ of Cragg's recovery – in his language, 'retrieval' – of what is of God in Islam that needs to be discovered and manifested in the Christian community.[573] This hospitality to the faith in Islam also brings the realization of disjunction between Christianity and Islam. For Gairdner, the 'reproach of Islam' 'calls us back to explore His forgotten secrets … to a closer association with Christ Himself'.[574]

The Christological disjunction between Islam and Christianity rebukes, in turn, an Islam that sees its realization in temporal power and the subordination of love to might. Thus, Gairdner can describe Islam and Christianity as 'incompatible', the *tawhīd*, or oneness of God, indicative of that which 'Islam simplifies with a vengeance!'[575] Gairdner provides a chilling cameo by way of illustration:

> Back to that Church-mosque at Damascus whence we took our start! See where a Cross once stood, and where there stands a Crescent to-day! That sight stands for, and typifies, what every Moslem sees inwardly, and believes he has the right to see actually, when he looks at the Cross on every continental Cathedral spire, every English Minster rising from the sweet silent Close, every village church, from whose belfry-tower the chimes come like a benediction over the hamlet nestling at its feet, and the meadow-lands smiling in the sunlight beyond …[576]

In Gairdner we find what may seem to be a deep contradiction: a spiritual sympathy with Islam and a rejection of the political means of Islam.

In Kenneth Cragg's own ministry there is a similar conflicted train of thought yet a determination to 'retrieve' within Islam that which is otherwise rejected: the kenosis of God in the cross and thus the rejection of power as the means to faithfulness. Thus, the Medinan turn in Islam is a decisive parting of the ways when understood in the light of the centrality of the cross for Christians.[577] It is not sufficient, though, for Cragg to stand aloof from Islam and condemn its will-to-power. The 'sympathy' with which Gairdner and he notice the central claim of Islam about 'letting God be God'[578] compels a Christian *embassy* within the texts and culture of Muslims. This embassy – the representative capacity of the Christian among Muslims speaking of Christ in the local language[579] – leads Cragg to advocate for the Meccan settlement from within the Qur'an and Islamic tradition. In this otherwise abrogated settlement of faithfulness to God in political weakness, the divine pathos might be seen and the Christ-prophet who suffers discovered in all his fullness.

The particular nature of Cragg's political theology will be presented in Chapter 8, but it is important to note the significance of a theology of kenosis to his response to Islam, and thence to the nature of Christian politics. Cragg admits his indebtedness to the *Lux Mundi* (1889) essays edited by Charles Gore and instrumental in an Anglican reawakening to engagement with modern scholarship.[580] Coincidentally, Cragg's doctoral research was written while living at the Longworth vicarage, which hosted the original *Lux Mundi* contributors. The *Lux Mundi* appraisal of contemporary scholarship was grounded in a theology of the incarnation; what became for Cragg a priority to see 'the role of the human in God's work of creation, revelation, and redemption.'[581] The focus on divine self-limitation foundational to the *Lux Mundi* school and Gore's essay, in particular, simultaneously allowed for Cragg a sympathy with Muslim hearers who would struggle with the idea of the deity of Jesus, alongside the radical departure of the incarnation within the godhead that he would commend to Muslims.[582]

Recovering the tradition of the Church Fathers and widening the canon of Anglican theological resources to include Eastern Orthodoxy, the incarnation was not to be seen as a one-off event in the life of Jesus but indicative of the nature of God. Thus Cragg can say, consistent with the project of the *Lux Mundi* school, that:

> every instance of human charisma in divine employ, every coinciding of historical event with heavenly intent, contains in its own measure, this mystery of the eternal and the temporal at rendezvous. To believe in the incarnation is not to exclusify that mystery. For it is relatively present everywhere in creation and without it this could not be the sort of world in which *the* incarnation could happen.[583]

The Christian encounter with the other is not primarily a doctrinal one but a sacramental relationship in a sacramental world. Reflecting on Cragg's Christmas poems, sent to friends in greetings cards, Richard Jones notices a particularly Anglican sensibility reflective of this kenotic tradition:

> As sermons in Anglican worship often do, a number of the poems mention the imminent sacrament of the Bread and Wine offered to renew in more than words – in our bodies – that same mystery inaugurated by Incarnation, the union of the human with the divine.[584]

Again, the eucharistic locus of Cragg's generative theology is revealed as consistent with the ecclesial turn of more recent Anglican perspectives on the Church and Islam.

It is perhaps surprising that Cragg's formative evangelicalism could embrace the liberal catholicism of the *Lux Mundi* school, with its associated indebtedness to the patristic inheritance. Setting Cragg in the context of the Christian Presence tradition of Anglican missionary endeavour serves to underline the theological resonances with a Catholic spirituality that is itself within a heritage of the Eastern Church. It must be noted that for Cragg, as with John V. Taylor and Max Warren, that wider ecclesial self-consciousness may not be explicit but the parallels are evident. We have already noted that the Vatican II sensibility was 'as one finding Christ even more than preaching him'.[585] The idea of Christian Presence had its equivalent in the theology of Jean Daniélou, so influential to the pronouncements of Vatican II. He was a member of the *nouvelle théologie* school that was energized by the recovery of the Church Fathers. This movement was in turn complemented by the modern Eastern Orthodox tradition's own explorations of ecclesial self-understanding.[586] For Daniélou, Christian Presence requires in the Christian a 'far-reaching dispossession' necessitating the Church continuing in its own life the incarnation of Christ.[587] What Daniélou calls a 'spirituality of incarnation' is alive to 'all that is good in these worlds' and 'must understand these lands, espouse their cultures, and we cannot afford to do this without genuine sympathy'.[588]

Daniélou was in turn influenced by Charles de Foucauld, who modelled a Christian presence of eucharistic witness in Algeria. We have already noted Ipgrave's role in contributing to the drafting of *Generous Love* and in highlighting the indebtedness of Anglican interreligious theology to Vatican II. Ipgrave's more Catholic Anglican sensibility leads him to draw from the example of the Christian Presence school of Catholicism. So in two articles about the 'provocation' of Christian–Muslim relations to holiness, de Foucauld and Massignon are cited as exemplars of a monastic tradition that helps the wider Church to encounter God in new ways from within a sacramental understanding of the world.[589] It seems, then, that Cragg, and the Anglican Christian Presence school, permit a widening of the canon of Anglican responses to Islam.

The 'Call to Understanding' advocated by 'The Way of Dialogue' is intrinsic to the Christian Presence school of Anglicans and Catholics alike. In Cragg's own *The Call of the Minaret*, he encourages 'entering into the soul of those to be served', an incarnational model congruent with the 'affirmation' and 'sharing' of 'The Way of Dialogue'.[590] In Max Warren's famous Introduction to the Christian Presence series of books, the nature of this incarnational understanding is dilated:

> Our first task in approaching another people, another culture, another religion, is to take off our shoes, for the place we are approaching is holy. Else we may find ourselves treading on men's dreams. More serious still, we may forget that God was here before our arrival.[591]

The costly identification with the religious other leads to the very discovery of God in the interreligious encounter. This echoes in turn the 'Indian vocation' of the Catholic missionary and friend of Henri de Lubac, Jules Monchanin. His was a personal exploration of Indian spirituality from within the practice of the eucharist as the mystery of Christ's presence. Jacques Prévotat describes both Monchanin and de Lubac, whose theology contributed so much to the climate of Vatican II, as having:

> a universal outlook, a shared desire to see Christianity enriched by other cultures. This inspiration rejoins the great tradition of the Church, expands it to worldwide dimensions, is favourable to a deepening of thought on doctrine, and paralyses the temptation of those who would like to harden it.[592]

Where some would seek to harden the borders between the Church and other religions, de Lubac and Monchanin, with Cragg and the Christian Presence school, are alert to the presence of Christ in the religious other. This is also true for de Foucauld, a direct influence on Louis Massignon. De Foucauld became, to his Muslim neighbours, a *marabout*, a holy man, mediating the sacrament of Christ's mystical body 'to offer a Christian presence in their midst'.[593]

A further illustration of the resonances across ecclesial traditions of Cragg and the Christian Presence school is in Paul Knitter's categorization of Cragg, Warren, Taylor and Roger Hooker as representative of a 'Catholic Model' of engagement with other faiths in contrast to his 'Conservative Evangelical' or 'Mainline Protestant' categories. Described in a section of his book *No Other Name?* as 'A Mainline Christian Model', this is a striking observation of the sacramentalism common to Cragg and Vatican II Catholicism.[594] As Graham Kings points out, 'this positioning is both ironic (in that they come from the evangelical Anglican tradition), but also perceptive in that they would not fit particularly easily into the Mainline Protestant model (where Knitter placed Lesslie Newbigin and Stephen Neill).'[595]

The sense that Cragg represents a sacramental theology that resonates ecumenically is confirmed by the high esteem accorded him by the French lay Russian Orthodox theologian Olivier Clément. In Clément's published dialogue with Mohamed Talbi, he speaks positively of Cragg's pioneering work and of the 'presence à-demi secrète de Jésus' ('a semi-secret presence of Jesus') he sees in Islam alongside the Catholic pioneer, Massignon.[596] Clément's sacramentalism finds an echo in Cragg's insistence on the 'traces' of Christ within Islam, similarly represented by the work of the Orthodox theologian George Khodr.[597] What this seems to confirm is that the attention given Cragg's theological account of Islam that I have identified is echoed in Eastern Christianity. It is this same Eastern Christian tradition that is drawn on to underpin the ecclesial turn more generally.

Despite the lack of an *explicit* retrieval of Eastern Orthodox theology in Cragg's writings, there is a notable respect for the Lebanese academic, President of the General Assembly of the United Nations and contributor to the Universal Declaration of Human Rights, Charles Malik (1906–87). Cragg and Malik worked as colleagues and friends at the American University of Beirut. In Malik, a Chalcedonian Orthodox Christian of the Middle East, Cragg identified an important voice from within a context familiar with Islam that needed to be heeded by the West: Malik 'gave utterance to an Arab Christianity which had stayed too long unidentified in the secular West'.[598]

For Cragg, Malik represented a 'reminder' of the significance of freedom in a Lebanon that had been able to model 'a state at once both Christian and composite, mediating between a nearer and a farther East'.[599] The retrieval I have identified that seeks to draw from the resources of Eastern Christians is seen to be emblematic of Malik. Though Cragg's evangelical heritage seems to inhibit his own self-conscious appropriation of tradition, there is an almost instinctive appreciation of a figure like Malik who can bridge the divide of East and West. Malik's 'reminder', reminiscent of Massignon's 'foil', is the challenge of atheism to the religious impulse to freedom, and a goad to the Church to be more fully itself, and also a provocation to Islam about the vulnerability of God in the incarnation. This is why Lamb can say of Cragg's appreciation of Malik's political and Eastern Orthodox sensibility that: 'We have seen the influence of a "kenotic" and incarnational theology on Cragg, and it is easy to see how Malik's thinking would have fitted into this growing pattern.'[600] It is intriguing to note an important and influential essay to Cragg written by Malik on 'The Orthodox Church' in the Middle East. While Cragg writes very little about ecclesial traditions, in contrast to Rowan Williams, it seems that Malik is the one who identifies the important heritages of Eastern Orthodoxy in the Middle East, its mysticism as a resource for engaging with Islam, and the particular place of Russian Orthodoxy in any retrieval of the East for the encounter with Islam:

> With respect to this dimension of transcendence Orthodoxy is at one with Islam, although of course it tempers it with God's humanity which Islam does not ... But for the Russian Orthodox Church, Orthodoxy in the Middle East would have been an orphan. The Churches of the West come to it as something alien: they want to change and convert it. Russian Orthodoxy comes to it as bone of its bones and flesh of its flesh.[601]

As Malik embodies a confluence of traditions, East and West, that engage sympathetically yet critically with Islam, so Cragg's temper of hospitality towards the Arab world provides a parallel point of confluence for Anglicanism. His hospitality towards Islam, the missionary impulse to identification, is a restraint: a disciplined listening that indeed hears Islam on its own terms. The 'space' carved out by this restraint does not engender a 'non-Christian' response, nor a new synthesis of the two faiths; rather, it is the place of meeting where a Christian presence is materially affected in relationship.

Jane Smith describes 'the persistence of his theme of perplexity'.[602] The perplexity, for Smith, is in the repeated effort to reconcile the two faiths around the cross of Christ, the cross that stands as ultimate departure from all that humanity wills. Throughout his writings, Cragg avoids the use of the phrase 'Abrahamic religion', while recognizing that there is a rich vein of insight to be mined from how the three faiths draw from Abraham in shared and contrasting ways. In an important chapter on Abraham in *The Privilege of Man*, Cragg notes the 'whole consensus of Semitic faiths ... [are] alike in esteeming Abraham as the first of the faith', yet he underlines 'significant differences of emphasis in the role of Abraham among the three systems'.[603] Interestingly, there is no reference to Massignon in this chapter, written as it was in the wake of Vatican II. Instead, there is a striking honesty about the questionable historical veracity of some of the respective claims on Abraham.

Cragg's method is, rather, to admit that 'Abraham is what Abraham's "family" say he is.'[604] It is in the *method*, rather, that I believe we find the real continuity between Massignon and Cragg. Writing of Constance Padwick in 1969, Cragg esteems her project of compiling Muslim prayers in *Muslim Devotions*. He compares her vision to that of Massignon, whose sympathy and imagination would enable him to 'recognize an ...

> ... observation of affinities
> In objects where no brotherhood exists
> To passive minds.[605]

This could easily be said of Cragg himself, who sought to discover resonances and convergences between faiths without occluding difference. Thus, his efforts to find Christian resonances within Muhammad have suggested to some that he is even arguing for acceptance of Muhammad's prophethood.[606] Aware that he will be criticized by both Christians and Muslims, I would suggest that it is an incorrect reading of Cragg to interpret an affirmative verdict on Muhammad's prophethood:

> In the command to 'let God be God' we can hardly fail to recognize each other. But it is just this significant 'agreement' and not some bent for insensitive hostility which requires a Christian's reservation about Muhammad … The Gospel represents what we must call a divine 'indicative', an initiative of self-disclosure on God's part by which His relation to our human situation is not only in law and education, but in grace and suffering.[607]

As Nick Wood concludes, 'Cragg represents the broadly inclusive stream of continuity, but recognizes the disjunction of the cross at the heart of the Gospel.'[608]

Throughout Cragg's writings there is repeated referencing of Scriptures; what he calls the 'ultimate court of appeal'.[609] Often convoluted, always eloquent and sometimes pedantic, Cragg provides a missionary theology of encounter with Islam that is respectful of founding texts and rooted in the Anglican tradition. He 'comes to his theological task as an Anglican bishop, with a clear view of authority',[610] yet willing to risk the challenge to his own inheritance. When Cragg says, in reference to the *hijra*, 'Muhammad was his own Constantine',[611] this is at once both a rebuke of the will-to-power in Islam and of the fusion of state and church interests in Christendom. The Christological imperative that runs through Cragg's theology prises open Anglicanism to discover the story of the Church worldwide. In opposition to the 'strongly domestic accent' of much of contemporary Christianity, 'embassy' involves also 'representing Christ but in full residential capacity, with credentials that, for all their authority, are subject to local presentation'.[612]

Considering the evolution of formal Anglican documents across the three Lambeth Conferences to 2008 and the pattern of developments within the Church of England, and across many other denominations, it seems that the work of Kenneth Cragg is in tune with the contemporary context of Christian–Muslim relations and rooted firmly in the Anglican tradition. As a sacramental theology of encounter, emphasizing the incarnation as a primary doctrine for understanding the work of God in the world, Cragg echoes a long-standing Anglican tradition reaffirmed by the *Lux Mundi* school and with antecedents to Richard Hooker. This tradition itself is reflective of an ecclesial turn, recovering a patristic ecclesiology consonant with the major developments of Vatican II in the Catholic Church.

Cragg's refusal to delineate or define Islam, on the one hand, and yet his ability to be hospitable to the religious impulse towards God that he encounters is indicative of the more recent rejection by the Church of England of a search for a 'common core' to the two faiths. Cragg's hospitality embraces the potential for the work of God in Islam, while always presenting the challenge of the cross: the 'embassy' of the missionary vocation. The recognition of the religious impulse posits the true ground of sharing in our common humanity: a humanity that must always be suspicious of 'systems' and of the trappings of power. The Church of England, established as the national Church but looking to an increasingly narrowed vista, stands in the tension evidenced in Cragg's critique of Medinan religion: power is not needed to serve God, but the service of God makes a difference to every power. How Cragg articulates a political theology in response to Islam will thus be a concluding analysis of the inquiry in Chapter 8, drawing together the influences and trajectories for contemporary Anglican Christian–Muslim encounters.

Archbishop Rowan Williams and Islam: trinitarian monotheism

Benjamin Myers has stated how Williams' early academic career was a 'decade-long immersion in the world of Russian Ortho-doxy'.[613] For Williams, it is the émigré school of Russian Orthodox theologians combined with his attentiveness to the Church Fathers that shapes his indebtedness to Eastern Christianity.[614] In demonstrating the ecclesial turn of Anglican Christian–Muslim relations that builds on the self-identity of the Church, Williams' leadership has been strikingly present in the resonances of Orthodox trinitarianism within *Generous Love*. Williams' rejection of an overriding schema of theology of religions in favour of theologies of relations that encourage unity *in difference* are a further imprint on the direction of the Church of England accounts that we have examined. How Williams has specifically spoken on Christian–Muslim relations is thus an important element of confirming the ecclesial turn as presented.

In this section we will not be analysing Williams' Shari'a law speech as that will be explored more fully in Chapter 8 on political theology. Rather, in two momentous lectures given to Muslims in vital centres of Islamic learning, I will highlight his consistent recourse to the Church Fathers in an explicit recasting of 'trinitarian monotheism'. How the themes of the trinity and the nature of the godhead, themes so intrinsic to Eastern Christianity, have shaped the corresponding Anglican ecclesial turn will become apparent in these two lectures.

In September 2004, Williams addressed an audience at al-Azhar al-Sharif, Cairo, one of the most important centres for Sunni Islamic learning in the world.[615] The symbolic significance of this event is given added freight by the fact that it was the third anniversary of the 9/11 atrocities. The first thing to note, and indicative of the trajectory of the Anglican Christian–Muslim relations we have outlined, is what Williams does *not* do. There is no appeal to an underlying synchronicity between the two faiths. There is no reference to 'Abrahamic religions' as the common language of Christianity and Islam. At the third anniversary of 9/11 in the heart of Sunni Islamic learning, Archbishop Rowan Williams talks about the *trinity* of the Christian faith. Neglecting any possible overarching scheme, Williams' avowed intent is that 'Christians and Muslims understand one another better'.[616]

To ground what becomes an articulation of the trinity, Williams begins with an assertion that both Christians and Muslims agree on: the unity or *tawhīd* of God. This is one of those points of *agreement* that can become a foundation that enables him then to express *disagreement*. Belief in the one God, as articulated by Vatican II, provides a deep affinity from which to talk about what it means to be accountable to God. As Michael Ipgrave states in his commentary on the al-Azhar address: 'Already this assumes the propriety, even the necessity, of cross-referencing between the divine as understood in Christianity and Islam.'[617] Clearing away the common Islamic misconception that Christians believe God literally had a son, Williams points out to his audience that in the history of the Church, there were many Christians who had the same reaction as Muslims to the erroneous idea of God's limitation in physical processes. This assertion becomes the opportunity for Williams to remind his audience that these Christian debates were at their richest among the Eastern Christians of Egypt.[618] This pointed aside roots him in the patristic milieu as well as situating himself in sympathy with the continuing and preceding Christian presence in North Africa.

Williams' approach is to make a defence of the trinity to Muslims by avoiding ambiguous language to which an Islamic audience may be especially sensitive. He is not expecting that the trinity will suddenly become palatable to Muslims ('There is, as you will have seen, a great difference between what I as a Christian must say and what the Muslim will say'[619]). Rather, his task is, as Ipgrave says, 'to illuminate, not to obliterate, the real differences which distinguish Christian belief from that of other ways of understanding the divine unity'.[620] Williams asserts the self-sufficiency or self-subsistence of God in common with Islam to then expand on the trinity as an account of this self-sufficiency in human experience.

Thus, Williams shuns the use of the word 'persons', the traditional grammar of trinity for the Church, and prefers to talk of God as a 'source' to which Jesus is the *expression* of that life, and the Holy Spirit the *sharing* of that life.[621] The role of the Holy Spirit in enabling the *participation* of the Church in the life of God resonates with the patristic sensibility already noted as intrinsic to Williams' theology and characteristic of the Anglican temper. Talking of God as the source of life echoes something of the work of the Church Father, Palamas, recovered by the émigré Russian Orthodox theologian John Meyendorff (1926–92). Palamas wrestled with attempts to explain the self-subsistence of God through the prism of trinitarian sociality where God was 'source'.[622]

Ipgrave sees a continuity in Williams' references to the trinity in 'Augustine's "psychological" analogies through to Barth's "circle of self-revelation"'.[623] What is evident, then, is that Williams is standing in a long tradition of trinitarian apologetic where the Church has had to make intelligible its most distinctive doctrine to the world. That God is the 'source of life', a shared commitment of Christians and Muslims, renews the possibilities for dialogue. The philosophical complexity of trinitarianism is no mere exercise in dogmatics but primarily an account that explains how Christians see themselves as responsible to Muslims, mutually, in God's created order. It is for this reason that Ipgrave, restating his own academic research on the earliest Christian–Muslim encounters and thus positioning Williams in the patristic inheritance, describes Williams' trinitarian model as one of 'divine plenitude'.[624] The radical disjunction of the trinity from Islam's understanding of God is paradoxically rich with potential for dialogue, empathy and indeed the discovery of God in the life of the other.

In a lecture at the 'Presence of Faith Conference', celebrating 100 years of Anglican interfaith relations, Williams explains his trinitarian impulse to interreligious dialogue to an audience of Christian scholars of other religions. This time content to use the word 'person' of the trinity, Williams is yet keen to avoid any sense of the atomization of the godhead, whether that be by severing the humanity of Jesus from the source of life that is God the Father, or unmooring an understanding of the Holy Spirit from the expression of that source in Jesus. Williams locates this theology in Richard Hooker, again referencing the patristic antecedents of this rationale.[625] What he describes as a 'sapiential theology':

> assumes that wherever we find ourselves in the universe the same pattern of immeasurable gift, mutual and harmonious interaction and an energy moving towards fulfilment is going to be at work: the Trinity is everywhere, active in a wholly consistent way, since there is no other ultimate agency and all finite occurrence happens because infinite energy has given the capacity for it.[626]

One again, the language of 'energy' and 'source' reflect Williams' Orthodox idioms that reassert God's unity while giving expression to the knowledge of God in the form of Christ; in Hooker's terms 'by way of conjunction' and 'by co-operation with Deity'.[627] In retrieving patristic and Eastern Christian sources, Williams is also retrieving that tradition of Anglicanism that was especially indebted to the Church Fathers and representing a reincorporation of Hooker's legacy. The essential otherness of God is experienced in the self-revelation of the trinity, making the human project a shared exercise in the discovery of the source of life in a shape that is always recognizably 'Christlike'. As Hans Urs von Balthasar says (another giant of Vatican II and the neo-patristic synthesis), all other religions and world views are 'christologies on the search'.[628] Rather than Christology and the trinity becoming an awkward impediment to relations with the religious other, they are the shape and impulse to such relations.

Rowan Williams' enthusiastic embrace of the historic, creedal significance of the trinity is evidenced in his lecture to the Islamic University in Islamabad in 2005. Again, addressing a Muslim audience, Williams is conscious of the need to explain and correct misperceptions about the nature of God's unity in Christianity. Importantly for the purposes of this inquiry, Williams' account of the Christian faith for Muslims, 'What is Christianity?', is situated in the context of the worshipping community of the Church. Williams invites the audience to imagine a stranger visiting Christians as they gather to sing hymns, read Scripture, declare creeds and, supremely, to break bread and drink wine.[629] A very Anglican sensibility of doctrine in practice is being modelled as the apologetic for Muslim students. Explaining how Christians talk of God, Williams again adopts the language of Eastern Christianity: 'We say rather that the one God is first the source of everything, the life from which everything flows out.'[630]

The Christian continuity with Judaism is noted with respect to the reading of the Old Testament and in the practice of the eucharist as a 'Christian version of the Passover'. The eucharistic ecclesiology of Anglicanism is unashamedly expressed in his statement that 'Just as Jesus' human flesh and blood is the place where God's power and Spirit are at work, so in this bread and wine, blessed in his memory, the same power and Spirit are active.'[631] The Church at the eucharist thus becomes a special locus for participation in the life of the godhead, repeating the themes of his al-Azhar address and *Generous Love*.

Williams concludes his lecture with a nod to the Desert Fathers and the mystical tradition of Orthodoxy, again evoking continuity with the Eastern Christian witness. In the 'darkness' of the apophatic experience, 'not because he does not want to communicate but because our minds and hearts are too small for him to enter fully', the goal of the beatific vision is commended to his Muslim audience.[632] The sophiology of Maximus the Confessor, as recapitulated by Sergei Bulgakov (1871–1944), is evident in this description of the Church's 'plenitude' within the trinity by way of the darkness of unknowing. Humanity is to be taken up into the life of the creator; the Church is the vanguard of this act of creation, incarnation and re-creation. This sophiology was:

a way of explaining how the Church can both be characterized by fullness and yet at the same time be a pilgrim people. The Church can be both if she in some sense embodies not only the eternal divine Wisdom but also the creaturely wisdom that is still in process of becoming.[633]

Williams' confident commendation of Christian doctrines is yet a means of generating a shared process of dialogue as humans responsible to a graced order of creation. It is worth mentioning Williams' epistemology of unity in difference. Williams is philosophically sympathetic to the Wittgensteinian turn that cultures are constructs of language and thus the 'other' can never be wholly known. Because languages are functions of our sociality, histories and communal practices, with all their heavily laden symbolism, human life bears the mark of repeated alienations.[634] The admission of such alienations is:

> neither a flight from relation, nor the quest for an impossible transparency or immediacy in relation … but that which equips us for knowing and being known humanly, taking time with the human world and not aiming to have done with knowing (and desiring).[635]

This sentiment is all of a piece with Rowan Williams' approach to Islam. He would not negate the 'self' in the effort to know the other, as continental philosophy might, but presents 'self' in a painstaking exercise of dialogue with the other that refuses closure. Much as Kenneth Cragg refuses the definition of Islam or the assessment of Muhammad's prophethood, so Williams resists the categorization of other religions. Instead, he prefers to reflect on those impulses in his own 'language of tradition' that he may be intelligible to the other by way of fostering and re-energizing continued dialogue and discovery. Those very impulses are kenotic and thus propel the Christian into a place of self-emptying, the place which is, in the grammar of Gillian Rose, a 'broken middle'.[636] The necessary 'mystery' of interfaith is, I believe, a vital connection between Rowan Williams' apophaticism and Kenneth Cragg's model of hospitality. Both are at turns restrained by and dilated by a high Christology.[637] In an interview with Williams in pursuance of this research, Williams was asked to comment on what he had learned from Cragg. The reply is a telling confirmation of the kenotic instincts of both Cragg and Williams: 'His constant attempt to refresh or reconstruct theological idiom in the language of another religion. "How might a Muslim say this?" which is always invariably searching or enlarging.'[638] Then Williams applauds Cragg's 'refusal of any "mega-theory"' of Islam; 'he continues to "do the work" on the frontier'.[639] Williams sees in Cragg a formative resource for the Anglican response to Islam precisely because he declines to abstract from the specific interreligious encounter into theories of religion that put oneself outside the traditioned community of theCchurch. Cragg's impulse is to re-present Christian truth in the language of Islam.

Jane Smith, in a perceptive essay in *A Faithful Presence*, has identified in Cragg the 'persistence of his theme of perplexity'.[640] While always locating his theology within a Christological orbit, there is a refusal to close down the nature of the encounter with the religious other. Essentially, any closure runs the danger that God, in the stranger, will be missed. The imperative to hospitality thus rests on a belief that the Church needs to risk itself in encounter after the pattern of Christ; the hopeful invitation we extend to the other always having the potential to become the place of invitation from God to us. Correspondingly, Williams can say that too often '"Incarnation" has become the ground of final valid-ation for the rights and authority of the new community; rather than serving as itself a sign of the dangers of religious self-enclosure and claims to control.'[641]

How Rowan Williams and Kenneth Cragg build on their re-spective understandings of Christian–Muslim relations from their trinitarian positions to propose a consequent political theology will be explored in Chapter 8.

Conclusion

Under the leadership of Williams, the presentation of 'trinitarian monotheism' has been indicative of efforts to make Christian doctrine intelligible to Muslims without the urge to seek an underlying synthesis of the two faiths. This instinct is consonant with the evident legacy of Cragg discernible in so many formal Anglican reflections on Islam.[642]

In returning to the original question of what an understanding of Islam may be to the Church of England, arguably the most unequivocal answer would be one of holy reticence. There are consistent efforts to see dialogue with Islam based on an appreciation of unity in difference, and there continue to be initiatives in both Christian and Muslim traditions that work towards a theological rapprochement that can reconfigure the respective faiths to a common core.[643] The originating stories of Abraham within the Bible and the Qur'an evidently provide an ongoing resource and obligation in relationship between Christians and Muslims. Whether the Church of England can say more than this without excluding the convictions of many Anglicans and presenting impediments to relations with other faiths is unclear. Certainly, though, any utilization of the Abrahamic motif cannot be made without reference to the vital relationship of the Christian faith to the Jewish faith, as underlined by Archbishop Rowan Williams in his response to *A Common Word*.[644] Furthermore, as Williams says, attention to Scripture, as Anglicans, will be a significant part of the process of theological reflection in the encounter with Islam for 'we are speaking *enough* of a common language'.[645]

For the Church of England, the process of negotiating the plurality of British life in the last 30 years seems to have begun to bring fresh realizations of what is essentially *distinctive* about the Christian faith moving from an earlier emphasis on the obligation to what is *shared* with the faith of Islam. Thus the motifs of hospitality and embassy, with the evocation of both dialogue and proclamation, have been reasserted in continuity with a distinguished tradition of scholarly Anglican missionary encounter with Islam, particularly of Bishop Kenneth Cragg. This theology is located in a sacramental tradition of incarnation consistent with Anglican self-understanding going back to Hooker and the

Church Fathers. Cragg's theology posits the Church as both host and guest in a truly relational dialectic with Muslims. The hospitality advocated by Kenneth Cragg is framed by a high Christology; God understood in his kenosis on the cross. This at turns compels an open identification with Islam and Muslims while challenging the will-to-power inherent in the Medinan economy.

Where earlier Anglican approaches included the trinity as but one element of controversy in the encounter with Islam, the ecclesial turn that I have outlined would suggest that the trinity provides the formative pattern for understanding relations with Islam. Nicholas Lossky reflected on how Anglicanism modelled the 'inseparable character of the Word of God and participation in the Sacrament of the Eucharist' in the Thirty-Nine Articles.[646] His comments seem pertinent to the ecclesial turn epitomized by *Generous Love*:

> The Holy Trinity should never be regarded as something like a mathematical formula that is reserved for academic, dogmatic, or even worse, 'systematic' theologians. The Holy Trinity concerns every aspect of every Christian's life. It is, or should be, the prototype of our relations within our community, our congregation, the gathering of the People of God.[647]

Where Lambeth 1988 revealed theologies of God in silos separated from the exposition of relations with other faiths, the Church of England now seems to be reflecting on relations with Islam with a greater degree of ecclesial and doctrinal cross-referencing.

When we consider the global and ecumenical context of the Church of England, an ecumenism rooted first and foremost in the Lambeth Communion, an attention to the diversity of encounters with Islam seems particularly significant. Across a wide range of traditions the primary theological drive seems to be less about finding novel theological schemes that conflate Christianity and Islam and more about using the essential characteristics of the Christian faith to forge shared notions of citizenship; indeed, of political theology. Throughout the history of Christian–Muslim relations and in the global context of today, the Church has had to reckon with the consequences of will-to-power; of persecution and isolationism. Both communities share a history of blame in this regard. The task then remains, if the Church of England is keen to assert difference as well as commonality with Islam, to develop a political theology whereby Christians and Muslims can overcome their differences in pursuit of the common good. How a trinitarian, participatory ontology might shape a corresponding political theology in response to Islam will be the subject of Chapter 8.

Anecdotes from the field: embracing mystery

In both Cragg and Williams there are philosophical and theological undercurrents that emphasize the mystery of the Christian–Muslim encounter and step back from circumscribing what Islam 'is' to Christians. They rather proffer a tentative and provisional spirituality that chimes with my own experience of encounters with Muslims. I am reminded of the Muslim colleague in North Africa who shared a dream that he had had. This colleague had been enchanted by the picture of Jesus he read of in the Qur'an and consequently obtained an Arabic New Testament. The dream that came to this man was of him walking up to a crossroads where someone waited, directing him to 'ask the British man in your office to show you the way'. How might we speak of this remarkable leading towards the Christian faith prompted by Islamic devotion?

I think of the young Muslim woman I met in Nottingham who had just completed a special Ramadan devotion, secluding herself in prayer in her bedroom for the month while her family provided food for the daily breaking of fast. How do I speak of this contemplative yearning when I encounter the visible radiance on her face and the palpable peace and transfiguration to which she witnessed?

Both these encounters are charged with the 'plenitude' of God but taken together are perplexing. Rather than seeking to delineate the parameters of the other's encounter with God, I can only witness to and discern what I understand of God in Christ, and affirm what I recognize as good, holy and true. It makes for a messier discipleship because the mystery both compels me to proclaim Christ and to acknowledge Christ in the other.

8

The Church of England, Islam and Theologies for the Public Square

Introduction

At the outset of this inquiry I defined 'political theology' according to Scott and Cavanaugh as an 'analysis and criticism of political arrangements ... from the perspective of differing interpretations of God's way with the world'.[648] Scott and Cavanaugh suggest that there are three broad trends within political theology of 'God's way with the world':

1.   On the basis that politics and theology were two distinct activities, 'the task of political theology might be to relate religious belief to larger societal issues while not confusing the proper autonomy of each.'

2.   Theology is a 'superstructure' to the material realities of socio-economic arrangements and thus acts as a means of critique of the justice of these arrangements.

3.   Both theology and politics have metaphysical properties that shape how life is to be lived and there are implicit conclusions for the embodiment of the political in Christian theology. So 'the task then might become one of exposing the false theologies underlying supposedly "secular" politics and promoting the true politics implicit in a true theology.'[649]

This study has sought to build on the primary 'theology' of 'God's way with the world' an articulation of what Islam, or Muslims, are

believed to be in relation to the Church of England. The analysis
has revealed an ecclesial turn in the Church of England as it relates
to other faiths and Islam in particular. This turn has sought to
ground relations with Islam in the identity of the Church and
recover a theology for interreligious relations in the prior understanding of the Church as participant in the life of the trinity.
Influenced by contemporary Eastern Orthodox and patristic
understandings of the trinity and incarnation, relations with Islam
flow from an appreciation of unity in difference, such that both
dialogue and proclamation are enabled.

It would seem, then, that a political theology appropriate to a
response to Islam might follow the ecclesial turn in interreligious
relations. If the third stream as described by Scott and Cavanaugh
contests any separation of religion and politics and believes that
'religious concepts, doctrines and institutions, such as God and
church, have political implications',[650] then this would seem to be
the area from which to pursue a consequent political theology. We
have already noted how the doctrine of the trinity seems to be
shaping a renewed ecclesial consciousness for Anglican interreligious relations. What might the political theology look like that
follows such an ecclesial turn?

Luke Bretherton has identified the ecclesial turn in political
theology (Scott and Cavanaugh's third stream), and noted how it
expresses a drive that the Church 'should not be policed or
determined by some external discourse'.[651] This is redolent of the
language we found in the contemporary suspicion of overarching
schemas for theologies of religion and some of the resistance to an
'Abrahamic' formula for relations with Islam within Anglicanism
and the broader Christian tradition. We have seen that Archbishop
Rowan Williams and Bishop Kenneth Cragg are two key contributors to the ecclesial turn in Anglican relations with Islam. I
will analyse more specifically their consequent 'political theologies',
assessing how they fit within the broader ecclesial turn and the
wider debate in political theology.[652]

Kenneth Cragg and political theology: *khilāfa* and dominion

It must be admitted that Cragg never uses the phrase 'political theology', yet his engagement with Islam persistently ranges into the nexus of religion and politics. Cragg's seminal 1956 work, *The Call of the Minaret*, was alert to the challenges of the political vision of Islam in relation to Christianity.[653] That Muhammad was 'from the outset its Constantine as well as its Prophet' marks out the *hijra* as the decisive and defining moment for political Islam.[654] The Islamic order is ordained by God 'because it stands under God's law', but this seeming statement of fact obscures the pressing need to be able to interpret and apply this law.[655] An impulse exists for the polity to be Islamic but the formative struggles over succession and authority continue to this day: 'Islam demands the entire allegiance of the believer and the state should insure as best as it may that those demands are satisfied ... Beyond that there is division.'[656]

That the Medinan moment at the *hijra* seems so decisive a departure for Cragg might be contradicted by Fred Donner's understanding of an early monotheistic reform movement that encompassed Jews and Christians even in Medina. However, in Cragg's analysis the Medinan turn is at least a motif for the political claims of Islam, with the Meccan origins as emblematic of the call to true worship. When Cragg juxtaposes the Meccan religious vision as foil to Medina, he is effectively articulating Donner's understanding of the believers movement's mission. As Donner says, 'The social dimensions of the message are undeniable and significant, but they are incidental to the central notions of the Qur'an, which are religious: Belief in the one God and righteous behaviour as proof of obedience to God's will.'[657]

It is from within this religious minding that Cragg seeks to 'retrieve' the Christ lost to Islam. This demands a responsive elucidation of the Christian faith to an Islam that otherwise judges the Church to be 'jejune, effete, misguided, and discredited'.[658] Thus, the incarnation, properly understood as the *sacramentalizing* of all physical life, can speak to an Islam concerned about the outward impact of religious faith. It is in the vision of a sacramentalized whole life that the influences of the Anglican *Lux Mundi* movement on Cragg's political theology can be discerned. In the kenosis of God, the twin truths of a graced created order and a necessarily vulnerable creator inform Cragg's response to political Islam. The radical 'called-out' community of believers speaks of the need for a redeemed society and not an internalized, individualistic gospel. However, a realistic assessment of the pervasive power of sin would guard against an idealism that might expect this order to be perfected in external terms. The retrieval of Christ to Muslims resonates with the spiritual challenge characteristic of Muhammad's Meccan vocation: the reform of religious life from a position of powerlessness.[659]

In defending the classic Christian inheritance of the doctrine of the two,[660] Cragg does not describe *how* church and temporal powers are to negotiate their respective responsibilities and opens himself up to the charge of pietism and naivety. As a Muslim critic of Cragg's work has observed:

Christianity wishes to leave unto Caesar what is Caesar's. In the absence of Christian guidance, a Christian ruler will follow not Christ but Machiavelli, whereas Islamic guidance to a ruler is as imperative as it is to one who prays and fasts.[661]

Cragg's dilemma is to express something of the political *implications* of the Christian faith at the same time as honouring a Christian suspicion of the power equation. In *Christianity in World Perspective*, Cragg draws a clear distinction between the 'creative trusteeship' of the Church and the 'custodian-mind'[662] of other religious communities. The Church itself is a body politic turned outwards to a sacramental creation. By contrast, Islam betrays a tendency to a 'custodian-mind' that is exclusionary and assertive.[663]

Trusteeship becomes an increasingly important motif for Cragg as he seeks to problematize the Medinan tendency – emblematic of the will-to-power – to self-assertion and exclusion. From drawing a sharp boundary between the Church's creative trusteeship, and other faiths, trusteeship is conceived as a universal vocation to humanity that can encompass Islamic self-understanding. Thus, the qur'anic principle of *khilāfa* is represented in terms akin to the Christian doctrine of humanity's dominion. Within the creation ordinance common to both Scriptures, God delegates a level of sovereignty to humanity, who is made accountable to God for this responsibility. God's appointment of a viceroy (*khalīfa*) on the earth in Q 2:30 is, for Cragg, an opportunity for Islam to discover the inclusive vicegerency of all humanity within the creation ordinance.[664] There is thus an appropriate realm of the 'secular' that is implicit in the delegation of authority: the trusteeship of the natural order.

From this shared scriptural foundation, Christians and Muslims can begin to talk together of the mutualities of political responsibility. Cragg believes there to be 'in the entire thrust of biblical or qur'anic Scripture', 'the option of *khilāfah*, there in the presentation to our intelligence of an intelligible world we are invited to inhabit and take up in act and will'.[665] This is at once a claim on the whole of life and society of the religious, *and* an admission that the 'religious' is always also bound to a higher court:

> This, then, is the Quranic caliphate – not some political institution, organized in single rulers to perpetuate Muhammad's legacy, but the whole, universal, plural dignity of all men, as men, in their empire over things and under God … Man has no sovereignty *over* the world, except in accountability *under* God.[666]

The human's responsibility to a creator God must relativize all created orders and strive to hallow all that is created: an 'autonomy thus pledged to the divine glory'.[667] By prioritizing this understanding of *khilāfa*, the caliphate as the idealized Islamic polity becomes an inhibition to true worship. The logic is that a 'reverse abrogation' to a Meccan Islam is called for.[668] With echoes of classic Augustinian theology, Cragg affirms that 'God's realm, being uncoercive, is not power-ensured'.[669] Cragg is, in effect, provoking

Islam to prove that there must be a way to worship God without the framework of an Islamic polity. Surely, the call to worship, *Allāhu Akbar*, makes a demand on every person, whatever their status and geography? As Cragg elsewhere says, 'every worshipper is an iconoclast'.[670] For him, the very Islamic call to submission has to prioritize the Meccan call to worship over the achievement of power.

That Islam could be conceived as not being 'power-ensured' raises questions about the integrity of Cragg's use of the term *khilāfa* as an inclusive domain of the secular that generates plural responsibilities to God. Within the qur'anic text itself, the supposed creative trusteeship in Q 2 contrasts with the Genesis account. Humanity is not tasked with naming the animals but Adam is *taught* the names by God (Q 2:31). *Khilāfa* in Q 22:65 is after the fact of God's prior 'dominion' of the earth, and humanity has merely to ensure what has already been realized. In Genesis, humanity is given the task of subduing creation.[671] The qur'anic pattern might be seen to offer a far more absolute notion of governance: Adam as a prophet receiving the law of God as the designated caliph in anticipation of ensuing prophets and ultimately the Muhammad of the Medinan Constitution.

Alister McGrath acknowledges that there is no equivalent notion of natural law in Islam; revelation is only accessible in the eternal word of the Qur'an.[672] Indeed, David Burrell asserts that the arena for experiencing the creative activity of God is in the verses (*ayāt*) of the Qur'an, due to the very absence of covenant and creation in Islam.[673] Has Cragg effectively Christianized *khilāfa* into a doctrine of natural law Islam cannot bear? Anver Emon contradicts the popular assumptions about Islam's rejection of natural law by tracing the doctrine's demise to the success of the Asharite school over the Mu'tazalites. For Emon, there is a classic inheritance of natural law to be reclaimed, and much of modernist, rationalistic Islamic thinking is rooted in this earlier tradition and ought to be given credence as 'orthodoxy'.[674]

Though Cragg's political theology displays all the characteristics of a natural law reading, he never uses the phrase itself. In many ways, the argument against Cragg's reading of *khilāfa* that Islam does not accept natural law is beside the point because what he is doing is taking the reading of the text seriously and critiquing it on its own terms. It is a generous reading because Cragg's logic of *khilāfa* and dominion is that the only way humanity can know anything about God in his otherness is by his self-disclosure in kenosis. Taking Alasdair MacIntyre's approach to dialogue between 'incommensurable' traditions, Cragg is exercising a rational enquiry into the problem of utter transcendence in Islam and probing its success in the terms of its foundational text.[675] The only 'logic', for Cragg, is that Islam must countenance divine vulnerability from within those texts of delegated sovereignty. The onus is then on Islam to rebut or agree the conclusion of that enquiry. That very discourse becomes an exercise of political theology: of seeking a shared truth about humanity's encounter with God's transcendence in a process of dialogue.

Cragg's reading of the Christological challenge to Medinan Islam has opened him up to the criticism that Christianity withdraws from the political realm. Maryam Jameelah observes that 'Since Christianity has ... had nothing but contempt for the religious law as spiritually useless, this means that there is no divine guidance for the Christian in his collective life, therefore politics ... are guided by opportunism and expediency.'[676] To conclude that Cragg is presenting an apolitical Christian faith would be a misreading of his work, though. As he states elsewhere, 'New Testament experience of grace does not deny Sinai; rather it retrieves its moral, without its ethnic, intention by other means.'[677] The key for Cragg is that political power is not an *aspiration* for the Church, neither is it the *decisive means* for the fullest Christian witness. Thus, the cross of Christ 'does not mean that Caesar's realm was one of divine indifference, an autonomy absolved of all transcendent reference.'[678] Indeed, 'it is not to say that, therefore, only perpetual minority status and persecution make for sincerity or that faith is only wholesome in catacombs.'[679] It is simply that there can never be a direct equation between the interests of human government and those of God. There must be a constant demurral of the ability of human government to be entirely trusted to implement the interests of God.

Timothy Winter refutes Cragg's critique of the Muhammadan decision, accusing him of a needless polarity that ignores the political and social implications of Jesus' prophethood.[680] But Cragg is not exempting 'the order of faith from the aegis of politics. Religion is right to equip itself with rulership.'[681] What he would bring to any religio-political project is the truth of the *complexity* involved in 'religion being wholly God's'.[682] Faith can be its own deception whereby 'Allah is great' too easily becomes 'Islam is great', and 'Jesus is Lord' becomes 'The Church is Lord'; all the more so in the appropriation of power. So the Medinan economy of dominance *has* to be qualified by the prior Meccan urge to worship of God *regardless* of social status.

An arguably more persuasive objection to Cragg's political theology is the consequent conclusion that the Church is never implicated in the sins of public life. When Cragg says that 'Christianity belongs to and inheres in people who believe. It is never coterminous with any given society',[683] there is a danger of idealizing Christian political presence. Where, for Cragg, Islam idealizes the ability of an Islamic political order to implement the will of God, there is a corresponding danger of idealizing the Church so that it does not have to bear responsibility for corrupting the will of God in the exercise of its power. Thus, Christopher Lamb can write: 'Christianity can in fact be exonerated from all the ills which its confessors may perpetrate, and remain innocent in any judgments delivered by history.'[684] In the end, though, the Christological departure from Islam ensures that the Church embodies in the very manner of its message the judgement of the cross and so can only speak with humility. History may reveal the failure of Christians to meet the demands of the faith they follow but that is an indictment of humanity not of the God-in-Christ. This is no tidy resolution to the failures of the Christian political project but of the essence of the eschatological dilemma of the politico-theological question.

In arguing for a Meccan interpretation of Muhammad's prophethood, Cragg identifies a new *hijra*, a 'departing' re-imagined without recourse to the establishment of a state.[685] David Marshall points out that a truly qur'anic reading of the *hijra* offers the Meccan paradigm as 'pragmatic necessity' rather than 'ultimate good', and is therefore rejecting the traditional Islamic view that minority status is a provisional stage.[686] Charles Adams has accused Cragg of 'Christianizing' Islam by interpreting the Islamic attitude to politics in terms sympathetic to New Testament theology, thereby doing violence to the Islamic tradition.[687] There is in this critique a very real challenge to Christian accounts of other faiths, especially when they otherwise espouse a hospitality that seeks to engage a tradition on its own terms. This hospitality, though, as David Marshall explains, 'need not require the surrender of one's own convictions and indeed can lead to a deeper understanding of them'.[688] In fact an honest appraisal of Islam by a Christian would conclude that the 'story we tell cannot be made to fit into Islamic categories'.[689] There is no 'view from nowhere', and no complete identification with Islam that stops short of becoming Muslim. Again, Cragg treads a path tense with the eschatological, 'already and not yet': the realized experience of the grace of God in Jesus and his people, the Church, and the 'not yet' of God's availability to all that call on him. In the cross of Christ there is the inference that 'the ground of hopefulness in Christian mission is one with the ground of hope in men (*sic*)'.[690] The cross as definitive doctrine and Christian distinctive is the lens with which true humanity is viewed, but this lens hobbles any doctrinaire closure about the activity of God within his creation.

The accusation that Cragg is Christianizing the Qur'an might be hard to reject but for his persistent recognition of the will-to-power within Islam.[691] Yet there are glimpses of divine self-limiting in the Qur'an that accord with the incarnation and allow Cragg to probe the coherence of a power-ensured faith. The demurral of the angels at the conferment of dominion on Adam in Q 2 hints at a risk taken by God: 'that the Divine lordship itself is in some sense staked in the human role'.[692] This is consonant with what Cragg calls 'the grand perhaps' of the Qur'an: '"Perhaps you may give thanks", "perhaps you may come to your senses", "perhaps you may ponder and consider".[693] In this economy, divine vulnerability can anticipate a Saviour who dies at the hands of political power. Arguably, what is most crucial to Cragg's engagement with Islamic polity is not his discussion of the respective structures of religious and secular power but his Christian convictions about the nature of the divine. A politics that is serious about the religious, for Cragg, demands a God who is not absolutely transcendent but somehow implicated in his creation, and even vulnerable to the sins of a fallen humanity. That there is enough within the Qur'an to suggest the penultimacy of temporal power and the possibility of divine restraint is confirmed by the temper of Shi'a martyrdom and Sufi mysticism.[694]

The belligerence and self-sufficiency evident in the archetype of the Medinan polity is countered in two ways, then: recognition of the pragmatic realities of the failure of religiously ordained politics; and an appeal to Islam's 'surer, saner, larger mind'.[695] What we have in Cragg's political theology is a deep suspicion of the will-to-power. Faith, even, can become a self-deception, and in the recognition of the one God, the 'surer, saner, larger mind' offers a constant rejoinder to self-satisfaction and self-legitimation. If the Muslim is 'perpetually mobilized to bring about the actualization of the absolute on earth', as al-Faruqi states, there is the internal paradox that God's unity would disqualify all absolutes.[696] Echoing Dag Hammarskjöld's sense of being 'responsible *for* God', there is an 'inter-liability between God and ourselves' that Cragg would see as intrinsic to true faith.[697]

In summary, then, Kenneth Cragg would seek to find *within* Islam reasons for a fully religious citizenship that can settle with minority status and a resistance to the power equation. The Christian grounds for advocating this stress the shared dominion of humanity and the corrosiveness of power to the religious sensibility. Thus, Christendom is an aberration; the state is always to be desacralized and relativized.

The two main avenues for Cragg's political theology, then, are creation and incarnation. Following the influence of the *Lux Mundi* school and consonant with the patristic legacy flowing through Hooker and Andrewes, a theology of natural law grounds an inclusive politics made distinct by its trinitarian impulses. First and foremost, Christians and Muslims are responsible to a creator God and given delegated sovereignty in the temporal realm. On that basis, there is the potential for shared endeavour: a politics of the common good. This common good is not specific; nowhere does Cragg provide content for such Christian–Muslim politics. Rather, he offers shared space for the conversation towards mutual politics that suggest a *heuristic* endeavour. In similar ways to Patrick Riordan's articulation of the common good as heuristic, Cragg encourages a politics 'which is to be discovered in the exploration of what is the human good'.[698]

The good order of creation of which Christians and Muslims are a part is one infused with the life of God. The participatory ontology of Richard Hooker and Eastern Orthodox understandings of God's kenosis operative in the life of the trinity that energizes all people are evident in Cragg's cosmology. As Eric Mascall, an Anglican scholar deeply influenced by Orthodoxy and the patristic tradition, says, 'Nature has, simply as nature, a *potentia oboedientialis* for the supernatural.'[699] The created order is, of necessity, always open to the creator, and hence the hopeful patience of the Christian Presence school of which Cragg was a part. This is why, as we noted in Chapter 7, Cragg's theology is given affirmation by an Orthodox scholar such as Olivier Clément,[700] and he is bracketed in the same category of such Catholic 'mainstream' scholars of religion as Jean Daniélou of the Christian Presence school within Catholicism.[701]

The doctrine of creation affirms that Christians and Muslims are exploring 'human good' in the political realm, while the doctrine of the incarnation permits this exploration to be practised responsively to God. A Reformed sensitivity to individual and structural sin undermines any sense of complacency in the exercise of political power. Thus, the cross of Christ acts as a constant challenge to Islam even if natural law propels Christians and Muslims to a joint trusteeship of creation. This is where Cragg's great theme of hospitality is most keenly apparent. For Cragg, hospitality is 'surely the closest of all analogies to the meaning of the Gospel'.[702] The concept of hospitality that we saw developing in Anglican documents of Christian–Muslim relations, epitomized by *Generous Love*, allows for the integrity of Christians and Muslims where *both* parties can become changed in the encounter. A politics of *khilāfa* and dominion allows Christians and Muslims to be mutually responsive in their exercise of the common good. The persistent 'cross reference' of Cragg retains the trinitarian, redemptive trajectory, while the consciousness of the will-to-power that can so easily supersede true faith guards against the self-validating totalizing of the other.

Robert Murray's *The Cosmic Covenant* provides an analogous account to Cragg's *khilāfa* and dominion of human stewardship based in the creation narratives of the Hebrew Bible. Murray's 'cosmic covenant' is a charge from the natural law tradition to a shared responsibility for the earth. In language reminiscent of Cragg, Murray speaks of humanity's 'viceregal' relationship to God.[703] As John Milbank points out, though, the emphasis on creation in Murray's account fails to incorporate the manifest and potential consequences of fallenness. Murray's preference for a strand of Judaic readings of sin as a dualistic constant back to the origins of creation both diminishes the Christian and Augustinian understanding of original sin and qualifies the perfection of the original creation.[704] Cragg decidedly does not make that mistake.

It is submitted that it is Cragg's redemptive trajectory, his attention to original sin, that distinguishes his political theology from the incarnationalist Anglican tradition. Where aspects of the *Lux Mundi* school saw the incarnation as the summit of God's revelation, and consequently the Christian Nation as the archetype of graced politics, Cragg's engagement with Islam produces a political theology that is always cross-referenced. That Cragg's political theology reflects the theme of hospitality and has such a Reformed flavour makes his vision comparable to that of the explicitly political theology of Oliver O'Donovan. O'Donovan too has exhibited what has been described as a political theology of 'hospitality' that follows MacIntyre in allowing the integrities of self and other while generating points of ad hoc commensurability.[705]

The relationship of the *ekklesia* to society is bound up in an understanding of the mission of God as the trinitarian life and hope of creation. Within this economy, the cross is set as a crucial event in the redemptive purposes of God for that creation. To that extent, Cragg's ambivalent defence of the Church of England's established status is more about its role in challenging the omnicompetent state than it is a conviction about its inherent worth.[706] Similarly, Michael Ipgrave argues for a 'hospitable establishment', after Archbishop George Carey, that is sensitive to the anxieties as to what might fill the vacuum of a post-establishment polity.[707]

The political theologian Oliver O'Donovan seeks to rehabilitate Christendom as, at least, a legitimate outcome of the success of the mission of the Western Church in a way that would make Cragg uncomfortable. O'Donovan provides an interesting counterpoint to Cragg from the discipline of political theology: they are both keen to stress the need for a transcendent accounting of secular sovereignty. A distinctive element of O'Donovan's political theology is his assertion that the juridical role of the state requires a moral foundation of specifically Christian character. The Christian faith is best fitted to ground the judgements of law, and any purported neutrality is merely a veiled absolutism that leads to atomized individualism.[708] O'Donovan's belief in the religious grounding of the juridical echoes something of Carl Schmitt's political theology.[709] However, he is not advocating a fixed shape to the political, merely asserting the philosophical logic that the law demands a moral foundation. It is only in that sense that O'Donovan could be said to advocate for the Christian Nation. The practice of hospitality is in the interplay of negotiations around the shared ends of ad hoc points of commensurability: in Cragg's terms, the delegated sovereignty that both Christians and Muslims believe in.

How law is grounded will be explored in the analysis of Rowan Williams' Shari'a law speech, but it is important to underline the resonances that Cragg's *khilāfa* and dominion themes hold within wider Anglican political theologies. Again, in Samuel Wells's *God's Companions* there is an emphasis on hospitality as a primary theme for Anglican social ethics shaped in the practice of the eucharist.[710] For O'Donovan, Wells and Cragg, the practice of hospitality does not give a programme for Anglican politics but an impulse to traditioned and open engagement with the other that can both challenge and receive, pastor and prophesy.

Rowan Williams: interactive pluralism and islam

Archbishop Rowan Williams' Shari'a law speech of 2008 sits at the intersection of the debate around the role of a church established by law and the recognition of the distinct nature of Islam in public life.[711] In many ways the speech was merely one of a number of lectures that presented Williams' vision of faith's relationship to the state: his argument for 'interactive pluralism'[712] following the political theology of Neville Figgis. Williams suggests that English law needed to give proper recognition to other religious communities, citing the case of Shari'a law. His argument has precedent in the accommodation of aspects of Orthodox Jewish law, but mention of Shari'a evoked images of Shari'a as violence and repression.[713] Williams was applying the work of Figgis to the contemporary issue of how space could be made for Islam in its fully political 'otherness', within the English legal system.

This otherness does not derive from any sense of Islam as an alien intrusion into British or European culture, rebutting the notion of a 'clash of civilizations'.[714] Williams admits a 'cultural mindset' deriving from the Christian influence on Europe whereby there is a marked separation of religious and secular governance. Islam's growing presence is thus a distinctive challenge as to how religion is now negotiated. Islam has brought a particular challenge to the West about the perceived individualism of the Christian faith whereby there is no apparent 'Christian law'.[715] The otherness of Islam is instead constituted in Williams' Eastern Orthodox cosmology: 'whenever I face another human being, I face a mystery.'[716] The participative ontology of the neo-patristic synthesis is readily apparent in his statement that 'every person is related to God before they are related to anything or anyone else.'[717] Thus, political structures setting up legal and territorial constraints on interrelationships can only be contingent. As Williams admits, there is a strain of 'negative theology' propelling his political theology, again echoing the influence of Vladimir Lossky.[718]

Williams advocates the primacy of the voluntary corporation. For Figgis this was an argument for the personality of the trade union. The state, then, has a relegated sovereignty and is thus merely an 'association of associations'. This assures the 'eschatological reserve' of the Augustinian doctrine of the two and gives space for the respective integrities of religious communities. In this economy, the liberalism of a genuine plurality stems from a corresponding ecclesiology of conciliarity, of unity in diversity:

> This relative independence – never absolute independence – of parish, of diocese of province, of local union, this organic and federalist conception of the whole, is at one with the facts of life in society of all kinds. We must remember that society does not cease to be society because it called itself the Church.[719]

Similarly, Williams emphasizes the sociality and diversity of the Church as an anticipation of the fully human: the intrinsic of true politics. Rooting himself in the ecclesial turn of political theology and commending a eucharistic centring of that life, Williams asserts that 'the future has arrived in the assembly of believers around Word and Sacrament.' That is alternately a claim about what it means to be fully human and a guard against supposing that that can be realized in the realm of political order. Indeed, when 'the Kingdom of God becomes a contender alongside others for the control of debated territory; it becomes less than itself'.[720] Interactive pluralism therefore demands a very Augustinian eschatological reserve over the temporal order of politics. As Williams states in an early essay on Augustine's *City of God*, 'Augustine's condemnation of "public life" in the classical world is, consistently, that it is not public enough.'[721] The Church is the repository of truly communal human flourishing but that can never be imposed or replicated in the provisional structures of the temporal state. The essentially incomplete nature of the visible Church that is constituted by a diverse authority means that politics, likewise, should follow that inherent belief in human sociality of which the *ekklesia* is the archetype. Thus, Williams can say that 'the whole idea of sacralized central authority, a single source of law, might be questionable, in the visible Church as much as in the state.'[722]

Even from the vantage point of early twentieth-century Britain, Figgis, the formative influence on Williams' political vision, had a clear-sighted view that 'English Society is ceasing to be Christian'[723] and that 'Our hopes will only be realized when we give up, as I have heard it put, "playing at being a majority".'[724] In Rupert Shortt's biography of Williams, a former colleague talks of previous archbishops wanting to 'give a moral and spiritual lead to the nation as a whole on particular issues'; '[Archbishop George] Carey shared that belief, but could not make it a reality. I question whether Rowan even wants to try.'[725] Williams displays a similar diffidence to Cragg about the will-to-power and a rejection of the idea that the Church should seek *any* privileged position of law in society. However, the Shari'a speech itself was notably about the legal system and *on behalf of* Muslims and by no means assumed a marginal role for the Church of England. A nuanced reading of Williams' interactive pluralism as it stands today would suggest that spiritual leadership is offered but not presumed, and that that leadership strives to find the common good with other communities of difference. The Church of England's role is then 'not to campaign for political control ... but for public visibility.'[726] This is no mere 'multiculturalism' that posits an anarchic accumulation of plural cultures and religions in parallel. As Mike Higton says, 'What Williams is asking for is a means of bringing this religious community more fully into public conversation.'[727] The best of the Christian inheritance of political theology, for Williams, decentres the legitimacy of communal identities and gives the state the role of brokering the acceptable limits of religious activity in the interactive negotiations across communities of difference. Rather than a supposed neutral state devolving what religious groups can and cannot do, traditions have a presupposed integrity. Deliberations over shared goods arbitrated by the state become the place for the establishment of the boundaries of those religious activities.[728]

There is no appeal to a purported universal realm of the 'secular' in Williams' ideas, such as Cragg invokes, rather an organic pluralism that realizes public religion in the dynamic interaction over shared goods. Thus, the distinctive nature of those religions is guarded and difference recognized and embraced within the unity of those shared goods. Figgis can say, then, while affirming public space for all 'associations', that 'The accent ought to be not on the likeness, but on the difference of Christianity from its rivals, whether philosophic or ethical or religious.'[729] Likewise, Williams states that 'I don't believe that religious dialogue is ever advanced by denying difference.'[730] Williams' political theology protects the integrities of Islam while, in the agonistic interaction over shared goods, it allows for the exploration of the limits of, say, Shari'a law, as they affect the most vulnerable, and recognizes the diversity of cultures and religions. It is across the dynamic of the primary units of religious communities, and not via a state apparatus that assumes a religious role, that the due limits of religious laws are realized. This political theology enables Williams to offer a critique to Islam as well as opening up deliberations of partnership. By acknowledging the essential otherness of Islam, the integrities of religious motivation and distinctives are guarded and these can be brought into the discourse of politics rather than bracketed out.

The question for this model of interactive pluralism, then, seems to be: what is to be done where those shared goods are not apparent or there is an insuperable conflict between communities about the ultimate ends of law?[731] The shortcomings of Figgis's ideas among the pluralists of the 1930s identified by Matthew Grimley seem relevant to Williams' contemporary account:

A society in which the main unit was the interest group would be prone to selfishness and conflict. In its way Figgis' pluralism was as dangerous as individualism, because like individualism it presented a fragmented and self-interested picture of social relations.[732]

A traditional criticism of the omnicompetent state was that it portrayed the individual in competition with the state, and thus in necessarily self-seeking mode: 'Man versus the state'. Figgis was countering this tendency by advocating for the strength of voluntary associations, recognized by the state. According to Grimley, Figgis may well have fallen into the trap of another relationship of self-aggrandisement: 'Groups versus the state'.[733] Has Williams merely replaced the old 'Man versus the state' distinction with 'Islam versus the state'? Thus, the public square becomes an arena for the competing self-interest of religious groups such as the Church, Islam and so on, with the inevitable problems of identifying which groups or leaders are appropriately representative of these constituencies. In this economy, the common good is in danger of taking second place to the selfish aspirations of religious communities. The ability of these respective groups to wield power and influence within a mode of competitive self-interest renders the public square more akin to a marketplace.

John Milbank warms to Williams' defence of corporatist religious identities but sees that defence as needing to be built on a single cultural foundation that is at least broadly Christian: 'We can only accommodate Islam on our own terms ... Something always rules, and this something is always substantive.' To recognize coercive religious law within the English legal system, as legal recognition of Shari'a presumes, would erode the liberties of both Christianity and Enlightenment as Islam is a 'rival universality to that of Christianity'.[734] It is *only* a Christian metaphysics, through its 'traditioned character of reason',[735] that can attain the sort of political legitimacy that provides public space for other religions, albeit in a qualified fashion. According to Milbank, the supersessionism of Islam and its absolutist conception of *tawhīd* militate against the absorption of cultural influences and underscore a violent totalizing of the other.[736] Milbank sees the European project as an essentially 'catholic' project of graced reason that recognizes universal humanity in a way that is alien to Islam and politically distinct. Again, the root theology of the respective understanding of divinity is crucial here:

Allah is impersonal; for the most orthodox Islamic theology he enjoys no beatitude (unlike the Christian God), much less suffers pain. And he certainly does not express himself internally in an image like the Christian *Logos*. Hence rule here on earth cannot reflect Allah.[737]

Islam's traditional non-sacramental nature mitigates against any rational space for the other. According to Milbank, where reason cannot offer any insights to the nature of God, natural law having to coincide with the revelation of the Qur'an, then the religious other becomes totalized into the political agenda of the revealed religion.

Milbank identifies a common ecclesiology with Williams but sees that what is missing in the Shari'a law speech is the confidence to assert the unique ability of the Christian metanarrative to ground religious plurality. Williams's admission that the gift of the European Christian inheritance is to qualify the claims of the state should, according to Milbank, alert him to its cultural significance as a hedge against totalitarianism. Rather than following through their shared identification with a eucharistic, integral theology to which the doctrine of the incarnation is vital, Williams has been tempted to 'consecrate uncertainty'.[738] In effect, Williams' use of 'liberalism' rather than 'Christendom' as a schema for the interactive pluralism he advocates in the Shari'a law lecture is a failure of nerve on his part. For Milbank, 'Not to believe in Christendom is not to believe in the Incarnation which (according to Maximus the Confessor) is a continuing dynamic reality.'[739] Milbank accuses Williams of exhibiting the inadequacies of the Anglican incarnationalist tendency in elevating the divine self-giving into a principle that effectively limits the godhead, collapsing into heterodoxy, and thereby 'bound to fail'.[740] Williams' agonistic epistemology that we noted in Chapter 7 is apparent in his advocacy of interactive pluralism: Gillian Rose's 'broken middle', the place where the other can be known.[741] It is ironic that Milbank accuses Williams of succumbing to the glorification of failure, a weakness Williams himself challenged in his observation of an absence of a redemptive trajectory in the *Lux Mundi* school. The neo-patristic synthesis exemplified by Henri de Lubac and Hans Urs von Balthasar is where Milbank would prefer to see Williams source and carry through his metaphysics.[742]

Milbank is effectively contending with Williams' unintentioned sacralization of the secular. Because Williams sees the state as holding the ring as broker of interactive pluralism, Milbank believes that, by the back door, his Augustinianism is compromised. That role is based on a vision of what it means to be fully human, and if divorced from Christian roots its 'liberalism' attains religious status. Thus, a nation that seeks to give space to the 'religious', for Milbank, 'has to be religious in a *specific* way'.[743] A truly incarnational theology would instead be able to embody the *victory* of the incarnation as embodied in Latin Catholicism's rebuttal of the sacral function of the secular.[744] Curiously for the Anglican Milbank, the role of the 'godly prince' that obtains in Anglican and Eastern Orthodox traditions is rejected in favour of the confident espousal of the primacy of the Christian culture of the Catholic Church exhibited in Pope Benedict XVI's Regensburg Address.[745]

This is where a distinction can be drawn between O'Donovan's rehabilitation of Christendom and Milbank's metaphysics. O'Donovan's assertion of evangelical freedom and the doctrine of the godly prince situate him in the Reformation tradition. His advocacy of the Christian roots to a state is a philosophical assertion of the *moral* basis for law. Milbank, with Benedict, is arguing for Christian *culture*. Williams, with Cragg, is all too conscious of the flip side of Christian culture and civilization; the fallenness that requires the judgement of a godly prince. Milbank's metaphysics seems overly idealized. Nigel Biggar critiques Milbank on this basis, arguing that he conflates Augustine's dual conception of the 'earthly city': the narrow, eschatological sense of 'the proud and selfish, those predestined to be damned' and the 'realm of the merely practical'.[746] The 'practical', or what Biggar also refers to as the very Anglican concern for the 'empirical', blurs the boundaries of what is indicative of 'Christ' and what is not. Agreeing with Eric Gregory, he believes that Milbank is too concerned with 'isms': 'totalitarianism, paganism, terrorism, materialism', and this is at the expense of stereotyping and caricaturing the other.[747] Noting Milbank's monolithic account of Islam, this critique seems to be well placed.[748]

From a legal standpoint, the simple polarity suggested by Milbank disguises the pragmatic realities of constitutional pluralism, further supporting the idea that the practical and empirical 'earthly city' has been conflated with the eschatological. Russell Sandberg, in his seminal account of religious law, responds to those critics of Williams who argued for the monist cultural roots of the legal system. The actual legal situation presents a far more variegated picture than the rhetoric of a unitary, binding culture would suggest:

> Religious law is already recognized in England and Wales in several different ways ... the rules and structures of religious associations are binding on assenting members through the doctrine of 'consensual compact'. Moreover, religious laws and practices are free to operate where the law of the State is silent.[749]

As Sandberg states elsewhere, 'the Archbishop's nuanced lecture deserves nuanced responses. And part of that nuance is the recognition of the complex ways in which Islam and the law already interact.'[750]

The original debate around the Shari'a law speech occurred within the context of the New Labour appeal to 'community cohesion'. Mark Chapman's warm endorsement of Williams' interactive pluralism concludes with a summary affirmation of the primacy of the association: 'The panacea for the problems of community cohesion lies in trusting the people.'[751] This would seem to suggest a degree of complacency unwarranted by either Williams' speech or Figgis's writings. In view of his comment that 'Without God, human society becomes barren and decays',[752] one wonders what Figgis would make of challenges to the Church of England today. He is most certainly alive to the dangers of a society or nation *without* any moral compass.[753] Williams too recognizes that:

> There has therefore to be some concept of common good that is not prescribed solely in terms of revealed Law, however provisional or imperfect such a situation is thought to be. And this implies in turn that the Muslim, even in a predominantly Muslim state, has something of a dual identity, as citizen and as believer within the community of the faithful.[754]

For Williams, though, there is a conscious avoidance of a description of what that common good *is* that might bind Christian and Muslim communities into a cohesive society.[755] Instead, the primary objective seems to be to ensure that religious language is acceptable in the public sphere, thereby challenging 'stateism' and the 'persistent and at the moment rather over anxious, social concern with preserving a kind of "neutrality" in the public sphere'.[756] Thus, like Cragg, he is alive to the need to retain the transcendent critique of temporal governance. That this flows from his prior Christian beliefs about what being fully human means is incontrovertible; and this is where Milbank's critique is surely apposite.[757]

Where Cragg's 'perplexity' stems from a hermeneutic of suspicion around the place of power in relation to religion, Williams' agonism seems to flow from his apophatic sensibility.[758] The interactive pluralism that is described is, at heart, the practice of 'contemplatives'. Williams' Eastern Orthodox sensibility and indebtedness to the Desert Fathers demands that 'the political calling of the Church' takes the *via negativa*.[759] It is instructive that Williams makes his discomfort with the language of Christian civilization and culture more explicit in an account of Thomas Merton's political theology. Seeing threads joining Olivier Clément and Paul Evdokimov, the 'eastern idiom' that has so shaped Williams, enables him to advocate a 'homelessness' that does not need to be nurtured in the 'static ideological construction' of the Church or the world. Only by fostering detachment such that it is accepted 'that Christendom will not return and there is only a minority future' can the true polis of the Church be a comprehensive blessing to the world. That is the great lesson of the contemplative tradition for Williams and vital to his political theology.[760]

The influence of the monastic and Eastern Orthodox tradition becomes decisive in Williams' rejection of the Christian Nation and Christian Civilization. His apophatic sensibility requires that there be no 'territorial anxiety', no need to see 'borders defended or patrolled'.[761] Instead, Williams posits an Anglican hospitality that risks the dynamic of relationship; of challenge and partnership, proclamation and dialogue. Thus, when asked to contribute to a collection of essays on 'Being British', Williams eschews any attempt to provide 'an essence of British identity' and emphasizes, rather, a 'history characterized by *unsuccessful* victories'.[762] Asked directly about how helpful the concept of the 'Christian Nation' is, Williams responds with a simple 'not very', and cautions that 'usually when we use Christian Nation it is generally used to bang someone over the head'.[763] Along with Cragg, any recourse to the Church's self-validation through the aegis of power denies the cruciform impulse at the Church's heart.

Conclusion

Kenneth Cragg does not write explicitly about political theology and is less concerned to situate his proposals in a wider tradition of political theory. However, his articulation of the principles of *khilāfa* and dominion depend on a belief in natural law for the pursuit of the shared good between Christians and Muslims. Cragg attempts to use Islamic tradition and texts in articulating this political theology, and thus risks Christianizing Islam. Drawing from the *Lux Mundi* school, kenosis becomes an important motif in discovering God at work in the world and in the other. It seems, though, that Cragg's evangelicalism and missionary sensibility dies hard because his sensitivity to the will-to-power makes him very attuned to the need for the cross. The dangers of power on the life of faith ensure that the Christian Nation concept can never be anything other than a pragmatic consequence of history, rather than a programmatic ideal. Ultimately, Cragg builds his political theology out of a keen awareness of the trinity, providing both continuity and discontinuity with the *Lux Mundi* school.

Rowan Williams' political theology draws from the pluralist stream of Anglicanism epitomized by Neville Figgis. This rejects the unitary personality of the state and any notion of the Christian Nation. For Williams, the Church's political theology allows for the foundational realities of traditioned communities, the state merely being an arbiter in the negotiation of shared goods and the limits of religious life that are prior to the state. This permits space for the integrity of Islam in its otherness. Williams seeks a more nuanced incarnationalism that is truer to the Church Fathers in its understanding of the trinity and thus seems to go back beyond Anglican reappropriations of that tradition. For Williams, the grammar of the trinity means that any overarching political scheme seeking to incorporate the other is illusory.

If the Church embodies the anticipation of the true humanity, the presumption of the ecclesial turn, then there is an eschatological value to what the Christian vision of the social life is to the whole world. However, paradoxically, Williams and Cragg converge to problematize also a high view of the Church in their attentiveness to the pragmatic realities of the Church's sin. They both commend a eucharistic centring of the Church's encounter with Islam that chimes with the broader ecclesial turn movement exemplified by O'Donovan and Milbank, but at the same time undermine the self-sufficiency of such political theologies. Underlying all their specific articulations of a political theology in response to Islam is a need to recognize the 'sacramental': at least some degree of natural law.

Anecdotes from the field: encountering a crisis

I have shared how the Sparkbrook church centre ministers from a conviction that evangelism and dialogue are part and parcel of the broader mission of the Church in this Muslim-majority community. Several summers ago, Sparkbrook was rocked by a drug-related murder just yards from the church. That evening, one of the local councillors called me to propose a gathering of community leaders and representatives of faith groups at the church in order to present a united front to the media and provide a ready source of moral leadership. This particular network had been instigated and convened by me as parish priest some months before and it was encouraging to see the usefulness of such a group at a time of crisis.

Evidently the church was seen as a safe, public space to base the subsequent television and radio interviews. Again, though, I was witnessing some of the fluidity of that interchange between host and guest. To some extent the inherited role of the Church of England was being played out, an example of the ecclesial turn that would see the Church informing and shaping public life. Yet at the same time, the Church was also on the edge, and receiving wisdom; indeed, itself being shaped. I was very conscious that the young man who had been murdered was a Muslim and that there were particularly deep feelings of grief and disturbance for the Muslim community. We are used to the photo opportunities at regional and national level that present Church of England representatives, invariably priests and bishops, at the centre of a line of community leaders from different faiths. On this day, it seemed of paramount importance *not* to be the lead person in drafting the public statement to the media, and *not* to be in the centre of the line even though the regional news coverage took place in the forecourt of the church. I was among people who were working in drug rehabilitation programmes as Muslims, who were close to the family of the victim, a man I did not know: there was wisdom and goodness available in this crisis beyond the church.

The often agonized and 'perplexing' political theologies suggested by Cragg and Williams speak to me of unpredictable encounter with a messy and variegated public square: another 'other', like Islam, which must allow for good and bad, grace and struggle. The inherited legacy of the Church of England parochial system offers opportunity to serve and bless but also to re-imagine encounters that reflect the increasingly diverse nature of public religion, albeit informed and energized by a eucharistic spirituality.

Final Thoughts

Last Christmas a Muslim in Sparkbrook came to the church and spoke to a colleague of mine about an elderly disabled neighbour who he had been told was a Christian and was in need of a visit. When I received the details of this woman, I went to her flat and was informed from an upstairs window by her adult son that she had just died. It transpires that this woman had been housebound for some years, looking after her son with learning difficulties and isolated from the rest of her family. The people who had been bringing her shopping for over five years and checking on her well-being were the Muslim next-door neighbours who had come to the church to ensure her spiritual needs were also being met. These same Muslim neighbours had made a collection to ensure that the woman had a proper funeral, inviting the church to lead prayers at this funeral, knowing that is what she would have wanted.

Such a story illustrates the possibilities for Christians to be challenged by and learn *from* Muslims: for there to be an encounter with the other where the Church listens and receives. This story also competes with stories of persecution, terrorism and religious extremism, but all come within the orbit of Christian–Muslim encounter. The challenge for theologies of Christian–Muslim relations, and for the public square that is the additional 'other' in such reflections, is to maintain a faithful Christian presence that does not predetermine the potential of each encounter. How might the Church of England maintain a parochial presence in the inner city, alive to the goodwill and constructive public life beyond the church as exemplified by the neighbours in Sparkbrook? The theologies I have identified in Kenneth Cragg and Rowan Williams resonate with wider theologies that are unashamedly 'traditioned': there is no search for an elusive common core to religions or a grand schema that defines the other. The other is always 'strange' but always capable of being a gift to us.

The Christian–Muslim encounters and consequent political theologies that they model, and that resonate with a thread of historical and ecumenical engagements, are both modest *and* ambitious. They are modest in assuming that Christians cannot say everything about the Muslim other nor shape the entirety of the public space, though they can say *something*. They are ambitious in risking a very Christian curiosity that pushes the Church into vulnerable, robust encounters when we may find ourselves being challenged, blessed and listening, as much as challenging, blessing and proclaiming.

The ecclesial turn I have identified in contemporary Anglican Christian–Muslim encounters suggests the need for a sacramental theology: a theology of natural law that gives space for finding Christ as well as proclaiming Christ. Such a theology of inter-religious relations finds its source and inspiration in a eucharistic spirituality that reminds us of the repeated failures of the Church while pointing to the hope of the world in Christ. The political implications of a sacramental theology are that our encounters in the public square matter: no relationship is devoid of the potential for divine encounter, and thus is gift and mystery. However, as William Cavanaugh notes, quoting de Lubac: 'A mystery is more of an action than a thing.'[764] The unravelling of Anglican mega-theories of religions for the more tentative ecclesial theologies of interrelating is not an excuse for withdrawing from movements for interfaith dialogue. Rather, the challenge is to embrace the complexity and unpredictability of traditioned encounters.

The financial vista of the Church of England suggests that many inner-city parishes for which that formative encounter with Islam is a daily reality are under real threat. Many of these parish churches have small, dwindling congregations and are in some of the most deprived communities in the country. There are very real possibilities that the unique ways that religion in the public square is negotiated in the Christian–Muslim encounter will be lost to the Church within a generation. This would be a travesty for any remaining integrity that the Church of England retains for speaking into the national consciousness, and demands creativity, imagination and strategic sacrifice in the training and deployment of ministers in the future. The question is perhaps not whether the Church of England can afford to be present in such areas, rather whether it can afford *not* to be present to the Christian–Muslim encounter in our inner cities and towns.

Throughout this book I have eschewed simple binaries in Christian–Muslim relations. I choose to resist judgemental categorizations of Islam, Muslims, the Church and the public square. The Islam that Christians encounter contains good and bad, as much as the Church that Muslims encounter. I cannot speak for what is 'true Islam' but rather point to the complex and variegated histories that inform our contemporary context. The sad reality is that there are those who would claim religious authority for terrorist atrocities, and it is a matter of 'when' not 'if' they succeed in further attacks in the UK. The ways Anglican and other Christian communities can respond in hope and love, often *with* Muslims, amid those realities, will be a measure of how seriously we have responded to that fundamental call to a Christian life made public.

Notes

1 J. Lewis, P. Mason and K. Moore, 2009, '"Islamic Terrorism" and the Repression of the Political', in Lee Marsden and Heather Savigny (eds), *Media, Religion and Conflict*, London: Ashgate, pp. 17–37, p. 33.

2 www.dailymail.co.uk/wires/ap/article-3730363/Ibtihaj-Muhammad-makes-US-history-wears-hijab-Olympics.html.

3 Julian Rivers, 2006, 'The Legal Status of Islam in Britain', Derecho Y Religion 1, pp. 144–64, p. 144.

4 For an account of British Islam and its history of immigration, see Humayun Ansari, 2004, *The Infidel Within: Muslims in Britain since 1800*, London: Hurst & Co.

5 *British Muslims in Number: A Demographic, Socio-economic and Health Profile of Muslims in Britain Drawing on the 2011 Census*, 2015, London: The Muslim Council of Britain.

6 Norman Doe, 1996, *The Legal Framework of the Church of England: A Critical Study in a Comparative Context*, Oxford: Clarendon Press, p. 19.

7 William Jacob, 2003, 'The Development of the Anglican Communion', in Stephen Platten (ed.), *Anglicanism and the Western Christian Tradition*, Norwich: Canterbury Press, pp. 192–206, p. 193.

8 Paul Avis, 2002, *Anglicanism and the Christian Church*, Edinburgh/New York: T. & T. Clark, p. 4.

9 Mark D. Chapman, 2008, 'The Dull Bits of History: Cautionary Tales for Anglicanism', in Mark D. Chapman (ed.), *The Anglican Covenant: Unity and Diversity in the Anglican Communion*, London/New York: Continuum, p. 95.

10 Paul Avis, 1998, 'What is Anglicanism?', in Stephen Sykes, John Booty and Jonathan Knight (eds), *The Study of Anglicanism*, rev. edn, London: SPCK, pp. 459–76, p. 461.

11 For a searing and sometimes polemical account of the decline and future unsustainability of the Church of England in its current form, see Linda Woodhead and Andrew Brown, 2016, *That Was the Church that Was: How the Church of England Lost the English People*, London: Bloomsbury.

12 Grace Davie, 2015, *Religion in Britain: A Persistent Paradox*, Oxford: Wiley-Blackwell.

13 In the burgeoning subject of political theology, a number of introductory and summary resources are available: Elaine Graham, 2013, *Between a Rock and*

a Hard Place: Public Theology in a Post-secular Age, London: SCM Press, 2013; Michael Kirwan, 2008, *Political Theology: A New Introduction*, London: Darton, Longman & Todd; Elizabeth Phillips, 2012, *Political Theology: A Guide for the Perplexed*, London: Bloomsbury.

14 Peter Scott and William T. Cavanaugh, 2007, 'Introduction', in Peter Scott and William T. Cavanaugh (eds), *The Blackwell Companion to Political Theology*, Oxford: Blackwell, pp. 2–4, p. 2.

15 Mona Siddiqui, 2008, 'Editorial', Political Theology 9:3, pp. 261–4, p. 261. See also A. al-Akiti and J. Hordern, 2016, 'New Conversations in Islamic and Christian Political Thought', Studies in Christian Ethics 29:2, pp. 131–4.

16 Kylie Baxter, 2006, 'From Migrants to Citizens: Muslims in Britain 1950s–1990s', Immigrants and Minorities 26:2, pp. 164–92.

17 Dilwar Hussain, 2004, 'Muslim Political Participation in Britain and the "Europeanisation" of Fiqh', *Welt des Islams* 44:33, pp. 376–401.

18 For example, Ron Geaves regards the Rushdie affair as the 'turning point and watershed in national Muslim participation'; Ron Geaves, 2005, 'Negotiating British Citizenship', in Tahir Abbas (ed.), *Muslim Britain: Communities Under Pressure*, London: Zed Books, pp. 66–77, p. 69.

19 Baxter, 'From Migrants to Citizens', p. 184.

20 For an example of this 'equalizing upwards' of religious recognition alongside the Church of England, and thus a Muslim argument for continued establishment, see Tariq Modood, 1997, 'Introduction: Establishment, Reform and Multiculturalism', in Tariq Modood (ed.), *Church, State and Religious Minorities*, London: Policy Studies Institute, pp. 3–15; and 1994, 'Establishment, Multiculturalism and British Citizenship', *Political Quarterly* 65:1, pp. 53–73.

21 Baxter, 'From Migrants to Citizens', p. 184.

22 For a comprehensive, contemporary account of the establishment debate, see R. M. Morris (ed.), 2009, *Church and State in 21st Century Britain: The Future of Church Establishment*, Basingstoke: Palgrave Macmillan.

23 Julian Rivers, 2010, *The Law of Organized Religions: Between Establishment and Secularism*, Oxford: Oxford University Press, p. 343.

24 Rivers, *Law of Organized Religions*, pp. 328–34.

25 Sophie Gilliat-Ray, 2000, *Religion in Higher Education: The Politics of the Multi-Faith Campus*, Aldershot: Ashgate, pp. 79–84.

26 Paul Weller, 2009, 'How Participation Changes Things: "Inter-Faith", "Multi-Faith" and a New Public Imaginary', in Adam Dinham, Robert Furbey and Vivien Lowndes (eds), *Faith in the Public Realm: Controversies, Policies and Practices*, Bristol: Policy Press, pp. 63–81, p. 71.

27 Philip Lewis, 2003, 'Christians and Muslims in the West: From Isolation to Shared Citizenship?', International Journal for the Study of the Christian Church 3:2, pp. 77–100, p. 92.

28 For a comparative study of Christian and Shi'a political theologies highlighting the precedence of the mujtahid as living representatives of the imamate for Shi'a Muslims in contrast to that of the Medinan polity to Sunni Muslims, see James A. Bill and John Alden Williams, 2002, *Roman Catholics and Shi'i Muslims: Prayer, Passion and Politics*, Chapel Hill, NC: University of North Carolina Press, pp. 93–116.

29 T. J. Winter, 2003, *British Muslim Identity: Past, Problems, Prospects*, Cambridge: Muslim Academic Trust. Tim Winter, as a convert to Islam, also writes as Abdal Hakim Murad (b. 1960). He is Shaykh Zayed Lecturer in Islamic Studies at Cambridge University and a significant interlocutor in British Christian–Muslim relations.

30 Abdullahi Ahmed An-Na'im, 1990, *Towards an Islamic Reformation: Civil Liberties, Human Rights and International Law*, New York: Syracuse University Press.

31 Farid Esack, 1997, *Qur'an, Liberation and Pluralism: An Islamic Perspective of Interreligious Solidarity Against Oppression*, Oxford: Oneworld.

32 Tariq Ramadan, 2004, *Western Muslims and the Future of Islam*, Oxford: Oxford University Press, pp. 72–5.

33 Mahmoud Mohamed Taha, 1987, *The Second Message of Islam*, trans. Abdullahi A. an-Na'im, New York: Syracuse University Press.

34 For a comparative study of Islamic political theology in history which highlights the unique challenges for Islam for religion in public life, see Michael Cook, 2014, *Ancient Religions, Modern Politics: The Islamic Case in Comparative Perspective*, Princeton, NJ: Princeton University Press.

35 For her analysis of the diversity of Islamist approaches within contemporary Egypt, see Rachel M. Scott, 2010, *The Challenge of Political Islam: Non-Muslims and the Egyptian State*, Stanford: Stanford University Press; also, Irfan Ahmad, 2009, *Islamism and Democracy in India: The Transformation of Jamaat-e-Islami*, Princeton, NJ: Princeton University Press, where an Islamist party has been seen to mutate from its Islamist agenda of establishing the caliphate in India towards defending secular democracy.

36 *Critical Muslim* is a quarterly magazine that seeks to 'look at everything and challenge traditionalist, modernist, fundamentalist and apologetic versions of Islam as well as the established conventions and orthodoxies of dominant cultures. We seek new readings of religion, culture and politics with the potential to transform the Muslim world and beyond'; from the back cover of the inaugural issue: Ziauddin Sardar and Robin Yassin-Kassab (eds), 2012, 'The Arabs Are Alive', *Critical Muslim*, January–March.

37 For an excellent, forensic analysis of different traditions within British Islam that helpfully conveys the complexities and light and shade in all the communities, see Innes Bowen, 2014, *Medina in Birmingham, Najaf in Brent: Inside British Islam*, London: Hurst & Co.

38 Jacques Waardenburg, 1997, 'Critical Issues in Muslim–Christian Relations:

Theoretical, Practical, Dialogical, Scholarly', *Islam and Christian–Muslim Relations* 8:1, pp. 9–26, p. 12.

39   For Sydney H. Griffith, 'the Qur'an and early Islam are literally unthinkable outside of the Judeo-Christian milieu in which Islam was born and grew to its maturity'; 2008, *The Church in the Shadow of the Mosque: Christians and Muslims in the World of Islam*, Princeton, NJ: Princeton University Press, p. 159.

40   Griffith, *The Church in the Shadow of the Mosque*, p. 159. This echoes Louis Massignon's sense that 'Islam is the divine lance, which, by the Holy War, has stigmatised Christianity', quoted in Sidney H. Griffith, 1997, 'Sharing the Faith of Abraham: The "Credo" of Louis Massignon', *Islam and Christian–Muslim Relations* 8:2, pp. 193–210, p. 202.

41   J. W. Sweetman, 1945, *Islam and Christian Theology: A Study of the Interpretation of Theological Ideas in the Two Religions, Part 1, Vol. 1*, London: Lutterworth Press, p. 57.

42   G. R. Hawting, 1999, *The Idea of Idolatry and the Emergence of Islam: From Polemic to History*, New York/Cambridge: Cambridge University Press.

43   J. M. Gaudeul, 2000, *Encounters and Clashes: Islam and Christianity in History I, A Survey*, Rome: Pontificio Istituto di Studie Arabi e d'Islamistica, p. 32.

44   Sweetman, *Islam and Christian Theology, Part 1, Vol. 1*, p. 65. It must also be noted, though, that Patricia Crone and Michael Cook have argued for the 'Hagarene' nomenclature as welcomed and indeed self-styled by Muhammad to claim the Abrahamic inheritance of an Islamic monotheism from within Judaic and Christian roots, though their more recent work has served to qualify this judgement: Patricia Crone and Michael Cook, 1977, *Hagarism: The Making of the Islamic World*, New York/Cambridge: Cambridge University Press.

45   Kenneth Cragg, 2006, *The Order of the Wounded Hands: Schooled in the East*, London: Melisende, pp. 97–8.

46   Cragg, *Order of the Wounded Hands*, p. 97.

47   Quoted in J. W. Sweetman, 1947, *Islam and Christian Theology: A Study of the Interpretation of Theological Ideas in the Two Religions, Part 1, Vol. 2*, London: Lutterworth Press, p. 1.

48   Gaudeul, *Encounters and Clashes*, p. 185. Timothy's response cleverly combines a theological rationale with the evidence of witnesses: 'So that this expectation of everlasting life and of the world to come be firmly impressed upon the people, therefore, it was fitting that Jesus Christ rise from the dead; and so that he rose from the dead, it was fitting and right that he first die; and so that he die it was right first that his death – also his resurrection – be witnessed by all.'

49   Griffith, *The Church in the Shadow of the Mosque*, p. 44.

50   Michael Ipgrave, 2003, *Trinity and Interfaith Dialogue: Plenitude and Plurality*, Bern: Peter Lang, p. 193.

51   Sweetman, *Islam and Christian Theology, Part 1, Vol. 1*, p. 87. A similar point about the Christian theology of the incarnation in relation to Islam is made by Ng

Kam Weng: 'Muslims rightly reject any attempt to ascribe ultimacy to anything outside of God. The Christian shares this insistence but goes further by insisting that such negation should be redemptive. In this regard, God's sovereignty should include his ability to enact the drama of redemption within the flux of history. Otherwise God would remain in splendid isolation and irrelevant to humankind': Ng Kam Weng, 2005, 'Jesus Christ – Eschatological Prophet and Incarnate Savior: A Christian Proposal to Muslims', in Sung Wook Chung (ed.), *Christ the One and Only: A Global Affirmation of the Uniqueness of Christ*, Milton Keynes: Paternoster Press, pp. 180–202, p. 200.

52 Griffith, *The Church in the Shadow of the Mosque*, p. 55.

53 Quoted in Anthony O'Mahony, 2004, 'Christianity, Interreligious Dialogue and Muslim–Christian Relations', in Anthony O'Mahony and Michael Kirwan (eds), *World Christianity: Politics, Theology, Dialogues*, London: Melisende, pp. 63–92, p. 85.

54 O'Mahony, 'Christianity, Interreligious Dialogue and Muslim–Christian Relations', p. 84.

55 Sweetman, *Islam and Christian Theology, Part 1, Vol. 2*, p. 80.

56 O'Mahony, 'Christianity, Interreligious Dialogue and Muslim–Christian Relations', p. 92.

57 Perhaps the towering influence in this regard is Kenneth Cragg, 1991, *The Arab Christian: A History in the Middle East*, Louisville, KY: Westminster/John Knox Press. Cragg's judgement that 'Islam was insistently set against what seemed to put in question divine sovereignty. The Christianity with which it cohabited so long gave its theology a temper of mind and an ambition of dogma ill-tuned to a vocation within Islam' (p. 89) epitomizes the perception that the earliest Christian encounters with Islam were inadequate to the task.

58 See Griffith, *The Church in the Shadow of the Mosque*, pp. 52–3 for details of the copy process that dates back to 877 CE.

59 Griffith, *The Church in the Shadow of the Mosque*, p. 58.

60 Griffith, *The Church in the Shadow of the Mosque*, p. 60.

61 Griffith, *The Church in the Shadow of the Mosque*, p. 75.

62 Griffith, *The Church in the Shadow of the Mosque*, pp. 93–4.

63 Sweetman, *Islam and Christian Theology, Part 1, Vol. 1*, pp. 65–6.

64 Griffith, *The Church in the Shadow of the Mosque*, pp. 83–5.

65 Rowan Williams, 2004, 'Archbishop's Address at al-Azhar al-Sharif, Cairo', Saturday 11 September 2004: www.archbishopofcanterbury.org/articles.php/1299/archbishops-address-at-al-azhar-al-sharif-cairo. Rowan Williams, 2005, 'What is Christianity?' A lecture on basic Christian beliefs and behaviour given by the Archbishop of Canterbury at the Islamic University, Islamabad, 23 November 2005: www.cte.org.uk/Articles/136370/Churches_Together_in/Working_To-gether/Inter_faith/Christian_Muslim_Relations/C_M_Archive/_What_is.aspx.

66 *Doctrina Jacobi Nuperbaptizati*: a text written in Greek by a Palestinian Jewish

convert to the Christian faith, Griffith, *The Church in the Shadow of the Mosque*, pp. 24–5.

67 Griffith, *The Church in the Shadow of the Mosque*, p. 25.

68 Griffith, *The Church in the Shadow of the Mosque*, p. 48.

69 Gaudeul, *Encounters and Clashes, Texts*, p. 248.

70 Gaudeul, *Encounters and Clashes, Texts*, p. 249.

71 Gaudeul, *Encounters and Clashes, Texts*, p. 251.

72 Gaudeul, *Encounters and Clashes, Texts*, p. 251.

73 Gaudeul, *Encounters and Clashes, Texts*, p. 69. Timothy goes on to say, 'Who will not praise, honour and exalt the one who not only fought for God in words, but showed also his zeal for Him in the sword?' We do not know whether this is a backhanded compliment casting common aspersions on the violent nature of Islam.

74 For an alternative, contemporary position that argues for a measure of Christian acknowledgement of the prophetic role of Muhammad, see David A. Kerr, 1995, '"He Walked in the Path of the Prophets": Toward Christian Theological Recognition of the Prophethood of Muhammad', in Yvonne Yazbeck Haddad and Wadi Zaidan Haddad (eds), *Christian–Muslim Encounters*, Gainesville, FL: University Press of Florida, pp. 426–46. Kerr analyses seven different Christian perspectives on Muhammad, including Kenneth Cragg, and concludes by suggesting that both Christians and Muslims need to come together for 'a new statement of the nature of revelation', revelation being the vital doctrine underpinning any assessment of prophethood (pp. 441–2).

75 J. W. Sweetman, 1955, *Islam and Christian Theology: A Study of the Interpretation of Theological Ideas in the Two Religions, Part 2, Vol. 1*, London: Lutterworth Press, p. 5.

76 Sweetman, *Islam and Christian Theology, Part 2, Vol. 1*, p. 9.

77 See, for example, John Wyclif's words on Islam in Gaudeul, *Encounters and Clashes I, A Survey*, p. 156: 'I am bold to say that this antireligion will grow until the clergy return to the poverty of Jesus Christ, and to its original state.'

78 Louis Massignon, 1948, 'Le Signe Marial', *Rhythmes du Monde* 3, pp. 7–16, p. 8.

79 Cragg, *The Arab Christian*, p. 31.

80 Sweetman, *Islam and Christian Theology, Part 1, Vol. 2*, pp. 12–13.

81 Sweetman, *Islam and Christian Theology, Part 1, Vol. 2*, pp. 57–8.

82 See Yohanan Friedmann, 2003, *Tolerance and Coercion in Islam: Interfaith Relations in the Muslim Tradition*, Cambridge: Cambridge University Press, pp. 13–86.

83 Friedmann, *Tolerance and Coercion*, p. 37.

84 'Most classical jurists agree that the execution of the unrepentant apostate is the proper punishment for his transgression': Friedmann, *Tolerance and Coercion*, p. 127.

85   Sydney Griffith is disparaging about the idea of *dhimmitude* equating to a form of citizenship: 'if the term "citizen" can even be meaningfully used of people whose presence in the body politic is merely tolerated': Griffith, *The Church in the Shadow of the Mosque*, p. 16.

86   Yohanan Friedmann, 1998, 'Classification of Unbelievers in Sunni Muslim Law and Tradition', *Jerusalem Studies in Arabic and Islam* 22, pp. 163–95, p. 191.

87   See, for example, Yahya Michot's commentary on Ibn Taymiyya's reflections on the status of Mardin, a mixed city outside of the then Islamic empire, to Muslims: Yahya Michot, 2006, *Muslims Under Non-Muslim Rule: Ibn Taymiyya on Fleeing from Sin; Kinds of Emigration; the Status of Mardin: Domain of Peace/ War, Domain Composite; the Conditions for Challenging Power*, Oxford/London: Interface Publications.

88   Friedmann, *Tolerance and Coercion*, p. 123.

89   David Burrell, 2008, 'Some Requisites for Interfaith Dialogue', *New Blackfriars* 89:1020, pp. 300–9, p. 304.

90   Quoted in Y. Courbage and P. Fargues, 1997, *Christians and Jews Under Islam*, London: I. B. Taurus, p. 44.

91   *Dhimmitude* is the status given to Christians and Jews within *Shari'a* law as a protection of their minority status within Islam. *Dhimmitude* required the payment of a tax (*jizya*) and penalties that reinforced the superior status of Muslims in the community. See Friedmann, *Tolerance and Coercion*, for a full account of formative *dhimmī* regulations.

92   Courbage and Fargues, *Christians and Jews Under Islam*, p. 51.

93   It must be remembered that *dhimmitude* afforded a degree of protection that the atrocities of Christian Crusaders often denied: 'the non-Muslim communities living under Islam experienced far less expulsions and persecutions than Jews, or "deviant" Christians, living under medieval Christendom': Friedmann, *Tolerance and Coercion*, p. 93.

94   Benjamin Z. Kedar, 1990, 'The Subjected Muslims of the Frankish Levant', in James M. Powell (ed.), *Muslims Under Latin Rule 1100–1300*, Princeton, NJ: Princeton University Press, pp. 135–74, pp. 148–9.

95   Kedar, 'Subjected Muslims', p. 157.

96   Kedar, 'Subjected Muslims', pp. 153–4, p. 156.

97   Kedar, 'Subjected Muslims', pp. 158–9.

98   Kedar, 'Subjected Muslims', pp. 160–1.

99   Kedar, 'Subjected Muslims', pp. 167–9.

100   Kedar, 'Subjected Muslims', pp. 139–40.

101   Kedar, 'Subjected Muslims', p. 145.

102   Andrew Wheatcroft, 2003, *Infidels: The Conflict between Christendom and Islam 638–2002*, London: Viking, pp. 73–81.

103   Wheatcroft, *Infidels*, p. 72.

104 Wheatcroft, *Infidels*, p. 96.

105 Wheatcroft, *Infidels*, p. 72.

106 Griffith, *The Church in the Shadow of the Mosque*, p. 22.

107 See, for example, Sweetman, *Islam and Christian Theology, Part 2, Vol. 1*, p. 64, which recounts the legend propagated by Jacob of Vitry that there was an image of Muhammad in the Mosque of 'Umar in Jerusalem. This is in stark contrast to Arabic Christians who were far better informed about the theological challenges of Islam and conscious of the rebuke of *tawhīd* to the Christian doctrine of the trinity. See Ipgrave, *Trinity and Interfaith Dialogue*, pp. 191–3.

108 Even though it may be argued that the Eastern Church's reservoir of theological resources for engagement with Islam was largely lost to the Latin Church, there remained exceptional models of enquiry and reflection, not least in the first Latin translation of the Qur'an (1143 CE), commissioned by Peter the Venerable and written by Robert of Ketton (*c*.1110–60 CE). This 'intelligent paraphrase' was still being cited in the seventeenth century by Hugo Grotius: C. E. Bosworth, 1997, 'The Study of Islam in British Scholarship', in Azim Nanji (ed.), *Mapping Islamic Studies: Genealogy, Continuity and Change*, Berlin/New York: Mouton de Gruyter, pp. 45–67, pp. 48–9.

109 See, for example, Hugh Goddard, 2000, *A History of Christian–Muslim Relations*, Edinburgh: Edinburgh University Press; Jonathan Riley-Smith, 1995, *The Oxford Illustrated History of the Crusades*, Oxford: Oxford University Press and 1996, *The First Crusade and the Idea of Crusading*, Cambridge: Cambridge University Press; Norman Daniel, 1960, *Islam and the West: The Making of an Image*, Edinburgh: Edinburgh University Press.

110 Francis Arinze, 2004, 'Christianity and the Realities of Life Today', in O'Mahony and Kirwan (eds), *World Christianity*, pp. 19–26: 'It was Islam, however, that presented a major challenge. At first considered a type of Christian heresy, it had to be accepted as a separate religion' (p. 22).

111 Michael Nazir-Ali, 'Extremism Flourished as UK Lost Christianity', *Daily Telegraph*, 11 January 2008, www.telegraph.co.uk/news/uknews/1574695/Extremism-flourished-as-UK-lost-Christianity.html.

112 Khaled Abou El Fadl, 1994, 'Islamic Law and Muslim Minorities: The Juristic Discourse on Muslim Minorities from the Second/Eighth to the Eleventh/Seventeenth Centuries', *Islamic Law and Society* 1:2, pp. 141–87, p. 181.

113 See in particular the work of Timothy Winter, 2003, *British Muslim Identity: Past, Problems, Prospects*, Cambridge: Muslim Academic Trust, 2003; 'Muslim Loyalty and Belonging: Some Reflections on the Psychosocial Background', in Mohammad Siddique Seddon, Dilwar Hussain and Nadeem Malik (eds), *British Muslims: Loyalty and Belonging*, Markfield: The Islamic Foundation, pp. 3–22 and Dilwar Hussain, 2008, 'Islam', in Zaki Cooper and Guy Lodge (eds), *Faith in the Nation: Religion, Identity and the Public Realm in Britain Today*, London: Institute for Public Policy Research, pp. 39–46. For a European perspective, see Ramadan, *Western Muslims and the Future of Islam*. El Fadl's own analysis of the

early years of Islam would indicate that the authoritative patterns suggest genuine diversity within Islamic schools and a level of pragmatism that provides grounds for a more contemporary application of rules governing Muslim minorities: El Fadl, 'Islamic Law and Muslim Minorities'.

114 Note the dangers of instrumentalizing a myth of St Francis to serve diverse contemporary agendas highlighted by J. Tolan, 2008, 'The Friar and the Sultan: Francis of Assisi's Mission to Egypt', *European Review* 16:1, pp. 115–26: 'The manipulation of this event tells us more about our own changing hopes and fears regarding Islam and East–West relations than it does about the historic Francis … If history is a mirror, it reflects above all a darkened and distorted image of our own worries and aspirations' (p. 126).

115 'The actions of many crusaders were individual expressions of a piety that may be alien to us but was very real to them': Jonathan Riley-Smith, 1992, *The Crusades: A Short History*, new edn, London: Athlone Press, p. 257.

116 Exemplified by Norman Daniel's argument that the 'closing victory' of the Crusades was in fact General Allenby's entry into Jerusalem in 1917: Norman Daniel, *Islam and the West*, p. 333.

117 Scott M. Thomas, 2008, 'The Way of St Francis? Catholic Approaches to Christian–Muslim Relations and Interreligious Dialogue', *The Downside Review* 126:444, pp. 157–68, pp. 160–2.

118 Thomas, 'Way of St Francis?', p. 160. When talking of 'thick' and 'thin' practices, Thomas is mobilizing the language of Alasdair Macintyre, 2007, *After Virtue: A Study in Moral Theory*, 3rd edn, London: Duckworth.

119 Sweetman, *Islam and Christian Theology, Part 2, Vol. 1*, p. 69.

120 Oliver O'Donovan and Joan Lockwood O'Donovan (eds), 1999, *From Irenaeus to Grotius: A Sourcebook in Christian Political Thought 100–1625*, Grand Rapids, MI/Cambridge: Eerdmans, p. 240.

121 Quoted in G. R. Evans and Robert J. Wright (eds), 1991, *The Anglican Tradition: A Handbook of Sources*, London: SPCK, p. 96. Interestingly, Pope Gregory VII concludes his letter by saying, 'And we pray in our hearts and with our lips that God may lead you to the abode of happiness, to the bosom of the holy patriarch Abraham, after long years of life here on earth.' The Abrahamic connection will become an increasingly significant motif for the establishment of peaceful relations between Christians and Muslims in later years.

122 Sweetman, *Islam and Christian Theology, Part 2, Vol. 1*, p. 69.

123 M. L. Fitzgerald and J. Borelli, 2006, *Interfaith Dialogue: A Catholic View*, London: SPCK, p. 109.

124 Ovey Mohammed, 1999, *Muslim–Christian Relations: Past, Present, Future*, Maryknoll, NY: Orbis Books, p. 46.

125 Sweetman, *Islam and Christian Theology, Part 2, Vol. 1*, p. 80.

126 Sweetman, *Islam and Christian Theology, Part 2, Vol. 1*, p. 71.

127 Ipgrave, *Trinity and Interfaith Dialogue*, p. 191.

128 Quoted in Chris McVey, 2008, 'The Land of Unlikeness: The Risk and Promise of Muslim–Christian Dialogue', *New Blackfriars* 89:1022, pp. 369–84, p. 378.

129 Sweetman, *Islam and Christian Theology, Part 2, Vol. 1*, p. 161.

130 Sweetman, *Islam and Christian Theology, Part 2, Vol. 1*, p. 161. This point is emphasized by Sweetman's reminder that Nicholas of Cusa had been a missionary in Constantinople and was writing his *De cribatione alchorani* at the time of the fall of Constantinople to the Turks; an event of shuddering import to Christendom.

131 Quoted in Sweetman, *Islam and Christian Theology, Part 1, Vol. 1*, p. 71.

132 *Summa Theologica* 2a2ae.10.10; 12.2. This argument is also used by the important Dominican scholar Francisco de Vitoria (*c.*1483–1546) in his influential work, *The American Indians*. See O'Donovan and Lockwood O'Donovan, *From Irenaeus to Grotius*, pp. 609–30.

133 Fitzgerald and Borelli, *Interfaith Dialogue*, p. 111.

134 Quoted in Mohammed, *Muslim–Christian Relations*, p. 46. It is worth noting that Aquinas's views here are very reminiscent of the sentiments of Emperor Manuel II Paleologus, from a dialogue of 1391, controversially quoted in Pope Benedict XVI's Regensburg Lecture.

135 David Burrell, 2004, 'Thomas Aquinas and Islam', *Modern Theology* 20:1, pp. 71–89, pp. 71–2.

136 David Burrell, 1986, *Knowing the Unknowable God: Ibn-Sina, Maimonides, Aquinas*, Notre Dame, IN: University of Notre Dame Press, p. 109. See also F. R. Sullivan, 1992, *Salvation Outside the Church? Tracing the History of the Catholic Response*, London: Geoffrey Chapman.

137 Jacques Dupuis, 2002, *Christianity and the Religions: From Confrontation to Dialogue*, Maryknoll, NY/London: Orbis Books and Darton, Longman & Todd, pp. 3 and 59.

138 *The Council of Vienne* in 1312 had called for the establishment of schools of Arabic at given European universities: Fitzgerald and Borelli, *Interfaith Dialogue*, p. 15. Peter the Venerable's translation of the Qur'an was supplemented by the more accurate translation by Ludovico Marracci in 1698 and a summary of Islamic belief, *De Religione Mohammedica*, by Hadrian Reland of Utrecht published in 1705. This was treated with suspicion by church authorities as being overly sympathetic to Islam: Mohammed, *Muslim–Christian Relations*, p. 46.

139 Susanna Throop, 2007, 'Combat and Conversation: Interfaith Dialogue in Twelfth-Century Crusading Narratives', *Medieval Encounters* 13:2, pp. 310–25, p. 325.

140 Wheatcroft, *Infidels*, p. 73.

141 With St Augustine, Oliver O'Donovan and Joan Lockwood O'Donovan can say of Aquinas that 'Together they ensured the classical cast of the Western political inheritance, its continuing conversations with Greek and Roman sources into the present': O'Donovan and Lockwood O'Donovan, *From Irenaeus to Grotius*, p. 320.

142 Paul Avis, 2013, *The Anglican Understanding of the Church: An Introduction*,

2nd edn, London: SPCK, p. 77; Mark Chapman, 2012, *Anglican Theology*, London: T. & T. Clark, pp. 103–25.

143 Jan Van Wiele, 2007, 'Neo-Thomism and the Theology of Religions: A Case Study on Belgian and U.S. Textbooks (1870–1950)', *Theological Studies* 68:4, pp. 780–807.

144 J. B. Trapnell, 2004, 'Catholic Engagement with India and Its Theological Implications: Jules Monchanin, Henri Le Saux, and Bede Griffiths', in O'Mahony and Kirwan, *World Christianity*, pp. 257–84, p. 259 and A. Lévy, 2008, 'Between Charybdis and Scylla: Catholic Theology and Interreligious Dialogue', *New Blackfriars* 89:1020, pp. 231–50, p. 234.

145 Trapnell, 'Catholic Engagement with India', p. 264: 'Christian mysticism is Trinitarian or it is nothing', quoting Monchanin.

146 Trapnell, 'Catholic Engagement with India', p. 261.

147 Anthony O'Mahony, 2008, 'The Influence of the Life and Thought of Louis Massignon on the Catholic Church's Relations with Islam', *The Downside Review* 126:444, pp. 169–92, p. 174.

148 Dupuis, *Christianity and the Religions*, p. 49. See Jean Daniélou, 1957, *God and Us*, London: Mowbray, and 1962, *The Salvation of the Nations*, Notre Dame, IN: University of Notre Dame Press.

149 Dupuis, *Christianity and the Religions*, p. 51.

150 Jacques Jomier, 1989, *How to Understand Islam*, London: SCM Press, p. 147.

151 Walter M. Abbott (ed.), 1966, *The Documents of Vatican II: With Notes and Comments by Catholic Protestant, and Orthodox Authorities*, London: Geoffrey Chapman, pp. 595–6.

152 A phrase borrowed from Karl Rahner: Dupuis, *Christianity and the Religions*, p. 64.

153 Abbott, *Documents of Vatican II*, p. 662.

154 Abbott, *Documents of Vatican II*, p. 662.

155 Dupuis, *Christianity and the Religions*, pp. 59–60.

156 Gavin D'Costa, 2011, 'Catholicism and the World Religions: A Theological and Phenomenological Account', in Gavin D'Costa (ed.), *The Catholic Church and the World Religions*, London/New York: T. & T. Clark, pp. 1–33, p. 19.

157 Abbott, *Documents of Vatican II*, p. 35.

158 Andrew Unsworth, 2008, 'Louis Massignon, The Holy See and the Ecclesial Transition from "*Immortale Dei*" to "*Nostra Aetate*": A Brief History of the Development of Catholic Church Teaching on Muslims and the Religion of Islam from 1883 to 1965', *ARAM* 20, pp. 299–316, pp. 308–9. Unsworth sees *Fidei Donum* as a 'bridge document' between earlier verdicts of Islam and the Vatican II trajectory.

159 This was renamed *The Pontifical Council for Inter-Religious Dialogue* in 1989, and then merged with the *Pontifical Council for Culture* in 2006.

160 Quoted in Unsworth, 'Louis Massignon, The Holy See', p. 305.

161 Dupuis, *Christianity and the Religions*, pp. 34–45 and McVey, 'The Land of Unlikeness', p. 247.

162 Dupuis, *Christianity and the Religions*, p. 45.

163 For an analysis of Dupuis' theology of religions in contrast to Karl Rahner and Jean Daniélou, key architects of Vatican II, see Adam Sparks, 2008, 'The Fulfilment Theology of Jean Daniélou, Karl Rahner and Jacques Dupuis', *New Blackfriars* 89:1024, pp. 633–56.

164 Thus, for example, *Lumen Gentium 16*, quoted earlier as opening up salvation to Muslims 'in the first place', concludes by seeing 'goodness and truth' in other faiths as a 'preparation for the gospel' necessitating that the 'Church painstakingly fosters her missionary work': Abbott, *Documents of Vatican II*, p. 35.

165 Andrew Unsworth, 2008, 'The Vatican, Islam and Muslim–Christian Relations', in Anthony O'Mahony and Emma Loosley (eds), *Christian Responses to Islam: Muslim–Christian Relations in the Modern World*, Manchester: Manchester University Press, pp. 54–65, p. 61.

166 He notes in particular *Evangelii Nuntiandi*, 1975, which reaffirms classic fulfilment theory contrasting the 'arms outstretched to heaven' of other religions with 'God's bending over towards humanity' of the Church in a document that talks of proclamation without mentioning interreligious dialogue: Dupuis, *Christianity and the Religions*, p. 68.

167 *Lumen gentium* acting arguably as the foundational encyclical to which the ensuing ecumenical (Decree on Ecumenism) and missional (*Ad gentes* and *Nostra aetate*) responsibilities flowed.

168 Gavin D'Costa, 2009, 'Hermeneutics and the Second Vatican Council's Teachings: Establishing Roman Catholic Grounds for Religious Freedoms in Relation to Islam. Continuity or Discontinuity in the Catholic Tradition?', *Islam and Christian–Muslim Relations* 20:3, pp. 277–90, pp. 278–9.

169 Anthony O'Mahony, 2007, 'Catholic Theological Perspectives on Islam at the Second Vatican Council', *New Blackfriars* 88:1016, pp. 385–98, p. 387.

170 John H. Watson, 2004, 'Christianity in the Middle East', in O'Mahony and Kirwan (eds), *World Christianity*, pp. 203–25, p. 215 and O'Mahony, 'The Influence', pp. 183–5.

171 Adrian Hastings, 1968, *A Concise Guide to the Documents of the Second Vatican Council, Volume One*, London: Darton, Longman & Todd, p. 198.

172 O'Mahony, 'The Influence', p. 181. See also David Burrell, 1998, 'Mind and Heart at the Service of Muslim–Christian Understanding: Louis Massignon as Trail Blazer', *The Muslim World* 88:3–4 , pp. 268–78: 'when we recall the prescient words of the Vatican II document, *Nostra Aetate*, on Islam, we can begin to see the fruits of the scholarship and especially of the person of Louis Massignon' (p. 275).

173 O'Mahony, 'Catholic Theological Perspectives', p. 392 and Unsworth, 'Louis Massignon, The Holy See', p. 313.

174 Anthony O'Mahony, 2010, 'Modern Catholic Thought on Islam and Christian–Muslim Relations', *One in Christ* 44:2, pp. 111–35, p. 127.

175 Fitzgerald and Borelli, *Interfaith Dialogue*, p. 117.

176 *Declaration on the Relation of the Church to Non-Christian Religions, Nostra Aetate, Proclaimed by His Holiness Pope Paul VI on October 28, 1965,* § 3: www.vatican.va/archive/hist_councils/ii_vatican_council/documents/vat-ii_decl_19651028_nostra-aetate_en.html.

177 Erik Borgman, 2005, 'The Transcendent and Present God as Space of Enlightenment: The Theological Dialogue between Christians and Muslims as a Contribution to Modernity', *Concilium* 2005:5, pp. 112–21, p. 120.

178 O'Mahony regards the latter as 'the most sensitive point for the Muslims'. To affirm Muhammad's prophethood would complete the Islamic creed, the *shahadah*; to clearly reject Muhammad's prophethood would be an offence to Muslims: O'Mahony, 'Catholic Theological Perspectives', p. 398.

179 Daniel Madigan, 2006, '*Nostra Aetate* and the Questions it Chose to Leave Open', *Gregorianum* 87:4, pp. 781–96, p. 789.

180 Madigan, '*Nostra Aetate*', p. 795.

181 F. Jourdan, 2008, *Dieu des chrétiens, Dieu des musulmans: des repères pour comprendre*, Paris: Éditions de l'Oeuvre, p. 33. For a recent defence of the proposal that Christians and Muslims worship the one God, see Miroslav Volf, 2011, *Allah: A Christian Response*, New York: HarperOne.

182 Burrell, *Knowing the Unknowable God*, p. 111.

183 For an outline of Massignon's life and ministry, see Anthony O'Mahony, 2006, 'Our Common Fidelity to Abraham is What Divides: Christianity and Islam in the Life and Thought of Louis Massignon', in Anthony O'Mahony and Peter Bowe (eds), *Catholics in Interreligious Dialogue: Studies in Monasticism, Theology and Spirituality*, Leominster: Gracewing, pp. 151–90, and 2007, 'Louis Massignon as Priest: Eastern Christianity and Islam', *Sobornost* 29:1, pp. 6–41.

184 O'Mahony, 'The Influence', p. 177.

185 See Anthony O'Mahony, 2004, 'Louis Massignon, the Seven Sleepers of Ephesus and the Christian–Muslim Pilgrimage at Vieux-Marché, Brittany', in Craig Bartholomew and Fred Hughes (eds), *Explorations in a Christian Theology of Pilgrimage*, Aldershot: Ashgate, pp. 126–46.

186 O'Mahony, 'The Influence', p. 175. See also Christian S. Krokus, 2012, 'Louis Massignon's Influence on the Teaching of Vatican II on Muslims and Islam', *Islam and Christian–Muslim Relations* 23:3, pp. 329–45.

187 Griffith, *The Church in the Shadow of the Mosque*, pp. 162–4.

188 Unsworth, 'The Vatican, Islam and Muslim–Christian Relations', p. 61.

189 O'Mahony, 'The Influence', p. 177.

190 Karl-Josef Kuschel, 1995, *Abraham: A Symbol of Hope for Jews, Christians and Muslims*, London: SCM Press, p. 231.

191 Kuschel, *Abraham*, p. 219.

192 O'Mahony, 'Our Common Fidelity', p. 158.

193 Roger Arnaldez, 1994, *Three Messengers for One God*, Notre Dame, IN: University of Notre Dame Press, p. 3.

194 Quoted in Pim Valkenberg, 2005, 'Does the Concept of "Abrahamic Religions" have a Future?', *Concilium* 2005:5, pp. 103–11, p. 108.

195 Michael Knowles, 2011, 'The Galatian Test: Is Islam an Abrahamic Religion?', *New Blackfriars* 92:1039, pp. 318–21.

196 'Their dialogue must never degenerate into a convivial get together, in which the existing relationships of power are left untouched': Valkenberg, 'Does the Concept of "Abrahamic Religions" have a Future?', p. 109, and see, for example, Mary Mills, 2008, 'The Story of Abraham and Models of Human Identity', *New Blackfriars* 89:1021, pp. 280–99 and 2004, 'Abraham: Man of Faith. A Catholic Perspective', in Anthony O'Mahony and Mohammad Ali Shomali (eds), *Catholics and Shi'a in Dialogue: Studies in Theology and Spirituality*, London: Melisende, pp. 308–20.

197 Mills, 'Story of Abraham', p. 299.

198 O'Mahony, 'The Influence', p. 178. Sydney Griffith describes Massignon's ideas as 'pre-theological', in Griffith, 'Sharing the Faith of Abraham', p. 205.

199 Burrell, 'Some Requisites for Interfaith Dialogue', p. 307.

200 Neal Robinson, 1991, 'Massignon, Vatican II and Islam as an Abrahamic Religion', *Islam and Christian–Muslim Relations* 2:2, pp. 182–205, p. 195.

201 Waardenburg, 'Critical Issues in Muslim–Christian Relations, p. 24.

202 Quoted in Unsworth, 'The Vatican, Islam and Muslim–Christian Relations', p. 59.

203 'There was a commonly held view that John Paul II was too irenic in his approach to global Islam, and that Benedict sees his role as one of tempering dialogical and evangelizing zeal of his predecessor with some much needed "realism"' (as per Robert Spencer, 'The Vatican's New Realism about Islam', FrontPageMagazine. com, 31 October 2003, as referenced in Barbara Wood and Andrew Unsworth, 2008, 'Before and After Regensburg: Pope Benedict XVI, Interreligious Dialogue and Islam', in Anthony O'Mahony, Timothy Wright and Mohammad Ali Shomali (eds), *A Catholic-Shi'a Dialogue: Ethics in Today's Society*, London: Melisende, pp. 44–68). The direct challenge of religious freedom to the Saudi government at the opening of a Saudi-financed mosque in Rome in 1995 and the championing of Christian minorities in Malaysia are two additional examples cited by Wood and Unsworth as evidence of John Paul II's robust pursuit of reciprocity as counter to this charge (pp. 60–2).

204 'John Paul II personalized inter-faith dialogue. His unprecedented travel schedule, meticulously chronicled by the media, sends a message of openness and determination about the importance of dialogue that no document has done or will ever be able to do in the same way. Putting flesh and blood into his commit-

ment is a symbolic act that speaks as no official statement on paper is able to do': Doris Donnelly, 2003, 'On Relationship as a Key to Interreligious Dialogue', in Daniel Kendall and Gerald O'Collins (eds), *In Many and Diverse Ways: In Honor of Jacques Dupuis*, Maryknoll, NY: Orbis Books, pp. 133–45, p. 136.

205 Hans Küng, 1987, *Christianity and the World Religions*, London: Collins, p. 26.

206 Küng, *Christianity and the World Religions*, p. 127.

207 This is exemplified by his speech as then Cardinal Ratzinger in 1996, entitled 'Relativism: The Central Problem for Faith Today', where he rejects the 'relativist dissolution of Christology, and even more of ecclesiology' and how these two moves become 'a central commandment of religion': Joseph Ratzinger, 2006, 'Relativism: The Central Problem for Faith Today', in John F. Thornton and Susan B. Varenne (eds), *The Essential Pope Benedict XVI: His Central Writings and Speeches*, New York: HarperOne, pp. 227–40, p. 231.

208 Daniel Madigan, 2005, 'Jesus and Muhammad: The Sufficiency of Prophecy', in Michael Ipgrave (ed.), *Bearing the Word: Prophecy in Biblical and Qur'anic Perspective*, London: Church House Publishing, pp. 90–9, pp. 93–6.

209 'Dialogue is possible because God's saving grace is not confined to the church alone. It is significant that at the Second Vatican Council the traditional dictum "outside the church there is no salvation" was never used': Stephen P. Bevans and Roger B. Schroeder, 2004, *Constants in Context: A Theology of Mission for Today*, Maryknoll, NY: Orbis Books, p. 379.

210 Diarmaid MacCulloch skilfully evokes the momentum of Reformation thought that was an *Ad fontes* cry, 'back to the sources', in 2004, *Reformation: Europe's House Divided, 1490–1700*, London: Penguin, pp. 76–87. MacCulloch notes the shifting boundaries of Europe in pp. 53–7 and how 'The fear which this Islamic aggression engendered in Europe was an essential background to the Reformation' (p. 57).

211 Katya Vehlow, 1995, 'The Swiss Reformers Zwingli, Bullinger and Bibliander and their Attitude to Islam (1520–1560)', *Islam and Christian–Muslim Relations* 6:2, pp. 229–54, p. 245.

212 Quoting from the Preface to Bibliander's translation of the Qur'an: Sarah Henrich and James L. Boyce, 1996, 'Martin Luther – Translations of Two Prefaces on Islam: *Prefaces to the Libellus de ritue et moribus Turcorum (1530)*, and *Preface to Bibliander's Edition of the Qur'an (1543)*', *Word and World* 16:2, pp. 250–66, p. 263.

213 Henrich and Boyce, 'Martin Luther', p. 259.

214 Henrich and Boyce, 'Martin Luther', p. 255. Note, too, the anticipation of Massignon's ideas about Islam being a 'foil' to the Christian faith.

215 Henrich and Boyce, 'Martin Luther', p. 259.

216 Vehlow, 'The Swiss Reformers', p. 243.

217 Vehlow, 'The Swiss Reformers', pp. 238–40.

218 Vehlow, 'The Swiss Reformers', pp. 236–44.

219 Mohammad, *Muslim–Christian Relations*, p. 46.

220 See, for example, O'Donovan and Lockwood O'Donovan, *From Irenaeus to Grotius*, pp. 581–4; W. D. J. Cargill Thompson, 1984, *The Political Thought of Martin Luther*, Brighton: Harvester Press and F. E. Cranz, 1959, *An Essay on the Development of Luther's Thoughts on Justification, Law, and Society*, Cambridge: Harvard University Press.

221 This strict separateness marks the key difference between Luther and Augustine's conception of the 'two cities'. See O'Donovan and Lockwood O'Donovan, *From Irenaeus to Grotius*, p. 582.

222 This was in marked contrast to Zwingli, who sought civil support for religious reforms: O'Donovan and Lockwood O'Donovan, *From Irenaeus to Grotius*, p. 582.

223 Andrew Bradstock, 2007, 'The Reformation', in Scott and Cavanaugh, *The Blackwell Companion to Political Theology*, p. 66.

224 Bradstock, 'The Reformation', p. 65.

225 Stanley Hauerwas, 2007, 'Dietrich Bonhoeffer', in Scott and Cavanaugh, *The Blackwell Companion to Political Theology*, pp. 136–49.

226 Kuschel, *Abraham*, p. 187.

227 See the report, *Guidelines for Inter Faith Encounter in the Churches of the Porvoo Communion*, Porvoo Communion Consultation on Inter Faith Relations, Oslo, 30 November to 3 December 2003: www.churchofengland.org/about-us/interfaith/resources.aspx.

228 *Guidelines for Inter Faith Encounter*, p. 2.

229 *Guidelines for Inter Faith Encounter*, p. 3.

230 Dupuis, *Christianity and the Religions*, p. 46.

231 Quoted in Kenneth Cragg, 2004, 'Responsible to Faith: Responsible for Faith', in O'Mahony and Kirwan, *World Christianity*, pp. 27–42, p. 34.

232 See Chapter 4 'Contemporary Issues in Christian–Muslim Encounter', including the literature on 'Islamo-fascism'.

233 Karl Barth, 1939, *The Church and the Political Problem of Our Day*, London: Hodder & Stoughton, p. 43.

234 Karl Barth, 1957, *Church Dogmatics: Volume II/1, The Doctrine of God*, Edinburgh: T. & T. Clark, pp. 448–9.

235 Glenn A. Chestnutt, 2012, 'Karl Barth and Islam', *Modern Theology* 28:2, pp. 278–302, p. 293.

236 George Lindbeck, 2002, *The Church in a Postliberal Age*, London: SCM Press, p. 232.

237 Incidentally, Lindbeck sees Islam as 'doubly' untranslatable because of the necessary Arabic idiom of the Qur'an: Lindbeck, *The Church*, p. 231.

238 Karl Barth, 2001, 'The Revelation of God as the Abolition of Religion', in John

Hick and Brian Hebblethwaite (eds), *Christianity and Other Religions: Selected Readings*, rev. edn, Oxford: Oneworld, pp. 5–18, p. 13.

239 Haddon Willmer, 2007, 'Karl Barth', in Scott and Cavanaugh, *The Blackwell Companion to Political Theology*, pp. 123–35, p. 125.

240 Willmer, 'Karl Barth', p. 125.

241 'Both the Peace of Augsburg (1555) and the Treaty of Westphalia a century later, by adopting the principle of "*cujus regio, ejus religio*" (the ruler determines the religion of his realm) made religious toleration and noninterference (on religious grounds) in the domestic affairs of other states – in other words, pluralism among states – one of the main principles of the modern international order' – Scott M. Thomas, 2005, *The Global Resurgence of Religion and the Transformation of International Relations: The Struggle for the Soul of the Twenty-First Century*, London: Palgrave-Macmillan, pp. 54–5.

242 Tom Greggs, 2008, 'Bringing Barth's Critique of Religion to the Inter-faith Table', *The Journal of Religion* 88:1, pp. 75–94, p. 85.

243 Glenn A. Chestnutt, 2010, *Challenging the Stereotype: The Theology of Karl Barth as a Resource for Inter-religious Encounter in a European Context*, Bern: Peter Lang.

244 Paul Brazier, 2005, 'Barth and Rome: A Critical Engagement with Catholic Thinkers', *The Downside Review* 123:430, pp. 137–53, p. 147.

245 See note 474 below.

246 See J. A. DiNoia, 2000, 'Religion and the Religions', in John Webster (ed.), *The Cambridge Companion to Karl Barth*, Cambridge: Cambridge University Press, pp. 243–57, and O'Mahony, 'Christianity, Interreligious Dialogue and Muslim–Christian Relations', pp. 69–70.

247 The idea of the 'anonymous Christian' was famously proposed by Karl Rahner as an inclusive theology of religions. See Karl Rahner, 1978, *Foundations of Christian Faith: An Introduction to the Idea of Christianity*, London: Darton, Longman & Todd.

248 Jürgen Moltmann, 'Dialogue or Mission?', in Hick and Hebblethwaite, *Christianity and Other Religions*, pp. 172–87, p. 186.

249 Mohammed, *Muslim–Christian Relations*, pp. 74–5.

250 Mohammed, *Muslim–Christian Relations*, p. 75.

251 *Issues in Christian–Muslim Relations: Ecumenical Considerations*, 1992, Geneva: WCC, pp. 9–14.

252 *Issues in Christian–Muslim Relations*, pp. 14–15.

253 Douglas Pratt, 2009, 'The World Council of Churches in Dialogue with Muslims: Retrospect and Prospect', *Islam and Christian–Muslim Relations* 20:1, pp. 21–42, pp. 31–4.

254 Pratt, 'World Council of Churches', p. 38.

255 'Christian Witness in a Multi-Religious World: Recommendations for Con-

duct', 2011: www.oikoumene.org/fileadmin/files/wcc-main/2011pdfs/Christian-Witness_recommendations.pdf.

256 'Christian Witness in a Multi-Religious World', p. 3.

257 John Hick and Paul Knitter (eds), 1987, *The Myth of Christian Uniqueness*, New York: Orbis Books.

258 John Hick, 1989, 'Trinity and Incarnation in the Light of Religious Pluralism', in John Hick and Edmund S. Meltzer (eds), *Three Faiths – One God: A Jewish, Christian, Muslim Encounter*, Basingstoke: Macmillan, pp. 197–210, p. 209.

259 McVey, 'The Land of Unlikeness', p. 378.

260 Sweetman, *Islam and Christian Theology, Part 1*, Vol. 2, p. 39.

261 Quoted in Dupuis, *Christianity and the Religions*, p. 377.

262 Wilfred Cantwell Smith, 1981, *Towards a World Theology: Faith and the Comparative History of Religion*, London: Macmillan.

263 Cantwell Smith, *Towards a World Theology*, p. 155.

264 Quoted in Cragg, 'Responsible to Faith', p. 38.

265 Kenneth Cragg, 1992, *Troubled By Truth: Life-Studies in Inter-Faith Concern*, Durham: Pentland Press, p. 255.

266 For a comparative study of Cragg and Cantwell Smith, see Bård Maeland, 2003, *Rewarding Encounters: Islam and the Comparative Theologies of Kenneth Cragg and Wilfred Cantwell Smith*, London: Melisende.

267 See, for example, Ipgrave, *Trinity and Interfaith Dialogue*.

268 George Lindbeck, 1984, *The Nature of Doctrine: Religion and Theology in a Postliberal Age*, Philadelphia, PA: Westminster Press, p. 6.

269 David Burrell, 1994, 'Preface', in Arnaldez, *Three Messengers for One God*, p. vii.

270 Alastair Hamilton, 1994, 'The English Interest in the Arabic-Speaking Christians', in G. A. Russell (ed.), *The 'Arabick' Interest of the Natural Philosophers in Seventeenth-Century England*, London/New York/Köln: E. J. Brill, pp. 30–4.

271 'One Tsar on earth corresponds with one God in heaven': Basil Cousins, 2004, 'Russian Orthodoxy: Contemporary Challenges in Society, Interreligious Encounters and Mission', in O'Mahony and Kirwan, *World Christianity*, pp. 308–46, p. 320.

272 Cousins, 'Russian Orthodoxy', p. 319.

273 See Adriano Garuti, 2005, *Libertà Religiosa Ed Ecumenismo: La Questione Del 'Territorio Canonico' in Russia*, Siena: Cantagalli, for an analysis of the Orthodox Church's concept of canonical territory and the impact of this on relations between the Russian Orthodox Church and the Roman Catholic Church following the latter's establishment of four Catholic dioceses in Russia in 2002.

274 Cousins, 'Russian Orthodoxy', p. 328.

275 According to the Pew Forum on Religion and Public Life, there were ap-

proximately 16 million Muslims in Russia in 2009, almost 12 per cent of the population, making it the country with the greatest number of Muslims in Europe: 'Mapping the Global Muslim Population: A Report on the Size and Distribution of the World's Muslim Population, October 2009', 2009, *The Pew Forum on Religion and Public Life*, pp. 7, pp. 21–2.

276 'Russian Orthodoxy still expends much effort in fighting off Catholicism when it should be tackling the advance of Islam': Cousins, 'Russian Orthodoxy', p. 323.

277 Basil Cousins, 2008, 'The Orthodox Church, Islam and Christian–Muslim relations in Russia', in O'Mahony and Loosley, *Christian Responses to Islam*, p. 51.

278 Jacques Waardenburg, 1998, 'European Civilisation and Islam in History', in Jørgen S. Nielsen (ed.), *The Christian–Muslim Frontier: Chaos, Clash or Dialogue?*, London: I. B. Taurus, pp. 5–23, p. 21.

279 Anthony O'Mahony, 2004, 'The Politics of Religious Renewal: Coptic Christianity in Egypt', in Anthony O'Mahony (ed.), *Eastern Christianity: Studies in Modern History, Religion and Politics*, London: Melisende, pp. 66–111.

280 Fiona McCallum, 2008, 'Muslim–Christian Relations in Egypt: Challenges for the Twenty-First Century', in O'Mahony and Loosley, *Christian Responses to Islam*, p. 81.

281 Garuti, *Libertà Religiosa ed Ecumenismo*.

282 Anthony O'Mahony, 2008, '"Between Rome and Constantinople": The Italian-Albanian Church: A Study in Eastern Catholic History and Ecclesiology', *International Journal for the Study of the Christian Church* 8:3, pp. 232–51.

283 Boris Bobrinskoy, 2008, 'God in Trinity', in Mary B. Cunningham and Elizabeth Theokritoff (eds), *The Cambridge Companion to Orthodox Christian Theology*, Cambridge: Cambridge University Press, pp. 49–62, p. 61.

284 Adrian Hastings, 1997, *The Construction of Nationhood: Ethnicity, Religion and Nationalism*, Cambridge: Cambridge University Press, p. 146.

285 Hastings, *Construction of Nationhood*, p. 202.

286 Victor Roudometof, 2008, 'Greek Orthodoxy, Territoriality, and Globality: Religious Responses and Institutional Disputes', *Sociology of Religion* 69:1, pp. 67–91. See also Stefanie Hugh-Donovan, 2010, 'Olivier Clément on Orthodox theological thought and ecclesiology in the West', *International Journal for the Study of the Christian Church* 10:2–3, pp. 116–29.

287 Charles Miller and Anthony O'Mahony, 2010, 'Guest Editorial: The Orthodox Church in Contemporary Contexts', *International Journal for the Study of the Christian Church* 10:2–3, pp. 82–9, p. 86.

288 Quoted in Nicolas Abou Mrad, 2008, 'The Witness of the Church in a Pluralistic World', in Cunningham and Theokritoff (eds), *The Cambridge Companion to Orthodox Christian Theology*, pp. 246–60, p. 256.

289 Bevans and Schroeder, *Constants in Context*, p. 288.

290 Ion Bria (ed.), 1996, *Go Forth in Peace: Orthodox Perspectives on Mission*, Geneva: WCC.

291 Jørgen S. Nielsen, 1997, 'Muslims in Europe: History Revisited or a Way Forward?', *Islam and Christian–Muslim Relations* 8:2, pp. 135–43, pp. 141–2.

292 Jørgen S. Nielsen, 2003, 'Is There an Escape from the History of Christian–Muslim Relations?', in David Thomas with Claire Amos (eds), *A Faithful Presence: Essays for Kenneth Cragg*, London: Melisende, pp. 350–61, p. 355.

293 Described and assessed in Philip Jenkins, 2002, *The Next Christendom: The Rise of Global Christianity*, Oxford: Oxford University Press.

294 Alister McGrath, 2004, 'The Future Configuration of a Global and Local Tradition', in O'Mahony and Kirwan, *World Christianity*, pp. 163–77, p. 163. It is important to acknowledge too, though, that Christian traditions from the 'south' that may be perceived to have a conservative approach to other religions can also be the source of creative and inclusive theologies. The Malaysian, Pentecostal theologian Amos Yong's 2003, *Beyond the Impasse: Toward a Pneumatological Theology of Religions*, Grand Rapids, MI: Baker Academic, is a fine example of this.

295 The work of the Gambian theologian Lamin Sanneh, himself a Christian convert from Islam, is perhaps notable in this regard. For a confident analysis of Christian–Muslim relations in West Africa encouraging a shared engagement in the public sphere, in partnership and dialogue, that accommodates the missionary demands of both faiths, see Lamin Sanneh, 1997, *The Crown and the Turban: Muslims and West African Pluralism*, Boulder, CO: Westview Press.

296 David Marshall, 2009, 'Christians, Muslims and Religious Freedom: A Christian Perspective', in Stephen R. Goodwin (ed.), *World Christianity in Muslim Encounter: Essays in Memory of David A. Kerr, Vol. 2*, London/New York: Continuum, pp. 115–27, p. 118.

297 Cragg, *The Order of the Wounded Hands*, p. 117.

298 Allen D. Hertzke and Daniel Philpott, 2000, 'Defending the Faiths', *National Interest* 61 (Fall), pp. 74–81.

299 Scott M. Thomas, 2010, 'A Globalized God: Religion's Growing Influence on International Politics', *Foreign Affairs* 89:6, pp. 93–101.

300 J. L. Hooper, 1993, 'General Introduction', in J. L. Hooper (ed.), *Religious Liberty: Catholic Struggles with Pluralism*, Louisville, KY: Westminster/John Knox Press, p. 13.

301 Defined as a 'twofold immunity: a man may not be coercively constrained to act against his conscience, nor may a man be coercively restrained or impeded from acting according to his conscience': J. C. Murray, 1993, 'The Problem of Religious Freedom', in Hooper (ed.), *Religious Liberty*, pp. 127–97, p. 142.

302 Brian J. Grim and Roger Finke, 2011, *The Price of Freedom Denied: Religious Persecution and Conflict in the Twenty-First Century*, Cambridge: Cambridge University Press, p. 185.

303 See Christopher Caldwell, 2009, *Reflections on the Revolution in Europe: Immigration, Islam and the West*, New York: Doubleday, who advocates a 'rational Islamophobia' in order to protect the liberties of a Christian heritage in Europe. For a counter-argument that resists the terminology of 'Christian Europe', recognizing the plurality of Christianity and Islam such that the removal of religious extremism is kept within the agenda of security services and not discourse about 'culture', see David Laitin, 2010, 'Rational Islamophobia', *European Journal of Sociology* 51:3, pp. 429–47.

304 In February 2006, an interesting coalition of atheist intellectuals and liberal Muslims (including Salman Rushdie, Bernard-Henri Levy, Irshad Manji and Ayaan Hirsi Ali) issued a manifesto against the 'reactionary ideology' of Islamism and its 'religious totalitarianism' as the new threat superseding Nazism and Stalinism: Salman Rushdie et al., 2006, 'Confronting Islamist Totalitarianism', *Middle East Quarterly* 13:3, pp. 82–3.

305 Exemplified by Emilio Gentile, 2000, 'The Sacralization of Politics: Definitions, Interpretations and Reflections on the Question of Secular Religion and Totalitarianism', *Totalitarian Movements and Political Religions* 1:1, pp. 18–55 and Roger Eatwell, 2004, 'Reflections on Fascism and Religion', in Leonard Weinberg and Ami Pedahzur (eds), *Religious Fundamentalism and Political Extremism*, London: Frank Cass, pp. 145–66.

306 Thomas, *The Global Resurgence of Religion*, p. 10.

307 A. I. Abushouk, 2006, 'Globalization and Muslim Identity Challenges and Prospects', *The Muslim World* 96:3, pp. 487–505, pp. 501–2.

308 Samuel Huntington, 1996, *The Clash of Civilizations and the Remaking of World Order*, London: Simon & Schuster.

309 Arnold Toynbee, 1948, *Civilization on Trial*, London: Oxford University Press, p. 209.

310 Arnold Toynbee, 1956, *An Historian's Approach to Religion*, London: Oxford University Press, p. 110.

311 Toynbee, *Civilization on Trial*, p. 237.

312 Olivier Roy, 2007, *The Failure of Political Islam*, new edn, London/New York: I. B. Tauris, p. 197.

313 H. G. Kippenberg and T. Seidensticker (eds), 2006, *The 9/11 Handbook: Annotated Translation and Interpretation of the Attackers' Spiritual Manual*, London: Equinox.

314 A phrase used by Robert Spencer in an article for FrontPageMagazine.com, quoted in Wood and Unsworth, 'Before and After Regensburg', p. 62.

315 Wood and Unsworth refute this accusation, affirming the ongoing priority of interreligious dialogue for Pope Benedict XVI and stressing the strategic significance of Michael Fitzgerald's new appointment in the pursuit of reciprocity in the Middle East: 'Before and After Regensburg', p. 67. Hugh Goddard rather sees the Regensburg Address as an 'own goal' for Christian–Muslim relations resulting

from the loss of key interfaith theological and public relations advisers from the papal staff: Hugh Goddard, 2009, 'Recent Developments in Christian–Muslim Relations', in Goodwin, *World Christianity in Muslim Encounter*, pp. 96–114, p. 102.

316 'Show me just what Muhammad brought that was new, and there you will only find things that are evil and inhuman, such as his command to spread by the sword the faith that he preached', quoted in Pope Benedict XVI, 2006, 'Faith, Reason and the University: Memories and Reflections', 12 September 2006: www.vatican.va/holy_father/benedict_xvi/speeches/2006/september/documents/hf_ben-xvi_spe_20060912_university-regensburg_en.html, p. 2.

317 Pope Benedict XVI, 'Faith, Reason and the University', p. 4.

318 Joseph Ratzinger, 2004, *Truth and Tolerance: Christian Belief and World Religions*, San Francisco, CA: Ignatius Press, p. 154.

319 Joseph Ratzinger, 2006, 'The Spiritual Roots of Europe: Yesterday, Today, and Tomorrow', in J. Ratzinger and M. Pera (eds), *Without Roots: The West, Relativism, Christianity, Islam*, New York: Basic Books, pp. 51–80, p. 78.

320 Michael Kirwan, 2004, 'Current Theological Themes in World Christianity', in O'Mahony and Kirwan, *World Christianity*, pp. 43–62, p. 46.

321 See Michael Sutton, 1997, 'John Paul II's Idea of Europe', *Religion, State and Society* 25:1, pp. 17–30.

322 Anthony O'Mahony, 2009, 'The Vatican and Europe: Political Theology and Ecclesiology in Papal Statements from Pius XII to Benedict XVI', *International Journal for the Study of the Christian Church* 9:3, pp. 177–94, p. 177.

323 O'Mahony, 'The Vatican and Europe', p. 190.

324 Kirwan, 'Current Theological Themes', p. 60. Political 'mythology' alludes to the pessimism described in Carl Schmitt's political theology. Schmitt assumed a *Freund/Feind* distinction as a basis for binding fragmentary groups into a cohesive nation. See Michael Hollerich, 2007, 'Carl Schmitt', in Scott and Cavanaugh, *The Blackwell Companion to Political Theology*, pp. 107–22.

325 George Sabra, 2006, 'Two Ways of Being a Christian in the Muslim Context of the Middle East', *Islam and Christian–Muslim Relations* 17:1, pp. 43–53.

326 Anthony O'Mahony, 2004, 'The Chaldean Catholic Church: The Politics of Church–State Relations in Modern Iraq', *The Heythrop Journal* 45:4, pp. 435–50 and 2008, 'Patriarchs and Politics: The Chaldean Catholic Church in Modern Iraq', in Anthony O'Mahony (ed), *Christianity in the Middle East: Studies in Modern History, Theology and Politics*, London: Melisende, pp. 105–42.

327 An ambiguity observed by Fiona McCallum within the Coptic Church in Egypt: 'Muslim–Christian relations in Egypt', p. 79.

328 Stanislaw Grodz, 2008, 'Christians and Muslims in West Africa', in O'Mahony and Loosley, *Christian Responses to Islam*, pp. 207–21, p. 216.

329 Grodz, 'Christians and Muslims in West Africa', p. 218.

330 "'If I am welcome only if I leave my religion at home, I cannot go, because that is who I am". Value "systems" with ideals for life and their norms for what we should and should not do are needed in the public domain, even though they can, and will, collide. Compromises cannot be discovered by the political system alone, because in the end political decisions depend on power relations whereas compromises on values need mutual understanding': Hendrik Vroom, 2008, 'Law, Muslim majority and the Implementation of Sharia in Northern Nigeria', *International Journal of Public Theology* 2:4, pp. 484–500, p. 499.

331 Rabiatu Ammah, 2007, 'Christian–Muslim Relations in Contemporary Sub-Saharan Africa', *Islam and Christian–Muslim Relations* 18:2, pp. 139–53.

332 Josiah Idowu-Fearon, 2004, 'Anglicans and Islam in Nigeria: Anglicans Encountering Difference', *Journal of Anglican Studies* 2:1, pp. 40–51.

333 Matthews A. Ojo has noted the growth in Pentecostal Christians in Nigeria and their renewed public and political discourse running counter to political Islam. The discourse is largely charged with very negative stereotyping of Muslims underscoring competition for public space. This highlights the need for a political theology that can embrace genuine plurality out of recognizably missionary claims: Matthews A. Ojo, 2007, 'Pentecostal Movements, Islam and the Contest for Public Space in Northern Nigeria', *Islam and Christian–Muslim Relations* 18:2, pp. 175–88.

334 E. Chukwudi Eza, 2008, 'Sources of Social and Political Theology: Interrogating the African Experience', *Transformation* 25:4, pp. 169–94, p. 188. See also Akintunde E. Akinade, 2009, 'Christian–Muslim Relations in Contemporary Nigeria: A Contextual Approach', in Goodwin, *World Christianity in Muslim Encounter, Vol. 2*, pp. 336–44: 'It is my contention that the present state of religious pluralism in contemporary Nigeria presents a real opportunity for celebration rather than a source for paranoia and violence. Through a dialogue of creative engagement, Christians and Muslims can create new tools for peacemaking, conflict resolution and community building. The agenda for this creative engagement must have cultural relevance, ecumenical vision, theological fidelity and existential implications' (p. 343).

335 Rocco Viviano, 2004, 'Responses of the Catholic Church to Islam in the Philippines from the Second Vatican Council to the Present-Day', in O'Mahony and Kirwan, *World Christianity*, pp. 372–415. This 'vocation' was expressed by Pope John Paul II in his visit of 1996 (pp. 387–8).

336 Rocco Viviano, 2008, 'Christian–Muslim relations in the Philippines', in O'Mahony and Loosley, *Christian Responses to Islam*, p. 137.

337 Viviano, 'Christian–Muslim relations in the Philippines', pp. 121–7.

338 Peter G. Riddell, 2004, 'Malaysian Christians and Islamisation', in O'Mahony and Kirwan, *World Christianity*, pp. 226–56, p. 253.

339 Peter G. Riddell, 2001, 'Muslims and Christians in Malaysia, Singapore and Brunei', in Anthony O'Mahony and Ataullah Siddiqui (eds), *Christians and Muslims in the Commonwealth: A Dynamic Role in the Future*, London: Altajir World

of Islam Trust, pp. 249–83, p. 283.

340 Anthony O'Mahony, 2001, 'Muslim–Christian Relations in India', in O'Mahony and Siddiqui, *Christians and Muslims in the Commonwealth*, pp. 212–48, pp. 238–9.

341 O'Mahony, 'Muslim–Christian Relations in India', p. 217.

342 Patrick Sookhdeo, 2009, *The Challenge of Islam to the Church and its Mission*, McLean, VA: Isaac Publishing, pp. 111–12. Sookhdeo here asserts the need for justice for Christians in Pakistan, mentioning also Egypt and the stand made there by the Anglican Bishop in Egypt.

343 Jan Slomp, 2009, 'Debates on Jesus and Muhammad in Europe, India and Pakistan', in Godowin, *World Christianity in Muslim Encounter, Vol. 2*, pp. 311–23, quoted anonymously on p. 321.

344 Jørgen S. Nielsen, 2010, 'Danish Cartoons and Christian–Muslim Relations in Denmark', *Exchange* 39:3, pp. 217–235.

345 Camilla Adang, 1999, 'Medieval Muslim Polemics against the Jewish Scriptures', in Jacques Waardenburg (ed.), *Muslim Perceptions of Other Religions: A Historical Survey*, New York/Oxford: Oxford University Press, pp. 143–59, p. 143.

346 Adang, 'Medieval Muslim Polemics', p. 145.

347 Gudrun Kramer, 2006, 'Anti-Semitism in the Muslim World: A Critical Review', *Die Welt des Islams* 46:3, pp. 143–276, pp. 267–70.

348 Kramer, 'Anti-Semitism in the Muslim World', p. 267.

349 Kramer, 'Anti-Semitism in the Muslim World', p. 273.

350 Hawting, *The Idea of Idolatry and the Emergence of Islam*, pp. 37–64.

351 It is the Jewish influence that seems especially pertinent and powerful in rooting Islamic identity: 'The source of this great similarity between the two cultures is the direct influence of Judaism on nascent Islam in the Arabian peninsula in the seventh century, and on the crystallization of its legal system in Babylon in the eighth century. Moreover, both religions drew from the civilizations that preceded them, while attempting to Judaize or Islamize this inheritance': H. Lazarus-Yafeh, 1984, 'Some Differences Between Judaism and Islam as Two Religions of Law', *Religion* 14:2, pp. 175–91, p. 177.

352 Fred Donner, 2010, *Muhammad and the Believers: At the Origins of Islam*, Cambridge, MA: The Belknap Press, p. 87.

353 T. J. Winter, 1999, 'The Last Trump Card: Islam and the Supercession of Other Faiths', *Studies in Interreligious Dialogue* 9:2, pp. 133–55, pp. 141–51.

354 Winter, 'The Last Trump Card', p. 141.

355 T. J. Winter, 2009, 'Jesus and Muhammad: New Convergences', *The Muslim World* 99:1, pp. 21–38.

356 Douglas Pratt, 2010, 'Muslim–Jewish Relations: Some Islamic Paradigms', *Islam and Christian Muslim Relations* 21:1, pp. 11–21.

357 Jacques Waardenburg, 2004, 'Christians, Muslims, Jews, and their Religions',

Islam and Christian–Muslim Relations 15:1, pp. 13–33.

358 See in particular Leonard Marsh, 2005, 'Palestinian Christianity – A Study in Religion and Politics', *International Journal for the Study of the Christian Church* 5:2, pp. 147–66; Anthony O'Mahony, 2005, 'Christianity and Jerusalem: Religion, Politics and Theology in the Modern Holy Land', *International Journal for the Study of the Christian Church* 5:2, pp. 86–102 and 2005, 'The Vatican, Jerusalem, the State of Israel, and Christianity in the Holy Land', *International Journal for the Study of the Christian Church* 5:2, pp. 123–46.

359 Watson, 'Christianity in the Middle East', pp. 211–14. The 'clash of civilizations' theory as classically proposed by the late Samuel Huntington (1996, *The Clash of Civilizations*) argued that there was an inevitable and inexorable confrontation between the cultures of the world, notably the West and Islam.

360 John Watson suggests there is a looming 'new apocalypse' for the Orthodox Christians in the Middle East: Watson, 'Christianity in the Middle East', pp. 224–5.

361 Jerome Murphy O'Connor describes the struggles between Christian traditions over holy places as a 'cacophony of warring chants': quoted in Watson, 'Christianity in the Middle East', p. 216.

362 Robert M. Johnson, 2010, 'The Jewish–Muslim Encounter in the Holy Land: The Theological and Political Implications for Christianity', in Anthony O'Mahony (ed.), *Christianity and Jerusalem: Studies in Modern Theology and Politics in the Holy Land*, Leominster: Gracewing, pp. 183–215, p. 197.

363 Anthony O'Mahony, 2008, 'Christianity and Islam: Between History and Theological Encounter', in O'Mahony and Loosley, *Christian Responses to Islam*, pp. 1–4, pp. 2–3.

364 Anthony O'Mahony, 2004, 'The Vatican, Jerusalem and the Palestinian Christians', in O'Mahony and Kirwan, *World Christianity*, pp. 416–48, p. 432.

365 Charles H. Miller, 2010, 'Jerusalem, the Holy City in Selected Documents of the Holy See and in Writings of Michel Sabba, Latin Patriarch of Jerusalem', in O'Mahony, *Christianity and Jerusalem*, pp. 216–44, p. 226: the 2009 invitation to the Synod of the Middle East accords with the formative pattern of papal concern for the 'Mother Church' of Christendom and its holy places manifest in documents of the Holy See.

366 Anthony O'Mahony, 2008, 'Introduction', in O'Mahony, *Christianity in the Middle East*, pp. 9–16, p. 16.

367 Johnson, 'Jewish–Muslim Encounter', p. 209.

368 Miller, 'Jerusalem, the Holy City', Appendix, p. 238.

369 Quoted in Bård Maeland, 2010, 'The Plural Significance of Jerusalem as Seen *Ex Infra*: Kenneth Cragg on the Interrelated Jerusalem', in O'Mahony, *Christianity and Jerusalem*, pp. 255–64, p. 261.

370 Kenneth Cragg, 1982, *This Year in Jerusalem: Israel in Experience*, London: Darton, Longman & Todd, pp. 125–6.

371 Michael Nazir-Ali, 2006, 'Jerusalem: The Christian Perspective', *Evangelical*

Quarterly 78:3, pp. 203–8, p. 208.

372 Cragg, *This Year in Jerusalem*, p. 50.

373 Kenneth Cragg, 1994, *Faith and Life Negotiate: A Christian Story-Study*, Norwich: Canterbury Press, pp. 154–78.

374 Cragg, *Faith and Life Negotiate*, p. 177.

375 Maeland, 'The Plural Significance of Jerusalem', pp. 251–8.

376 See Michael Marten, 2010, 'Indigenization and Contextualization – the Example of Anglican and Presbyterian Churches in the Holy Land', in O'Mahony, *Christianity and Jerusalem*, pp. 115–37; Thomas Hummel, 2003, 'Between Eastern and Western Christendom: The Anglican Presence in Jerusalem', in Anthony O'Mahony (ed.), *The Christian Communities of Jerusalem and the Holy Land*, Cardiff: University of Wales Press, pp. 147–70.

377 Marten, 'Indigenization and Contextualization', p. 129.

378 'Profile: Archbishop John Sentamu', *BBC News*: http://news.bbc.co.uk/1/hi/uk/4102960.stm.

379 Pratt, 'Muslim–Jewish Relations', p. 11.

380 For two thorough, critical analyses of Christian Zionism in historical context, see Colin Chapman, 2002, *Whose Promised Land?*, rev. edn, Oxford: Lion and Stephen Sizer, 2007, *Zion's Christian Soldiers? The Bible, Israel and the Church*, Leicester: InterVarsity Press. Christian Zionism is particularly prevalent in evangelical circles and it is from within evangelicalism that these two authors write their critiques.

381 This is now known as the Church's Ministry Among Jewish People, 'CMJ'.

382 Marten, 'Indigenization and Contextualization', pp. 118–19.

383 Miller, 'Jerusalem, the Holy City', Appendix, pp. 238–44.

384 Humuyan Ansari, 2005, 'Attitudes to Jihad, Martyrdom and Terrorism among British Muslims', in Abbas, *Muslim Britain:*, pp. 144–63; S. Sayyid, 2003, 'Muslims in Britain: Towards a Political Agenda', in Seddon, Hussain and Malik, *British Muslims*, pp. 87–94. Bemoaning the lack of any coherent British Muslim political agenda, the latter essay highlights the critique of Zionism as the one, unifying cause for Muslims (p. 91).

385 Muzaffar Iqbal, 2001, 'Islam and the West in the Emerging World Order', in Zafar Ishaq Ansari and John L. Esposito (eds), *Muslims and the West: Encounter and Dialogue*, Islamabad: Islamic Research Institute, pp. 232–73, p. 247.

386 Iqbal, 'Islam and the West', p. 271.

387 For an analysis of the ways Christian values may be informing British foreign policy, see the collection of essays in Timothy Blewitt, Adrian Hyde-Price and Wyn Rees (eds), 2008, *British Foreign Policy and the Anglican Church: Christian Engagement with the Contemporary World*, Aldershot: Ashgate.

388 Laura C. Robson, 2010, 'Palestinian Liberation Theology, Muslim–Christian Relations and the Arab–Israeli Conflict', *Islam and Christian–Muslim Relations* 21:1, pp. 39–50.

389 'Palestine/Israel, Resolution 25', 1987, *Anglican Consultative Council – ACC7*: www.anglicancommunion.org/communion/acc/meetings/acc7/resolutions.cfm#s25.

390 Marcus Braybrooke, 1990, *Time to Meet: Towards a Deeper Relationship between Jews and Christians*, London: SCM Press; Richard Harries, 2003, *After the Evil: Christianity and Judaism in the Shadow of the Holocaust*, Oxford: Oxford University Press.

391 Daniel R. Langton, 2006, 'Relations Between Christians and Jews, 1914–2000', in Hugh McLeod (ed.), *The Cambridge History of Christianity: Vol. 9, World Christianities c.1914–c.2000*, Cambridge: Cambridge University Press, pp. 483–93, p. 493.

392 *Sharing One Hope? The Church of England and Christian–Jewish Relations: A Contribution to a Continuing Debate*, 2001, London: Church House Publishing.

393 *Communique of the Anglican Jewish Commission of the Archbishop of Canterbury and the Chief Rabbinate of Israel*, 23 July 2008: www. google.co.uk/url?sa=t&rct=j&q=&esrc=s&source=web&cd=4&ved=-0CEEQFjAD&url=http%3A%2F%2Fwww.fodip.org%2Farticles%2FAnglican%-2520Commission%2520communique.doc&ei=Ph9kUZTzC4aD4AShxYA4&us-g=AFQjCNHuP4tCEd0–UuC4BaFeoupZKpazQQ&bvm=bv.44990110,d.d2k.

394 *Sharing One Hope?*, p. 20.

395 Two contrasting Anglican positions are evident in the work of Richard Harries and Kenneth Cragg. Richard Harries argues for a dual covenant that would negate the need for evangelism of the Jews: Harries, *After the Evil*. Kenneth Cragg seeks to establish a 'Christian Judaica' that is responsive and responsible to its Jewish heritage yet faithful to 'the mind of their own Scripture and the ground of their own genesis in Christ' in bringing a gospel challenge to Judaism: Cragg, *Faith and Life Negotiate*, pp. 179–203, p. 184.

396 Rowan Williams, 1999, *Sergeii Bulgakov: Towards a Russian Political Theology*, Edinburgh: T. & T. Clark, p. 300.

397 *A Common Word between Us and You*, 2007: www.acommonword.com/index.php?lang=en&page=option1. In October 2007, 138 Muslim scholars and religious leaders wrote an open letter to Christian leaders, worldwide, entitled *A Common Word between Us and You*. This remarkable and unprecedented letter proposed a shared basis for dialogue and cooperation between Muslims and Christians; that is, a theological rationale was proposed that could be foundational for the goodwill and collaboration between the two faiths: love of God and love of neighbour.

398 See *The Guardian* newspaper's coverage of the phenomenon of conversions to Christianity among the refugee community: Nazeen Parveen, 2016: www. theguardian.com/world/2016/jul/18/this-is-what-im-meant-to-be-doing-the-vicar-welcoming-muslims-to-church?CMP=Share_iOSApp_Other.

399 The Marrakech Declaration, 2016: http://marrakeshdeclaration.org/about.html.

400 For an analysis of the development away from this characterization of Jews in the liturgy of the Church of England Prayer Book, see Harries, *After the Evil*.

401 On the significance of the threat of the 'Turk' in framing the context of Reformation across Europe, see MacCulloch, *Reformation*, pp. 53–7 and 550–5.

402 Quoted in Nabil Matar, 1997, 'Muslims in Seventeenth-Century England', *Journal of Islamic Studies* 8:1, pp. 63–82, pp. 63–4.

403 Bosworth, 'The Study of Islam in British Scholarship', pp. 46–7.

404 Matar, 'Muslims in Seventeenth-Century England'.

405 Nabil Matar, 1998, *Islam in Britain 1558–1685*, Cambridge: Cambridge University Press, pp. 21–49.

406 Matar, 'Muslims in Seventeenth-Century England', p. 82.

407 Nabil Matar, 1994, '"Turning Turk": Conversion to Islam in English Renaissance Thought', *Durham University Journal* 86, pp. 33–43, p. 33.

408 Matar, *Islam in Britain 1558–1685*, pp. 50–72.

409 Ansari, *The Infidel Within*.

410 Nabil Matar, 1991, 'John Locke and the "Turbanned Nations"', *Journal of Islamic Studies* 2:1, pp. 67–77.

411 Matar, 'John Locke', p. 72.

412 Matar, 'John Locke', p. 74.

413 The belief that the Second Coming of Jesus would be heralded by the return of Jews to the homeland of Israel and the mass conversion of Jews to Christianity.

414 Nabil Matar, 1985, 'The Idea of the Restoration of the Jews in English Protestant Thought: Between the Reformation and 1660', *Durham University Journal* 78, pp. 23–35, 1985; 'The Idea of the Restoration of the Jews in English Protestant Thought, 1661–1701', *Harvard Theological Review* 78:1–2, pp. 115–48; 1988, 'The Controversy over the Restoration of the Jews in English Protestant Thought: 1701–1753', *Durham University Journal* 80, pp. 241–56; 1990, 'The Controversy over the Restoration of the Jews: From 1754 until the London Society for Promoting Christianity Among Jews', *Durham University Journal* 87, pp. 29–44.

415 Samir Khalaf, 1997, 'Protestant Images of Islam: Disparaging Stereotypes Reconfirmed', *Islam and Christian–Muslim Relations* 8:2, pp. 211–29, p. 215.

416 Shereen Khairallah, 1988, 'Arabic Studies in Europe with an Accent on England', *Theological Review* 9:1, pp. 6–27.

417 Khairallah, 'Arabic Studies in Europe', p. 12.

418 Khairallah, 'Arabic Studies in Europe', p. 13.

419 Bernard Lewis, 1941, *British Contributions to Arabic Studies*, London: Longmans, Green & Co., p. 12.

420 Nielsen, 'Is There an Escape from the History of Christian–Muslim Relations?', p. 351.

421 Quoted from *The True Nature of Imposture Fully Displayed in the Life of*

Mahomet. With a Discourse Annexed for the Vindication of Christianity from this Charge. Offered to the Consideration of the Deists of the Present Age (1697), in Bosworth, 'The Study of Islam', p. 54.

422 See G. J. Toomer, 1996, *Eastern Wisedome and Learning: The Study of Arabic in Seventeenth-Century England*, Oxford: Clarendon Press.

423 Kenneth Cragg, 1969, 'The Anglican Church', in A. J. Arberry (ed.), *Religion in the Middle East: Three Religions in Concord and Conflict*, Cambridge: Cambridge University Press, pp. 570–95, p. 573.

424 Khalaf, 'Protestant Images of Islam', p. 211.

425 Clinton Bennett, 1992, *Victorian Images of Islam*, London: Grey Seal Books, pp. 28–9.

426 W. R. W. Stephens, 1877, *Christianity and Islam: The Bible and the Koran*, London: Richard Bentley & Son, p. 168.

427 Quoted in Ansari, 'The Infidel Within', p. 61.

428 Ansari, 'The Infidel Within', p. 61.

429 Ansari, 'The Infidel Within', p. 61.

430 Jane Smith, 1997, 'Some Contemporary Protestant Theological Reflections on Pluralism: Implications for Christian–Muslim Understanding', *Islam and Christian–Muslim Relations* 8:1, pp. 67–83, p. 68.

431 See Avril Ann Powell, 1993, *Muslims and Missionaries in Pre-Mutiny India*, Richmond: Curzon Press.

432 Michael T. Shelley, 1999, 'Temple Gairdner of Cairo Revisited', *Islam and Christian–Muslim Relations* 10:3, pp. 261–78.

433 C. E. Padwick, 1961, *Temple Gairdner of Cairo*, London: SPCK; 1961, *Muslim Devotions: A Study of Prayer-Manuals in Common Use*, London: SPCK. See also Jane Smith, 1998, 'Christian Missionary Views of Islam in the Nineteenth and Twentieth Centuries', *Islam and Christian–Muslim Relations* 9:3, pp. 357–73 and Catriona Laing, 2012, 'Print, Prayer and Presence: Constance Padwick's Model for Christian Encounter with Islam', unpublished PhD thesis, University of Cambridge.

434 Joan Lockwood O'Donovan, 2004, 'The Church of England and the Anglican Communion: A Timely Engagement with the National Church Tradition?', *Scottish Journal of Theology* 57:3, pp. 313–37, p. 325.

435 It is beyond the scope of this study to assess the legitimacy of the Anglican triad of Scripture, reason and tradition, though worth noting Lesslie Newbigin's Barthian critique of the distinct nature of these sources in Lesslie Newbigin, 1999, *The Gospel in a Pluralist Society*, London: SPCK, pp. 52–65. For Newbigin, there has been a split between faith and reason, dating back to Aquinas and responsible for modernity's 'classical distinction between theory and practice', which operates to the detriment of embodied, local witness: D. Le Roy Stults, 2009, *Grasping Truth and Reality: Lesslie Newbigin's Theology of Mission to the Western World*, Cambridge: James Clarke, p. 131.

436 Michael Ipgrave, 2008, 'Understanding, Affirmation, Sharing: *Nostra Aetate* and an Anglican Approach to Inter-Faith Relations', *Journal of Ecumenical Studies* 43:1, pp. 1–16, p. 2. For a comparative study of ecclesial accounts of relations with Islam within the Catholic Church, see Unsworth, 'Louis Massignon, The Holy See', pp. 299–316.

437 'Encyclical Letter, *Lambeth Conference, 1897*', 1991, in G. R. Evans and J. Robert Wright (eds), *The Anglican Tradition: A Handbook of Sources*, London: SPCK, p. 360.

438 D. J. Bosch, 1991, *Transforming Mission: Paradigm Shifts in Theology of Mission*, Maryknoll, NY: Orbis Books, p. 338.

439 Bosch, *Transforming Mission*, p. 336.

440 Bosch, *Transforming Mission*, pp. 334–41. Bosch identifies Edinburgh 1910 as the source of the rebirthed ecumenical movement. The challenges to Enlightenment optimism of two world wars have accelerated the cause of unity that has been embodied in the dichotomy of unity and mission at the inception of the World Council of Churches in 1948 (pp. 457–61).

441 Padwick, *Temple Gairdner of Cairo*, p. 198.

442 Temple Gairdner, 1910, *Edinburgh 1910: An Account and Interpretation of the World Missionary Conference*, Edinburgh: Oliphant, pp. 128–9.

443 'Encyclical Letter, *Lambeth Conference, 1930*', in Evans and Wright, p. 389.

444 'Encyclical Letter, *Lambeth Conference, 1930*', p. 391.

445 For two classic, theological accounts of Marxism, see Nicholas Lash, 1981, *Matter of Hope: Theologian's Reflections on the Thoughts of Karl Marx*, London: Darton, Longman & Todd, and Denys Turner, 1968, *On the Philosophy of Karl Marx*, Dublin: Sceptre Publishers.

446 For extracts of Lambeth Conference resolutions on interfaith matters to 1988, see Michael Ingham, 1997, *Mansions of the Spirit: The Gospel in a Multi-Faith World*, Toronto: Anglican Book Centre, pp. 141–3.

447 Ipgrave, 'Understanding, Affirmation, Sharing', p. 2. Michael Ipgrave was the Secretary to the Churches' Commission on Inter Faith Relations and Inter Faith Relations Adviser for the Archbishops' Council (Church of England) from 1999 to 2004. This post, employed by the General Synod of the Church of England, was initiated in 1992. Christopher Lamb was the first such adviser, from 1992 to 1999. The post was reconfigured when Guy Wilkinson took up his position in 2005. Wilkinson was appointed the National Inter Faith Relations Adviser and Secretary for Inter Faith Relations to the Archbishop of Canterbury. The significance of this shift is that the role is now positioned within Lambeth Palace, accountable and responsive to the Archbishop of Canterbury in his pivotal role within the Anglican Communion. This arguably reflects a growing recognition of the global sensitivities of the interreligious questions. Guy Wilkinson resigned from his post in 2010. His successor, Toby Howarth, was appointed in May 2011. As a former employee of the celebrated evangelical scholar John Stott, Howarth

represents a tradition that would maintain moves to keep evangelism and dialogue as combined responsibilities in the interreligious encounter. In 2015, he was appointed Bishop of Bradford and succeeded in his post by Mark Poulson, another evangelical parish priest.

448 'Jews, Christians and Muslims: The Way of Dialogue', 1988, Appendix 6 in *The Truth Shall Make You Free: The Lambeth Conference 1988: The Reports, Resolutions and Pastoral Letters from the Bishops*, London: Anglican Consultative Council, pp. 299–308, p. 299

449 'The Way of Dialogue', p. 299.

450 Ipgrave, 'Understanding, Affirmation, Sharing'.

451 Hastings, *A Concise Guide, Volume One*, p. 198.

452 Ipgrave, 'Understanding, Affirmation, Sharing', p. 6.

453 'Nostra aetate 3', 1966, in Abbott, *The Documents of Vatican II*, p. 663.

454 'Lumen Gentium 16', *The Documents of Vatican II*, p. 35.

455 Unsworth, 'The Vatican, Islam and Muslim–Christian Relations', p. 61.

456 O'Mahony, 'Catholic Theological Perspectives on Islam at the Second Vatican Council', p. 392.

457 Galatians 3.7 in this vein refers to those 'who believe' as 'children of Abraham'.

458 Knowles, 'The Galatian Test: Is Islam an Abrahamic Religion?', pp. 318–21.

459 'In Britain, Christian–Muslim relations cannot be isolated from a context of religious diversity, which encompasses both the oldest religious minority – the Jews – and Sikh and Hindu communities formed since the Second World War, part of that larger flow of migrants from former British colonies invited to fill the labour shortages ... Much of the institutionalisation of Christian–Muslim relations is part of this larger reality': Philip Lewis, 2001, 'Christian–Muslim Relations in Britain: Between the Local and the Global', in O'Mahony and Siddiqui, *Christians and Muslims in the Commonwealth*, pp. 182–97, p. 182.

460 Anil Bhanot, 2007, *The Advancement of Dharma: A Discussion Paper for Faith Leaders*, London: Hindu Council UK, p. 10.

461 For a Catholic reflection of the Abrahamic faiths motif that shuns the reductionism of a 'common core' theology, see Arnaldez, *Three Messengers for One God*. For an alternative advocacy of a complementary and unitary core Abrahamic theology, see Kuschel, *Abraham*.

462 For an annotated commentary of 'The Way of Dialogue' informed by contemporaneous notes of discussions and the records of the principal drafter, Bert Breiner, I am indebted to Lucinda Mosher's unpublished historical-critical analysis of 1997 for the General Theological Seminary, New York: Lucinda Mosher, 1997, '"Christ and People of Other Faiths" and "Jews, Christians and Muslims: The Way of Dialogue," the Statements on Interfaith Relations of The Anglican Communion prepared by The Dogmatic and Pastoral Concerns Section, Lambeth Conference 1988'.

463 Ipgrave, 'Understanding, Affirmation, Sharing', p. 7. This 'affective' identification with the faith of the author, as Ipgrave points out, was famously described in Max Warren's introduction to Bishop Kenneth Cragg's 1959 *Sandals at the Mosque: Christian Presence amid Islam* (London: SCM Press), a part of Warren's 'Christian Presence' series: 'Our first task in approaching another people, another culture, another religion, is to take off our shoes, for the place where we are approaching is holy. Else we may find ourselves treading on men's dreams' (p. 9).

464 For an account of Temple Gairdner's own influence on the work of Bishop Kenneth Cragg, see Christopher Lamb, 1997, *The Call to Retrieval: Kenneth Cragg's Christian Vocation to Islam*, London: Grey Seal, and 2003, 'Kenneth Cragg's Understanding of Christian Mission to Islam', in Thomas with Amos, *A Faithful Presence*, pp. 121–49.

465 Graham Kings, 2000, 'Mission and the Meeting of Faiths: The Theologies of Max Warren and John V. Taylor', in K. Ward and B. Stanley (eds), *The Church Mission Society and World Christianity, 1799–1999*, Grand Rapids, MI/Cambridge: Eerdmans, pp. 285–318.

466 'The Way of Dialogue' §8, pp. 300–1.

467 'The Way of Dialogue' §9, p. 301.

468 'The Way of Dialogue' §11, p. 302.

469 'The Way of Dialogue' §19, pp. 303–4.

470 Mosher, 'Christ and People of Other Faiths', p. 14. Michael Nazir-Ali (b. 1947) was born in Pakistan, son of a father who had converted from Islam, and became Bishop of Raiwind in 1984. Following threats to his life, Archbishop Robert Runcie invited him to Lambeth to assist him in his work, taking a significant role in the planning for the 1988 Lambeth Conference before becoming General Secretary of the Church Missionary Society. In 1994 he became the Bishop of Rochester until his resignation in September 2009.

471 Mosher, 'Christ and People of Other Faiths', p. 15.

472 'The Way of Dialogue' §33 *and* §28 , pp. 305–6.

473 *Towards a Theology for Inter-Faith Dialogue*, 1984, Leominster: Orphans Press; hereafter designated '*TTID*'.

474 Exclusivism, inclusivism, pluralism. This typology is typically associated with Alan Race, 1983, *Christians and Religious Pluralism*, London: SCM Press.

475 *TTID*, pp. 7–10. It is perhaps noticeable that Alan Race, an exponent of pluralist theologies of religion, was a member of the working group that produced *TTID*, as was the Methodist pluralist, Kenneth Cracknell.

476 *TTID*, pp. 20–1.

477 For a brief discussion of the Eastern Orthodox challenge to Latin Christian theologies of religions, see Dupuis, *Christianity and the Religions*, pp. 178–82. For two classic Eastern Orthodox texts on the understanding of God in *perichoresis*, see Vladimir Lossky, 1963, *The Vision of God*, London: The Faith Press, and 1957, *The Mystical Theology of the Eastern Church*, Cambridge: James Clarke.

478 *TTID*, 1986, 2nd edn, London: Church House Publishing.

479 Michael Nazir-Ali, 1986, 'That which is not to be Found but which Finds us', in *TTID*, 2nd edn, London: Church House Publishing, p. 47.

480 *TTID*, 2nd edn, p. 20.

481 Nazir-Ali, 'That which is not to be Found', p. 48.

482 C. J. H. Wright, 1984, 'Interfaith Dialogue', *Anvil* 1:3, pp. 231–58, p. 256.

483 Wright, 'Interfaith Dialogue', p. 257.

484 Christopher Lamb, 1984, 'Interfaith Dialogue', *Anvil* 1:3, pp. 259–60, p. 259. Christopher Lamb was the first Secretary to the Churches' Commission on Inter Faith Relations and Inter Faith Relations Adviser for the Archbishop's Council (Church of England) from 1992 to 1999. Lamb served with the Anglican Church Missionary Society in Lahore, Pakistan for six years and his 1997 *The Call to Retrieval* is probably the most authoritative account of Cragg's engagement with Islam.

485 'Extracts from "Bonds of Affection"', 1986, in *TTID*, 2nd edn, London: Church House Publishing, p. 39.

486 *TTID*, 2nd edn, pp. 5–6.

487 Roger Hooker and Christopher Lamb, 1986, *Love the Stranger: Ministry in Multi-Faith Areas*, London: SPCK.

488 Hooker and Lamb, *Love the Stranger*, p. 47.

489 Hooker and Lamb, *Love the Stranger*, p. 12.

490 Hooker and Lamb, *Love the Stranger*, p. 35.

491 'What is the controlling image of that which is great, and good and desirable, for men and for women and for nations? There is no avoiding religious language and religious issues here': Hooker and Lamb, *Love the Stranger*, p. 117.

492 Ipgrave, 'Understanding, Affirmation, Sharing', pp. 1–16, p. 4.

493 *The Official Report of the Lambeth Conference 1998*, 1999, Harrisburg, PA: Morehouse, pp. 268–327.

494 *Official Report of the Lambeth Conference 1998*, p. 273.

495 Christopher Lamb quotes Cragg stating that 'Hospitality' is 'surely the closest of all analogies to the meaning of the Gospel' as the key to understanding Kenneth Cragg's Christian vocation to Islam: Lamb, *The Call to Retrieval*, p. 102. Kenneth Cragg saw the Christian mission to Islam as 'conceived in terms of residence, hospitality, embassy and retrieval' (p. 114).

496 Michael Nazir-Ali, 1999, 'Embassy, Hospitality and Dialogue: Christians and People of Other Faiths', in *Official Report of the Lambeth Conference 1998*, p. 312.

497 Nazir-Ali, 'Embassy, Hospitality and Dialogue', p. 312.

498 Nazir-Ali, 'Embassy, Hospitality and Dialogue', p. 315.

499 *Communities and Buildings: Church of England Premises and Other Faiths.*

A Report prepared for the General Synod of the Church of England by the Board of Mission's Inter-Faith Consultative Group, 1996, London: Church House Publishing, p. 43.

500 *Communities and Buildings*, p. 54.

501 Chad F. Emmett, 2009, 'The Siting of Churches and Mosques as an Indicator of Christian–Muslim Relations', *Islam and Christian–Muslim Relations* 20:4, pp. 451–76.

502 Ipgrave, 'Understanding, Affirmation, Sharing', pp. 4–5.

503 D'Costa, 'Hermeneutics and the Second Vatican Council's Teachings', pp. 277–90

504 See Christian W. Troll, 2011, 'Catholicism and Islam', in D'Costa (ed.), *The Catholic Church and the World Religions*, pp. 71–105.

505 *TTID*, 2nd edn, p. 19.

506 *The Mystery of Salvation*, 1995, London: Church House Publishing, pp. 40–1. See also the excerpt in Andrew Wingate, 'Salvation and Other Faiths – An Anglican Perspective', in Andrew Wingate, Kevin Ward, Carrie Pemberton and Wilson Sitshebo (eds), 1998, *Anglicanism: A Global Communion*, London: Mowbray.

507 Martin Davie, 2009, *A Church of England Approach to the Unique Significance of Jesus Christ*, Oxford: Church Mission Society.

508 *Sharing the Gospel of Salvation*, 2010, London: Church House Publishing, Foreword.

509 *Sharing the Gospel of Salvation*, p. 1.

510 From the Foreword to *Sharing the Gospel of Salvation*.

511 *Generous Love: The Truth of the Gospel and the Call to Dialogue*. A report from the Anglican Communion Network for Inter Faith Concerns, 2008, www.presenceandengagement.org.uk/generous-love.

512 *Generous Love*, from the Foreword by Rowan Williams, p. v.

513 In assessing the immediate context to *Generous Love* I am indebted to Michael Ipgrave, who has kindly conveyed the influences (textual, theological and political), informing the drafting of the document in a conversation dated 29 March 2010. It is worth noting, in the light of subsequent analysis, that Ipgrave's doctoral research reflected on the significance of the doctrine of the trinity to the earliest Christian–Muslim encounters. See Ipgrave, *Trinity and Inter Faith Dialogue*.

514 Jacques Dupuis expresses his 'disillusionment and dissatisfaction' with a perceived hardening of position towards other religions within conciliar documents in the 40 years since Vatican II, hoping that some of the ambiguities of *Nostra aetate* would have led to a more pluralist assessment of God's revelation: Dupuis, *Christianity and the Religions*, p. 66.

515 Gavin D'Costa (ed.), 1990, *Christian Uniqueness Reconsidered: The Myth of a Pluralistic Theology of Religions*, Maryknoll, NY: Orbis Books. Significantly, this

collection contains essays by Rowan Williams and John Milbank that contradict the pluralism of John Hick and argue for a more ecclesio-centric vision of religion.

516 *Generous Love*, from the Foreword by Rowan Williams, p. v.

517 *Generous Love*, p. 1.

518 *Generous Love*, p. 1.

519 *Guidelines for Inter Faith Encounter.*

520 For Michael Ipgrave, this is about 'setting interfaith within the language and context of mission: mission understood in an inclusive sense': quoting from a conversation with Michael Ipgrave dated 29 March 2010.

521 Mosher, 'Christ and People of Other Faiths', p. 6.

522 *Generous Love*, p. 15.

523 *The Church of the Triune God: The Cyprus Statement Agreed by the International Commission for Anglican–Orthodox Theological Dialogue*, 2006, London: The Anglican Communion Office, Section II.5.

524 Mosher, 'Christ and People of Other Faiths', p. 6.

525 John Zizioulas, 1985, *Being as Communion*, London: Darton, Longman & Todd, provides an influential counterpoint to Russian Orthodox eucharistic ecclesiology from within the Greek Orthodox tradition.

526 *Generous Love*, pp. 3–4.

527 A creative analogy is made here between the theology of the Church of England and English common law 'with its appeal to precedents at the same time as its openness to new applications in new cases': *Generous Love*, note 10, p. 17.

528 The key text referenced is D. F. Ford and C. C. Pecknold (eds), 2006, *A Handbook for Scriptural Reasoning*, Oxford: Blackwell.

529 See Michael Ipgrave, 2011, 'The Use of Scripture in *Generous Love*', in David Marshall (ed.) *Communicating the Word: Revelation, Translation, and Interpretation in Christianity and Islam*, Washington DC: Georgetown University Press, pp. 142–62.

530 *Generous Love*, quoted on p. 5.

531 *Generous Love*, pp. 13–14.

532 *Generous Love*, p. 13.

533 Michael Barnes, 2003, *Theology and the Dialogue of Religions*, Cambridge: Cambridge University Press, p. 192.

534 Clare Amos was, from 2001 to 2011, the Director of Theological Studies for the Anglican Communion, and Coordinator for the Network for Inter-faith Concerns for the Anglican Communion ('NIFCON') as well as part of the working party that produced *Generous Love*.

535 Jonathan Sacks, 2007, *The Home We Build Together*, London: Continuum. Sacks offers three models for religious diversity. The 'hotel' would be the picture best suited to multiculturalism, where groups are present in one place but do

not interact and have little attachment to the common place of residence. The 'country house' assumes one dominant culture that welcomes and includes the 'guests' or strangers. For Sacks, the 'home we build together' presents the third, best and most suitable aspiration for Britain's contemporary situation.

536 Christopher Lamb, speaking of Kenneth Cragg: 'The language of hospitality is always in his mind: "Are we not ourselves the guests of God in Christ?"': Lamb, 'Kenneth Cragg's Understanding of Christian Mission to Islam', p. 124.

537 Kenneth Cragg, 1984, *Muhammad and the Christian: A Question of Response*, London: Darton, Longman & Todd, p. 139.

538 *Generous Love*, p. 10.

539 Lewis, 2001, 'Christian–Muslim Relations in Britain', p. 189.

540 For a perspective on the Church of England's contribution to relations with Islam from the context of Bradford, see Philip Lewis, 1993, 'Beyond Babel: An Anglican Perspective in Bradford. The Eighth Lambeth Interfaith Lecture', *Islam and Christian–Muslim Relations* 4:1, pp. 118–38.

541 Barbara Mitchell, 2008, 'The Response of the Church of England, Islam and Muslim–Christian Relations in Contemporary Britain', in O'Mahony and Loosley, *Christian Responses to Islam*, pp. 21–37.

542 David Brown, 1976, *A New Threshold: Guidelines for the Churches in their Relations with Muslim Communities*, London: British Council of Churches.

543 Brown, *New Threshold*, Preface by T. Carlisle Patterson and Harry O. Morton, p. v.

544 Brown, *New Threshold*, p. 8.

545 Brown, *New Threshold*, p. 11.

546 Brown, *New Threshold*, pp. 13–17.

547 Brown, *New Threshold*, pp. 15–17.

548 Brown, *New Threshold*, pp. 22–5.

549 Brown, *New Threshold*, pp. 23–5.

550 Brown, *New Threshold*, p. 25.

551 Brown, *New Threshold*, pp. 26–9.

552 Michael Ipgrave, 2005, 'Anglican Approaches to Christian–Muslim Dialogue', *Journal of Anglican Studies* 3:2, pp. 219–36, p. 228.

553 Among the ongoing published 'Building Bridges' seminars are: Michael Ipgrave (ed.), 2002, *The Road Ahead: A Christian–Muslim Dialogue*, London: Church House Publishing; 2004, *Scriptures in Dialogue: Christians and Muslims studying the Bible and the Qur'an Together*, London: Church House Publishing; *Bearing the Word*; 2008, *Building a Better Bridge: Muslims, Christians, and the Common Good*, Washington DC: Georgetown University Press; 2009, *Justice and Rights: Christian and Muslim Perspectives*, Washington DC: Georgetown University Press; Michael Ipgrave and David Marshall (eds), 2011, *Humanity: Texts and Contexts. Christian and Muslim Perspectives*, Washington DC: Georgetown

University Press; Marshall, *Communicating the Word*; 2012, *Science and Religion: Christian and Muslim Perspectives*, Washington DC: Georgetown University Press.

554 *Presence and Engagement: The Churches' Task in a Multi Faith Society*, 2005, London: Church House Publishing, p. 8, commended by General Synod in July 2005.

555 *Presence and Engagement*, p. 27.

556 *Presence and Engagement*, p. 50.

557 See the Forum website for details of the aims and objectives, events and statements: www.christianmuslimforum.org.

558 'Religious Festivals and Celebrations', released by Bishop David Gillett, the then chair of the national Christian Muslim Forum and Dr Ataullah Siddiqui, then Vice Chair of the Forum: www.christianmuslimforum.org/subpage.asp?id=269.

559 The lurid headlines of the following two articles are typical of some of the fears expressed by a constituency seeking to shore up the Christian heritage of the nation: Peter Hitchens, 2008, 'A Merry Christmas Before it's Abolished', *Mail on Sunday*, 22 December 2008: www.dailymail.co.uk/debate/columnists/article-152406/A-Merry-Christmas-abolished.html, and J. Henry and V. Miller, 'School Nativity Plays Under Threat', 2007, *The Telegraph*, 2 December 2007: www.telegraph.co.uk/news/uknews/1571187/School-nativity-plays-under-threat.html.

560 *Ethical Witness?*, 2009, Christian Muslim Forum 22 June 2009: www.christianmuslimforum.org/downloads/Ethical_Guidelines_for_Witness.pdf.

561 Subsequent developments within the Roman Catholic Church confirm the conviction that both dialogue and proclamation are to be addressed. See the 1991 Vatican document *Dialogue and Proclamation*, discussed with reference to Christian–Muslim relations by Archbishop Michael Fitzgerald, 2003, '"Dialogue and Proclamation": A Reading in the Perspective of Christian–Muslim Relations', in Kendall and O'Collins, *In Many and Diverse Ways*, pp. 181–93. See also Richard Sudworth, 2015, 'Anglican Interreligious Relations in *Generous Love*: Indebted to and Moving from Vatican II', in D. Pratt, J. Hoover, J. Davies and J. Chesworth (eds), *The Character of Christian–Muslim Encounter: Essays in Honour of David Thomas*, Leiden/Boston, MA: Brill, pp. 527–43.

562 Philip Lewis, 2015, 'The Civic, Religious and Political Incorporation of British Muslims and the Role of the Anglican Church: Whose Incorporation, Which Islam?', *Journal of Anglican Studies* 13:2, pp. 189–214.

563 Samuel Wells, 2015, *A Nazareth Manifesto: Being with God*, Oxford: Wiley-Blackwell.

564 For biographical information and a theological assessment on Bishop Kenneth Cragg, see Lamb, *The Call to Retrieval*. A 'partly autobiographical' account of his life and influences is Kenneth Cragg, *Faith and Life Negotiate*. For comparative accounts of Cragg's theology, see Nicholas J. Wood, 2009, *Faiths and Faithfulness: Pluralism, Dialogue and Mission in the Work of Kenneth Cragg and Lesslie Newbigin*, Milton Keynes: Paternoster, and Maeland, *Rewarding Encounters*.

565 Kenneth Cragg, 1986, *The Call of the Minaret*, new edn, Glasgow: Collins, 1959; *Sandals at the Mosque.*

566 Christopher Brown, 2009, 'Kenneth Cragg on Shi'a Islam and Iran: An Anglican Theological Response to Political Islam', *ARAM* 20, pp. 375–91, p. 377.

567 E. Pisani, 2009, 'Bulletin d'islamologie (IV)', *Revue Thomiste* 109:3, pp. 467–96, p. 492.

568 Lamb, *Call to Retrieval*, p. 173.

569 See in particular Kenneth Cragg, 1981, 'Temple Gairdner's Legacy', *International Bulletin of Missionary Research* 5:4, pp. 164–7; 1992, 'Constance E. Padwick: Through Liturgy to Islam', in Cragg, *Troubled By Truth*, pp. 52–73.

570 Lamb, 'Kenneth Cragg's Understanding of Christian Mission to Islam', pp. 121–49, p. 122.

571 Gairdner, *Edinburgh 1910*, p. 148.

572 Gairdner, *Edinburgh 1910*, pp. 148–9.

573 Notice, too, the similarities to Louis Massignon's belief of Islam as 'foil' to the Church.

574 Temple Gairdner, 1909, *The Reproach of Islam*, London: Church Missionary Society, p. 335.

575 Gairdner, *Reproach of Islam*, p. 315.

576 Gairdner, *Reproach of Islam*, pp. 313–14.

577 Kenneth Cragg, 2004, *A Certain Sympathy of Scriptures: Biblical and Quranic*, Brighton: Sussex Academic Press, pp. 44–5.

578 Kenneth Cragg, 1968, *Christianity in World Perspective*, London: Lutterworth Press, pp. 119–20.

579 Lamb, *Call to Retrieval*, pp. 103–5.

580 Charles Gore (ed.), 1909, *Lux Mundi: A Series of Studies in the Religion of the Incarnation*, 10th edn, London: John Murray.

581 Richard J. Jones, 2003, 'Singing of God's Incarnation', in David Thomas with Amos, *A Faithful Presence*, p. 98.

582 Lamb, *Call to Retrieval*, p. 15.

583 Kenneth Cragg, 1974, 'Islam and Incarnation', in John Hick (ed.), *Truth and Dialogue: The Relationship Between World Religions*, London: Sheldon Press, pp. 126–39, p. 134.

584 Jones, 'Singing of God's Incarnation', pp. 107–8.

585 O'Mahony, 'Our Common Fidelity', p. 152.

586 Tracey Rowland, 2003, *Culture and the Thomist Tradition After Vatican II*, London/New York: Routledge.

587 Daniélou, *The Salvation of the Nations*, p. 59. See also his *God and Us.*

588 Daniélou, *Salvation of the Nations*, pp. 48–9.

589 Michael Ipgrave, 2011, 'The God who Provokes us all to Holiness', *Monastic Interreligious Dialogue*: http://themathesontrust.org/papers/christianity/DC-Ipgrave-Provokes.pdf; 2010, 'Provocation and Resonance: Sacramental Spirituality in the Context of Islam', *Campion Hall Seminars*: http://repository.berkleycenter.georgetown.edu/120711IpgraveProvocationResonanceSacramentalSpiritualityContextIslam.pdf.

590 Cragg, *Call of the Minaret*, p. ix.

591 Max Warren, 1959, 'General Introduction', in Cragg, *Sandals at the Mosque*, pp. 9–10.

592 Jacques Prévotat, 2001, 'Henri de Lubac and Jules Monchanin', in *Jules Monchanin (1895–1957): As Seen from East and West. Acts of the Colloquium Held in Lyon-Fleurie, France and in Shantivanam-Tannirpalli, India (April–July 1995), Vol. 1: Lyon-Fleurie*, Delhi: Saccidananda Ashram/ISPCK, pp. 58–71, pp. 62–3.

593 Robert Ellsberg, 1999, 'Introduction', in *Charles de Foucauld: Essential Writings*, Maryknoll, NY: Orbis Books, p. 21. See also Hughes Didier, 2008, 'Louis Massignon and Charles de Foucauld', *ARAM* 20, pp. 337–53 and Ariana Patey, 2011, 'Sanctity and Mission in the Life of Charles de Foucauld', *Studies in Church History* 47, pp. 365–75.

594 Paul F. Knitter, 1985, *No Other Name? A Critical Survey of Christian Attitudes Toward the World Religions*, Maryknoll, NY: Orbis Books.

595 Graham Kings, 2002, *Christianity Connected: Hindus, Muslims and the World in the Letters of Max Warren and Roger Hooker*, Zoetermeer: Uitgeverij Boekencentrum, p. 146. I am grateful to a conversation with Bishop Graham Kings for pointing out this categorization of Cragg, Hooker and Taylor by Paul Knitter.

596 Olivier Clément, 1989, in Mohamed Talbi and Olivier Clément, *Un respect têtu*, Paris: Nouvelle Cité, pp. 272–3. See also Stefanie Hugh-Donovan's series of studies, 2010, 'Olivier Clément on Orthodox Theological Thought and Ecclesiology in the West'; 2011, 'Ecclesial Thought and Life Trajectories: An Ecumenical Dialogue. Part 1: Olivier Clément and Thomas Merton', *One in Christ* 45:1, pp. 35–53; 2011, 'Ecclesial Thought and Life Trajectories: An Ecumenical Dialogue. Part 2: Olivier Clément and Paul Evdokimov: *Deux Passeurs*', *One in Christ* 45:2, pp. 297–311; 2011, 'An Eastern Orthodox Perspective on Europe and Catholicism. A Study in the Thought of Olivier Clément', *Journal of Eastern Christian Studies* 63:1–2, pp. 233–54. These articles draw important threads between Western and Eastern sacramentalism and locate resonances between the theologies of Merton, Evdokimov and Clément that find expression in the theological approach of Rowan Williams.

597 Clément, in *Un respect têtu*, p. 276.

598 Kenneth Cragg, 2011, 'Charles Malik and the Meaning of Lebanon: *In Media Res*', *Journal of Eastern Christian Studies* 63:1–2: pp. 251–62, p. 261.

599 Cragg, 'Charles Malik', p. 257.

600 Lamb, *Call to Retrieval*, p. 21.

601 Charles Malik, 1969, 'The Orthodox Church', in Arberry, *Religion in the Middle East*, pp. 297–346, pp. 310–11.

602 Jane Smith, 2003, 'Balancing Divergence and Convergence, or "Is God the Author of Confusion?" An Essay on Kenneth Cragg', in Thomas with Amos, *A Faithful Presence*, pp. 29–41, p. 40.

603 Kenneth Cragg, 1968, *The Privilege of Man: A Theme in Judaism, Islam and Christianity*, London: Athlone Press, p. 51.

604 Cragg, *Privilege of Man*, p. 54.

605 Kenneth Cragg, 1969, 'Constance E. Padwick 1886–1968', *The Muslim World* 59:4, pp. 29–39, p. 37.

606 Kerr, '"He Walked in the Path of the Prophets"', pp. 426–46; 2000, 'Muhammad: Prophet of Liberation – A Christian Perspective from Political Theology', *Studies in World Christianity* 6:2, pp. 139–74, and Keith Ward, 2005, 'Muhammad from a Christian perspective', in Norman Solomon, Richard Harries and Tim Winter (eds), *Abraham's Children*, London: T. & T. Clark, pp. 124–31.

607 Cragg, *Muhammad and the Christian*, p. 158.

608 Wood, *Faiths and Faithfulness*, p. 204.

609 Cragg, *A Certain Sympathy of Scriptures*, p. vii.

610 Brown, 'Kenneth Cragg on Shi'a Islam and Iran', p. 381.

611 Wood, *Faiths and Faithfulness*, p. 72.

612 Cragg, *Christianity in World Perspective*, p. 198.

613 Benjamin Myers, 2012, *Christ the Stranger: The Theology of Rowan Williams*, London: T. & T. Clark, p. 43.

614 For an important account of the earliest debates on the nature of the godhead, see Rowan Williams, 2001, *Arius: Heresy and Tradition*, 2nd edn, London: SCM Press.

615 Williams, 'Archbishop's Address at al-Azhar al-Sharif'.

616 Williams, 'Archbishop's Address at al-Azhar al-Sharif', p. 1.

617 Michael Ipgrave, 2005, 'God who is Trinity: Speaking with Muslims, Reflections on an Anglican Contribution by Archbishop Rowan Williams': www.anglicanism.org/admin/docs/ipgrave_trinity.pdf.

618 Williams, 'Archbishop's Address at al-Azhar al-Sharif', p 2.

619 Williams, 'Archbishop's Address at al-Azhar al-Sharif', p. 3.

620 Ipgrave, 'God who is Trinity', p. 6.

621 Williams, 'Archbishop's Address at al-Azhar al-Sharif', p. 2.

622 John Meyendorff, 1964, *A Study of Gregory Palamas*, Leighton Buzzard: Faith Press. See Aidan Nichols' essay on Meyendorff, in 1995, *Light from the East: Authors and Themes in Orthodox Theology*, London: Sheed & Ward, pp. 41–56, including the discussion of contemporary critiques of 'neo-Palamism' for Williams' own reservations about the Palamite proposal of the distinction between

God's substance and essence in 'energies'.

623 Ipgrave 'God who is Trinity', p. 4.

624 Ipgrave, 'God who is Trinity', p. 11, also echoing the title of his doctoral thesis published as Ipgrave, *Trinity and Interfaith Dialogue*.

625 Rowan Williams, 2011, 'Christology and Inter Religious Dialogue', *Presence of Faith Conference*, Lambeth Palace, 8 December 2011, author's transcript, pp. 1–2.

626 Williams, 'Christology and Inter Religious Dialogue', p. 2.

627 Richard Hooker, 1841, *The Works of that Learned and Judicious Divine Mr Richard Hooker in Two Volumes*, Oxford: Oxford University Press, 1841 edn, Vol. I, Book V. LV, pp. 7–8.

628 Hans Urs von Balthasar, 1986, *New Elucidations*, San Francisco, CA: Ignatius Press, p. 76.

629 Williams, 'What is Christianity?'

630 Williams, 'What is Christianity?', p. 2.

631 Williams, 'What is Christianity?', p. 8.

632 Williams, 'What is Christianity?', p. 10.

633 Aidan Nichols, 2005, *Wisdom from Above: A Primer in the Theology of Father Sergei Bulgakov*, Leominster: Gracewing, p. 199. See also J. Pain and N. Zernov (eds), 1976, *A Bulgakov Anthology*, London: SPCK, and Williams, *Sergeii Bulgakov*.

634 Rowan Williams, 2007, 'Between Politics and Metaphysics: Reflections in the Wake of Gillian Rose' and 'The Suspicion of Suspicion: Wittgenstein and Bonhoeffer', in Mike Higton (ed.), *Wrestling with Angels: Conversations in Modern Theology*, London: SCM Press, pp. 53–76 and 186–202 respectively. For an important assessment of Wittgenstein's philosophy for theological practice, warmly commended by Williams, see also Fergus Kerr, 1986, *Theology after Wittgenstein*, Oxford: Blackwell.

635 Williams, 'Suspicion of Suspicion', p. 199.

636 Gillian Rose (1947–95) was a Jewish philosopher and friend of Rowan Williams who made a deathbed conversion to the Church of England. Rowan Williams' own interest in her work is evidenced in his essay 'Between Politics and Metaphysics: Reflections in the Wake of Gillian Rose', and a testimony to their friendship is his poem '*Winterreise*: for Gillian Rose, 9 December 1995', in 2002, *The Poems of Rowan Williams*, Oxford: Perpetua Press.

637 See, for example, Rowan Williams, 2010, 'The Finality of Christ in a Plural World', 2 March 2010: http://rowanwilliams.archbishopofcanterbury.org/articles. php/585/the-finality-of-christ-in-a-pluralist-world. This lecture rejects a narrow construal of Jesus' finality in terms of the damnation of adherents of other religions in favour of Christology as a means of speaking about 'hope for the entire human family' such that it impels a 'generous desire to share' and a 'humble desire to learn'.

638 From an interview with Archbishop Rowan Williams by Richard Sudworth and Stefanie Hugh-Donovan, Lambeth Palace 6 September 2012, author's transcript.

639 Interview with Rowan Williams, author's transcript.

640 Smith, 'Balancing Divergence and Convergence', p. 40.

641 Rowan Williams, 2000, 'The Finality of Christ', in *On Christian Theology*, Oxford: Blackwell, pp. 93–106, p. 99.

642 Richard Sudworth, 2014, 'Hospitality and Embassy: The Persistent Influence of Kenneth Cragg on Anglican Theologies of Interfaith Relations', *Anglican Theological Review* 96:1, pp. 73–89. For a comparative study of Cragg and Williams in dialogue with Louis Massignon, see also Richard Sudworth, 2014, 'Responding to Islam as Priests, Mystics and Trail Blazers: Louis Massignon, Kenneth Cragg and Rowan Williams', *Logos* 55:3–4, pp. 451–72.

643 See David Thomas's assessment of this process in the work of John Hick and Mohammed Arkoun in David Thomas, 2007, 'The Past and the Future in Christian–Muslim Relations', *Islam and Christian–Muslim Relations* 18:1, pp. 33–42. Thomas argues instead for a 'respectful, agnostic, inquisitiveness' (p. 41). The plea for a creative theological convergence between Islam and Christianity is argued by the Muslim scholar Mohammed Arkoun, 1989, 'New Perspectives for a Jewish–Christian–Muslim Dialogue', *Journal of Ecumenical Studies* 26:3, pp. 523–9.

644 Rowan Williams, 2008, *A Common Word for the Common Good*: www.acommonword.com/lib/downloads/Common-Good-Canterbury-FINAL-assent-14-7-08-1.pdf. It is instructive that Rowan Williams mentions Judaism where the original *A Common Word* document omitted it: 'And for Christians and Muslims together addressing our scriptures in this way, it is essential also to take account of the place of the Jewish people and of the Hebrew scriptures in our encounter, since we both look to our origins in that history of divine revelation and action' (p. 16).

645 Williams, *Common Word for the Common Good*, p. 2; my italics.

646 Nicholas Lossky, 2010, 'Orthodoxy and the Western European Reformation Tradition: A Memoir', *International Journal for the Study of the Christian Church* 10:2–3, pp. 90–6, p. 93. In highlighting the reciprocal indebtedness of Eastern Christianity to Anglicanism, see also Nicholas Lossky, 1998, 'The Anglican Contribution to the Ecumenical Age: A Non-Anglican View', *Anglican Theological Review* 80:2, pp. 250–5; 1971, 'An Orthodox Approach to Anglicanism', *Sobornost* 6:2, pp. 78–88; 2010, 'Nicholas Lossky: An Interview', *One in Christ* 44:2, pp. 101–9. This is supremely exemplified in Lossky's authoritative account of the theology of Lancelot Andrewes: Nicolas Lossky, 1991, *Lancelot Andrewes the Preacher (1555–1626): The Origins of the Mystical Theology of the Church of England*, Oxford: Clarendon Press.

647 Lossky, 'Orthodoxy', p. 95.

648 Scott and Cavanaugh, 'Introduction', p. 2.

649 Scott and Cavanaugh, 'Introduction', p. 3.

650 Kirwan, *Political Theology*, p. 8.

651 Luke Bretherton, 2008, 'Introduction: Oliver O'Donovan's Political Theology and the Liberal Imperative', *Political Theology* 9:3, pp. 265–71, p. 269.

652 Richard Sudworth, 2013, 'Christian Responses to the Political Challenge of Islam', *Islam and Christian–Muslim Relations* 4:2, pp. 191–211.

653 For an overview of Cragg's political theology, see Brown, 'Kenneth Cragg on Shi'a Islam and Iran',: 'Cragg believes that religious faith could and should renounce all power-complex and physical militancy without abandoning political duties' (p. 390).

654 Kenneth Cragg, 1964, *The Call of the Minaret*, 2nd edn, Oxford/New York: Oxford University Press, p. 256.

655 Cragg, *Call of the Minaret*, p. 161.

656 Cragg, *Call of the Minaret*, p. 162.

657 Donner, *Muhammad and the Believers*, p. 89.

658 Cragg, *Call of the Minaret*, p. 248.

659 Cragg, *Call of the Minaret*, pp. 319–31.

660 Oliver O'Donovan, 2003, *The Desire of the Nations*, Cambridge: Cambridge University Press, pp. 82–119. The 'doctrine of the two' describes the high tradition of political theology epitomized by St Augustine that asserts the presence of two kingdoms of social rule to which God's people are simultaneously called to account: the kingdom of God's rule of love and that of the 'secular' founded on coercion. These realms are both separate yet overlapping, the challenge of political theology one of discerning the implications of the eschatological fulfilment of God's rule for the temporal rule of the secular: 'Proclaiming the unity of God's rule in Christ is the task of Christian witness; understanding the duality is the chief assistance rendered by Christian reflection' (p. 82).

661 From a critical review of *The Call of the Minaret* by the Pakistani scholar Hamidullah, quoted in Lamb, *The Call to Retrieval*, p. 86.

662 Cragg, *Christianity in World Perspective*, pp. 56–74.

663 Cragg, *Christianity in World Perspective*, p. 74.

664 This idea is a consistent theme throughout Kenneth Cragg's writings but is given particular attention in Cragg, *The Privilege of Man* (see ch. 2, '"God is, and Man is His Caliph": A Quranic View', pp. 51–75), and *A Certain Sympathy of Scriptures*.

665 Cragg, *Certain Sympathy of Scriptures*, p. 8.

666 Cragg, *Privilege of Man*, p. 40; emphasis original.

667 Cragg, *Certain Sympathy of Scriptures*, p. 38.

668 Cragg, *Certain Sympathy of Scriptures*, p. 84.

669 Cragg, *Certain Sympathy of Scriptures*, p. 59.

670 Kenneth Cragg, 1971, *The Event of the Qur'an: Islam in its Scripture*, London: Allen & Unwin, p. 73.

671 For a view that disputes Cragg's rendering of *khilāfa*, see Rémi Brague, 2007, *The Law of God: The Philosophical History of an Idea*, Chicago, IL/London: University of Chicago Press, p. 79.

672 Alister McGrath, 2008, *The Open Secret: A New Vision for Natural Theology*, Oxford: Blackwell, pp. 181–2.

673 Burrell, 'Thomas Aquinas and Islam', p. 83.

674 Anver M. Emon, 2010, *Islamic Natural Law Theories*, Oxford: Oxford University Press. See also Ramadan, *Western Muslims and the Future of Islam*, p. 13.

675 Alasdair MacIntyre, 2009, 'Intractable Moral Disagreements', in Lawrence S. Cunningham (ed.), *Intractable Disputes About the Natural Law*, Notre Dame, IN: Notre Dame University Press, pp. 1–52, pp. 32–6: 'For insofar as each enquiry is a genuinely rational enquiry, those who participate in it are bound to ask – and we who have imaginatively identified with their standpoint, at least for the moment, are also bound to ask – just how successful by their own standards their tradition has been and is at resolving the various issues that have arisen and do arise for it, issues that are problematic by its own standards and in its own terms' (p. 34). Cragg, I believe, is 'imaginatively' taking the standpoint of a serious reader of the text of the Qur'an and engaging with the issues that have and continue to arise over the utter transcendence of God in Islam.

676 Quoted in Lamb, *Call to Retrieval*, p. 125.

677 Cragg, *Muhammad and the Christian*, p. 157.

678 Cragg, *Muhammad and the Christian*, p. 159.

679 Cragg, *Muhammad and the Christian*, p. 47.

680 Winter, 'Jesus and Muhammad', pp. 22–6.

681 Kenneth Cragg, 2008, 'The Cross and Power: The Parting of the Ways', in David Emmanuel Singh (ed.), *Jesus and the Cross: Reflections of Christians from Islamic Contexts*, Eugene, OR: Wipf & Stock, pp. 33–46, p. 38.

682 Cragg, *Christianity in World Perspective*, p. 129.

683 Cragg, *Call of the Minaret*, p. 295.

684 Lamb, *Call to Retrieval*, p. 87.

685 Cragg, *The Event of the Qur'an*, p. 132.

686 David Marshall, 1999, *God, Muhammad and the Unbelievers*, Richmond: Curzon Press, pp. 196 and 193.

687 Charles Adams, 1976, 'Islamic Religious Tradition', in L. Binder (ed.), *The Study of the Middle East*, New York: Wiley, p. 39.

688 David Marshall, 2006, *Learning from How Muslims See Christianity*, Cambridge: Grove Books, p. 4.

689 Marshall, *Learning from How Muslims See Christianity*, p. 16.

690 Cragg, *Christianity in World Perspective*, p. 217.

691 See Lamb, *Call to Retrieval*, pp. 123–49, for a summary of objections to Cragg's writings, especially from Islamic critics. For Hamidullah, Cragg offers a 'sugar-coated pill' (p. 123).

692 Cragg, *Privilege of Man*, pp. 27–8.

693 Cragg, *Privilege of Man*, p. 33.

694 Kenneth Cragg, 2006, *God's Wrong is Most of All: Divine Capacity*, Brighton: Sussex Academic Press, pp. 115–16.

695 Kenneth Cragg, 2005, *The Qur'an and the West: Some Minding Between*, London: Melisende, p. 1.

696 Quoted in Kenneth Cragg, 1992, 'Isma'il al-Faruqi (1921–1986)', in Cragg, *Troubled by Truth*, pp. 127–46, p. 127.

697 Cragg, *Qur'an and the West*, p. 80.

698 Patrick Riordan, 2008, *A Grammar of the Common Good: Speaking of Globalization*, London/New York: Continuum, p. 27.

699 E. L. Mascall, *The Openness of Being*, London: Darton, Longman & Todd, p. 146.

700 Olivier Clément, in Talbi and Clément, *Un Respect têtu*, pp. 272–3.

701 Paul F. Knitter, 1985, *No Other Name? A Critical Survey of Christian Attitudes Toward the World Religions*, Maryknoll, NY: Orbis Books, p. 135.

702 Cragg, *Christianity in World Perspective*, p. 71.

703 Robert Murray, 1992, *The Cosmic Covenant: Biblical Themes of Justice, Peace and the Integrity of Creation*, London: Sheed & Ward, p. 98.

704 John Milbank, 1997, *The Word Made Strange: Theology, Language, Culture*, Oxford: Blackwell, p. 263.

705 For accounts of O'Donovan that characterize his approach as one of 'hospitality', see Luke Bretherton, 2006, *Hospitality as Holiness: Christian Witness Amid Moral Diversity*, Aldershot: Ashgate, and 2009, 'Translation, Conversation, or Hospitality? Approaches to Theological Reasons in Public Deliberation', in Nigel Biggar and Linda Hogan (eds), *Religious Voices in Public Places*, Oxford: Oxford University Press, pp. 85–109.

706 Kenneth Cragg, 1997, *Defending (the) Faith*, London: New Millennium, pp. 167–78.

707 Michael Ipgrave, 2004, '*Fidei Defensor* Revisited: Church and State in a Religiously Plural Society', in Nazila Ghanea (ed.), *The Challenge of Religious Discrimination at the Dawn of the New Millennium*, Leiden: Martinus Nijhoff, pp. 207–22, p. 220.

708 See Oliver O'Donovan, 2005, *The Ways of Judgment*, Grand Rapids, MI/ Cambridge: Eerdmans. For a debate about Oliver O'Donovan's political theology, see *Political Theology* 9:3 (2008). O'Donovan's response engages with the various nuanced critiques from Jonathan Chaplin, Nigel Biggar, John Rist, David Novak

and Robert Markus: 2008, 'Judgment, Tradition and Reason: A Response', *Political Theology* 9:3, pp. 395–414.

709 Carl Schmitt, 2007, *The Concept of the Political*, Chicago, IL: University of Chicago Press.

710 Samuel Wells, 2006, *God's Companions: Reimagining Christian Ethics*, Oxford: Blackwell.

711 Rowan Williams, 2008, 'Civil and Religious Law in England: A Religious Perspective', *Ecclesiastical Law Journal* 10:3, pp. 262–82.

712 Rowan Williams, 2005, 'Religion, Culture, Diversity and Tolerance – Shaping the New Europe', Address at the European Policy Centre, Brussels, 7 November 2005: www.archbishopofcanterbury.org/articles.php/1179/religion-culture-diversity-and-tolerance-shaping-the-new-europe-address-at-the-european-policy-centr, p. 3. See also 2004, 'States Need to be Comfortable with Public Faith, Archbishop's Chatham Lecture', 29 October 2004: www.archbishopofcanterbury.org/articles.php/1561/states-need-to-be-comfortable-with-public-faith-archbishops-chatham-lecture; 2005, 'David Nicholls Memorial Lecture: Law, Power and Peace: Christian Perspectives on Sovereignty': www.archbishopofcanterbury.org/articles.php/1181/david-nicholls-memorial-lecture-law-power-and-peace-christian-perspectives-on-sovereignty; 2007, 'Christianity: Public Religion and the Common Good': www.archbishopofcanterbury.org/articles.php/1165/christianity-public-religion-and-the-common-good; 2008, 'Archbishop's Liverpool Lecture: Europe, Faith and Culture': www.archbishopofcanterbury.org/articles.php/1164/archbishops-liverpool-lecture-europe-faith-and-culture.

713 Myers, *Christ the Stranger*, p. 63: 'His remarks on Islamic sharia law were greeted with cries of alarm and incredulity: tabloid papers ran hysterical headlines about a "victory for terrorists" or "a victory for al Qaeda", while one Home Office minister complained that Williams wanted "to fundamentally change the rule of law"'.

714 'Islam has long been bound up with Europe's internal identity as a matter of simple historical fact, and it stands on a cultural continuum with Christianity, not in some completely different frame': Williams, 'Europe, Faith and Culture', p. 4.

715 Rowan Williams, 2007, *Islam, Christianity and Pluralism*, Richmond: AMSS UK, pp. 10–11.

716 Williams, 'Christianity: Public Religion and the Common Good', p. 2.

717 Williams, 'Christianity: Public Religion and the Common Good', p. 2. Andrew Louth characterizes the neo-patristic synthesis, the retrieval of the Church Fathers in an engagement with contemporary issues, for Vladimir Lossky and Georges Florovsky, as 'an insistence that theology springs from an encounter with God, manifest in the Incarnation, found in the Church': Andrew Louth, 2008, 'The Patristic Revival and its Protagonists', in Cunningham and Theokritoff, *The Cambridge Companion to Orthodox Christian Theology*, pp. 188–202, p. 195.

718 Williams, 'Europe, Faith and Culture', p. 5.

719 John Neville Figgis, 1919, *Hopes for English Religion*, London: Longmans, Green & Co., p. 80.

720 Williams, 'Law, Power and Peace', p. 4.

721 See Rowan Williams, 1987, 'Politics and the Soul: A Reading of the City of God', *Milltown Studies* 19/20, pp. 55–72, p. 68.

722 Williams, 'Law, Power and Peace', p. 2.

723 John Neville Figgis, 1911, *Religion and English Society: Two Addresses Delivered at a Conference Held in London November 9th and 10th, 1910*, London: Longmans, Green & Co., p. v.

724 Figgis, *Religion and English Society*, p. vii. See also his 1913, *Churches in the Modern State*, London: Longmans, Green & Co.

725 Rupert Shortt, 2008, *Rowan's Rule: The Biography of the Archbishop*, London: Hodder & Stoughton, p. 315.

726 Williams, 'Christianity: Public Religion and the Common Good', p. 3.

727 Mike Higton, 2008, 'Rowan Williams and Sharia: Defending the Secular', *International Journal of Public Theology* 2:4, pp. 400–17, p. 414.

728 See Mark D. Chapman, 2011, 'Rowan Williams's Political Theology: Multiculturalism and Interactive Pluralism', *Journal of Anglican Studies* 9:1, pp. 61–79.

729 John Neville Figgis, 1910, *The Gospel and Human Need: Being the Hulsean Lectures Delivered before the University of Cambridge, 1908–9*, London: Longmans, Green and Co., p. viii.

730 Williams, *Islam, Christianity and Pluralism*, p. 2.

731 See Bernard Jackson, 2009, '"Transformative Accommodation" and Religious Law', *Ecclesiastical Law Journal* 11:2, pp. 131–53, which questions Williams' lecture from a Jewish perspective, arguing that the 'transformative accommodation' that Williams proposes, in the case of Jewish marriage, results in the conflation of civic and religious institutions.

732 Matthew Grimley, 2004, *Citizenship, Community, and the Church of England: Liberal Anglican Theories of the State from Between the Wars*, Oxford/New York: Oxford University Press, p. 77.

733 Grimley, *Citizenship, Community, and the Church of England*, p. 77.

734 John Milbank, 2010, 'Shari'a and the True Basis of Group Rights: Islam, the West, and Liberalism', in Rex Ahdar and Nicholas Aroney (eds), *Shari'a in the West*, Oxford: Oxford University Press, pp. 135–57, p. 146.

735 John Milbank, 2009, 'Multiculturalism in Britain and the Political Identity of Europe', *International Journal for the Study of the Christian Church* 9:4, pp. 268–81, p. 277.

736 Milbank, 'Multiculturalism in Britain', p. 278.

737 John Milbank, 2009, 'Geopolitical Theology: Economy, Religion and Empire After 9/11': www.scribd.com/doc/19773671/John-Milbank-Geopolitical-Economy-Religion-and-Empire-after-911n, p. 84.

738 John Milbank, 2010, 'The Archbishop of Canterbury: The Man and the Theology Behind the Shari'a Lecture', in Ahdar and Aroney, *Shari'a in the West*, pp. 43–57, p. 52.

739 Milbank, 'Shari'a and the True Basis of Group Rights', p. 155.

740 Milbank, 'Archbishop of Canterbury', pp. 48–9.

741 Vincent Lloyd, 2009, 'Complex Space or Broken Middle? Milbank, Rose, and the Sharia Controversy', *Political Theology* 10:2, pp. 225–45.

742 The metaphysical, Platonic roots of Radical Orthodoxy and the political derivations of this into 'Red Toryism' are described in Nathan Coombs, 2011, 'The Political Theology of Red Toryism', *Journal of Political Ideologies* 16:1, pp. 79–96.

743 Milbank, 'Shari'a and the True Basis of Group Rights', p. 138.

744 For a Catholic incarnational political theology that echoes the logic of Milbank's position, see Aidan Nichols, 1999, *Christendom Awake: On Re-energising the Church in Culture*, Edinburgh: T. & T. Clark.

745 Milbank, 'The Archbishop of Canterbury'. 'From this [Milbank's] point of view, the Anglican Church simply is the Catholic Church in England' (p. 51). For a Catholic critique of Milbank's political theology, see Mary Doak, 2007, 'The Politics of Radical Orthodoxy: A Catholic Critique', *Theological Studies* 68:2, pp. 368–93.

746 Nigel Biggar, 2011, *Behaving in Public: How to Do Christian Ethics*, Grand Rapids, MI: Eerdmans, p. 97.

747 Biggar, *Behaving in Public*, pp. 98–9, quoting Eric Gregory, 2008, *Politics and the Order of Love: An Augustinian Ethic of Democratic Citizenship*, Chicago, IL: University of Chicago Press.

748 Paul Hedges, 2010, 'Is John Milbank's Radical Orthodoxy a Form of Liberal Theology? A Rhetorical Counter', *Heythrop Journal* 51:5, pp. 795–818. Hedges critiques Milbank from a liberal perspective, accusing him of a monolithic approach to modernism.

749 Russell Sandberg, 2011, *Law and Religion*, Cambridge: Cambridge University Press, p. 182.

750 Russell Sandberg, 2010, 'Islam and English Law', *Law and Justice* 164, pp. 27–44, p. 43.

751 Mark D. Chapman, 2008, *Doing God: Religion and Public Policy in Brown's Britain*, London: Darton, Longman & Todd, p. 122.

752 Figgis, *Hopes for English Religion*, p. 132.

753 'The higher goods even of human culture will not persist apart from a spiritual ideal': Figgis, *Hopes for English Religion*, p. 132.

754 Williams, 'Civil and Religious Law in England'.

755 For Milbank, it is a 'teleological ethics' that is missing from Williams' account: what is the group *goal* for the whole society? In Milbank's account, though,

only the catholic spirit can found an inclusive common good: Milbank, 'Multiculturalism in Britain', p. 275.

756 Williams, *Islam, Christianity and Pluralism*, p. 12.

757 See also Rowan Williams, 2012, 'Monastic Virtue and Ecumenical Hopes: The Archbishop of Canterbury's Address at San Gregorio al Celio, 11 March 2012', *One in Christ* 46:2, pp. 306–13.

758 Richard Sudworth, 2013, 'Eastern Orthodoxy, Rowan Williams, and Islam: Exploring the Impact of Eastern Orthodoxy on Rowan Williams' Anglican Engagement with Islam', *ARAM* 25, pp. 501–18.

759 Rowan Williams, 2011, 'Relations between the Church and State Today: What is the Role of the Christian Citizen?', 1 March 2011: www.archbishopofcanterbury. org/articles.php/2009/relations-between-the-church-and-state-today-what-is-the-role-of-the-christian-citizen, p. 4.

760 Rowan Williams, 2011, '"The Only Real City": Monasticism and the Social Vision', in Rowan Williams, *A Silent Action: Engagements with Thomas Merton*, Louisville, KY: Fons Vitae, pp. 55–68.

761 Rowan Williams, 2008, 'Epilogue', in Samuel Wells and Sarah Coakley (eds), *Praying for England: Priestly Presence in Contemporary Culture*, London: Continuum, pp. 171–82, p. 177.

762 Rowan Williams, 2009, 'The Scepter'd Isle: Culture and Power in an Offshore Setting', in Matthew D'Ancona (ed.), *Being British: The Search for the Values that Bind the Nation*, Edinburgh: Mainstream, pp. 145–53. This is in marked contrast to his predecessor George Carey, who writes in the same volume: 'The deepest marks on this nation's landscape have been left by the Church and the Christian faith': George Carey, 2009, 'Great Britain: A Disintegrating Kingdom?', in D'Ancona, *Being British*, pp. 215–24, p. 224.

763 Interview with Archbishop Rowan Williams by Richard Sudworth and Stefanie Hugh-Donovan, Lambeth Palace, 6 September 2012.

764 William T. Cavanaugh, 2016, *Field Hospital: The Church's Engagement with a Wounded World*, Grand Rapids, MI/Cambridge: Eerdmans, p. 116. The essays in this collection are, in many ways, an extended meditation on the need for a sacramental theology in the articulation of political theology.